Taking Steps to End H **W9-DCC-457**

Advance Praise for *Crossing the Line: Taking Steps to End Home...*

"Read this book. Diane Nilan has spent a distinguished lifetime helping the homeless. She writes beautifully, from the heart, and will help you feel from your own heart not only the desperation of homeless persons but their particular strengths as well. You might even start daring to hope that the plight of homelessness might someday be solved."
—Richard R. Guzman, Professor of English, Director of the Master of Arts in Liberal Studies, and the Master of Leadership Studies, North Central College

"Diane Nilan's fire for this issue and these folks shines brightly in every portrait she sketches in this important book about a subject that has slipped off the American social radar."
—Marcia Z. Nelson, journalist, author of *God of Second Chances, Come and Sit: A Week Inside Meditation Centers*, and *The Gospel According to Oprah*

"Diane skillfully and poignantly takes us where many of us are reluctant to go–into the lives of homeless people. Her insights into the massive and heartbreaking problem of homelessness in the richest country on Earth must bring even the stoic among us to tears, and more importantly, to action. Diane masterfully tells this true story without sugarcoating the reasons or the solutions. You will be changed, as I was, after reading her book."
—Barbara Mang Kois, author of *Help Wanted for Busy Moms*

"I'm not a book person, but I read the first page and was surprised to find myself smirking. Several pages into it, I was laughing. Chapters later, I felt a tear on my cheek. After 72 hours of sneaking in more pages around doing the dishes and playdates, I put it down, thinking that I wish I felt glued to more books, but don't because their authors can't write like Diane Nilan."
—Jan Hamilton, freelance journalist, mom, Sunday school teacher, current PADS volunteer, former AIDS hospice support manager for Vets in Chicago

"I had a big problem as I critiqued your book. I became so engrossed in the content that I had to disengage myself to provide any needed correction or comment. Diane, your writing tells the stories vividly. I wouldn't change your style or your vocabulary one bit. The organization is good, the writing flows smoothly, and the topic is absorbing.... As I read, I cried..."
—Bonnie Kendall, author, editor, community volunteer

Crossing the Line:

Taking Steps to End Homelessness

By Diane D. Nilan

Copyright © 2005 Diane D. Nilan, HEAR US Inc.

ISBN 1-59113-836-1 / 978-1-59113-836-5

Printed in the United States of America.

Proceeds from this book will benefit HEAR US Inc. 1163 E. Ogden Ave., #705-329, Naperville, IL 60563, a not-for-profit organization dedicated to raising awareness of and sensitivity to homelessness. More information, contact Bookinfo@hearus.us

www.hearus.us

Dedication

My "homies" who keep me from being bored,
and infuse me with passion,

My family whose genetic composition makes me proud,

My friends who keep me from giving up,

My adversaries and naysayers who motivate me,

And all those who will find themselves without a place to call home...

Acknowledgements

Now I know how important the seemingly innocuous "Acknowledgements" sections are in books I've read. Trying to list everyone who helped will prove that my reputed "system" for keeping track of things is faulty. But, my old and new friends who assisted me so much deserve their name in print (and on the wall of a spectacular monument, maybe "The Bean" in Chicago's Millennium Park.) So here goes…

- For Karen Turk's patient encouragement and support before, during and after this process…
- For Jen and Elijah's understanding of my seemingly unsociable manner…
- For my initial gang of readers and encouragers: Tom Parisi, Barbara Duffield, Christi Parsons, Jen Turk, Ken Johnson, Helen Jilek osb, Pat Van Doren, Liz Lipford, Christine Moyes, Jesse Hernandez, Mom and even my Dad!
- For those who helped immeasurably with in-depth editing and encouragement, honoring my style but finding my gaffes: Tom Johnson, Sally Strosahl-Johnson, Marcia Nelson, Barbara Kois, Mary Lou Cowlishaw, Richard Guzman, Jan Hamilton and Bonnie Kendall. Special mention to Sr. Paula Bingert, OSF, my freshman English teacher who also added her edits and praise.
- For the HEAR US Board's support of this project and the pursuit of my dream mission.
- For Mary Ellen Durbin's nudge that plunged me into social justice work, and her steadfast efforts that keeps me inspired.
- For Nancy Manzie who knows how much I need her humorous encouragement.
- *Most importantly, for the thousands of homeless children and adults I've had the honor of knowing…*

Crossing the Line:

Taking Steps to End Homelessness

By Diane D. Nilan

Table of Contents

Introduction

Homeless shelter director. Not on my career plan. In my wildest dreams I would never have imagined the path that led me to this place.

Nor would I believe the day-to-day drama of running a homeless shelter if portrayed on TV. However, the reality show genre could use a dose of unique adventure called "A Day In the Life of a Homeless Shelter Director." It could include drama, comedy, music, and athletics; "home" repair and maintenance lessons; and "interesting" visits from police, fire, and FBI. Missing would be boredom. And routine. And predictability.

Writing a book never occurred to me during my 15 years of running homeless shelters. I didn't have time to think about it. Neither must have any other shelter director, because it seems no book like this exists. From my viewpoint, all you can hope to do is cope with masses of people seeking help—try to keep them alive—while juggling myriad survival challenges to keeping your program alive.

The human drama, which unfolds daily and nightly at shelters, is a story begging to be told, if by no one else than the estimated 3+ million homeless men, women and children in this country who experience this macabre reality theater. Many loved ones and family members of homeless persons also would want the story told, if for nothing else than to dispel myths swirling around "the homeless." Stories about homelessness, especially how it affects people in a homeless situation, rarely make it into the media anymore. Homelessness, far from understood, has for the most part fallen off our list of issues to address—on a personal, community or national level. In the meantime, more and more people find themselves in this wretched condition.[1]

I could tell countless poignant stories about heroic efforts of people working with homeless persons—tireless shelter staff, determined mental health professionals, medical workers, dedicated volunteers, fervent clergy and myriad unidentified helpers who see beyond the all-but-faded headlines on homelessness. Powerful interactions between helper and helpee occur on a daily and nightly basis on streets and in shelters across the land. These relationships offer life-sustaining hope to those who find themselves swirling in despair, without homes, disregarded by family, friends and society. Ironically, the lives most transformed often are the lives of the helpers.

This book will mention some of my favorite champions. However, the substance of this book will simply portray persons without homes that have a profound effect on my life. Yes, society's homeless "pariahs" touched me deeply with their lives and deaths. Those with so little have so much, and those of us blessed enough to walk with them clamor to tell the story. The opportunity came my way. This is my humble effort.

Most names of real persons in this book have been changed to protect their privacy, indicated by quotes on the first use. Those who gave me permission to use their real names know that I can be trusted to represent them truthfully. The stories represent my best recollections of events in order to share my memories and appreciation of very special people.

About the Author

*D*uring Diane Nilan's 20 years of working with homeless people, including as a homeless shelter director, she ventured into the urban wilderness known only to the nameless. As of November 2005 she faces homelessness (albeit a less dire form) because of her relentless pursuit of justice on behalf of homeless kids.

For two decades, Nilan created and operated hectic shelters and vital services to address myriad causes of homelessness, thus earning the right to offer her obstinate insights. She earned her position as a respected and relentless advocate on the national, state and local level.

Nilan continues to issue an unmistakable call for action to address the injustice and suffering endemic to homelessness, particularly for children and teens that get turned away from school because of homelessness.

She recently plunged too close for comfort to homelessness, a result of her steadfast position on the worthiness of homeless students' educational rights. That compelled her to start a not-for-profit organization in July 2005 called HEAR US (Homeless Education Awareness Raising in the US). In November 2005 she will begin a unique odyssey across America's back roads in search of homeless kids who want a means to be heard by school personnel nationwide. She will travel in an RV to areas not thought of having homelessness—rural areas, small towns, and mid-sized affluent communities.

The primary purpose of her journey is to invite homeless children and youth to speak on film about homelessness, particularly as it applies to education. HEAR US will produce three short training films to be used in educator trainings on the issue of homelessness. Along the way she will address audiences on homelessness.

Proceeds from the sale of this book will fund HEAR US*. Hopefully that will keep Diane off the streets in the worst sense of homelessness.

*HEAR US Inc., a not-for-profit organization with the mission to "To raise awareness and sensitivity about homelessness in order to inspire actions to ease and/or end it."

Donations to HEAR US are tax deductible as allowed by law.

www.hearus.us

PART 1—
WHAT'S A PERSON LIKE ME
DOING IN A PLACE LIKE THIS?

**"Do what you can
with what you have
where you are."**

Theodore Roosevelt

1. Landing on My Feet

Social worker I'm not. Missionary neither. Naïve do-gooder doesn't fit. Malcontent? Nope. I'm too optimistic. So how did a person like me—a non-conforming, plucky "ballsy-bitch" end up working with homeless people?

My moderately moneyed south Florida upbringing offers clues if one digs enough. Poverty, not on our family radar screen, despite what my hard-working parents felt as they toiled to provide for us 5 kids— somehow hung on the edges of mine. St. Francis of Assisi, champion of the poor, became my de facto role model in the personhood of the Franciscan sisters who taught us in grade and high school. A non-conformist by genetic determination, I figured that the life of a nun would be the path I would travel and from the time I was able to make decisions for myself, at the early age of 12, I began preparing myself for this vocation.

Of course, it wasn't all prayers, penance and preparation for "nun-dom." School and I didn't get along. The traditional approach to education—study and homework—seemed too mundane. I'd rather be playing football, soccer, baseball and dodgeball with our neighborhood "gang" that consisted of the oldest 3 kids from our family, eventual pro football players Danny and Johnny from down the block, and a rotating cast of kids that genuinely enjoyed our time outside together. Sports became my passion as I joined whatever team available to girls in the early 60s—basketball, volleyball and softball were my favorites—and my skills were only surpassed by a fierce sense of competition supplemented by my willingness to take hard shots from opponents attempting physical intimidation. Such "training" came in handy in my later careers.

Had I spent as much time studying as I did practicing free throws I'd probably have been college scholarship material. With my sights on the convent walls in Joliet, IL, I slogged through most subjects at high school but developed some healthy and diverse experiences: being the youngest catechism teacher at our parish, with 66 10-year olds depending on me for their religious upbringing (very scary as I think about it now!); working with migrant children during summers; playing guitar and singing before audiences of all sizes; honing my athletic ability and competitive nature; developing my photography and journalism aptitude through our excellent high school newspaper; enhancing leadership skills as I taught swimming to kids and adults, and helped oversee a Brownie troop.

The mid-60s found the nation torn by the struggle for civil rights. Even in my hometown of Pompano Beach, FL, riots erupted and caused great controversy for those of us on the edge of the skin-colored unrest. My avid reading exposed me to theories that we were all created equal. Our family dynamics challenged that principle—my "Archie Bunker"-like father decried any call for equality and my mom seemed to go along (to get along, it turns out). This, the beginning of my non-conformist shaping, put me at odds with those I was closest to—my parents. I was right and they were wrong I stridently, but internally, maintained. Provoking my father's ire would be unwise, though unavoidable as I aged. I managed to do so with some frequency, gaining a healthy dose of lack of respect for the "because I said so" authority.

Learning to Cross the Line

Courage to step over the line of "acceptable behavior" and explore life on the other side of material comfort began during my formative early teen years. Minnie, our loving Aunt Jemimah-like maid, ruled our roost consisting of my 2 brothers, 2 sisters and me while my Mom worked with my Dad in our family gift sales business. Minnie's competent way of getting us to obey was natural to her. She and her thirteen children managed to survive their dire living conditions on the edge of Pompano Beach. She applied valuable child-raising skills to us, and despite her intolerance for misbehavior my respect for her as an authority figure grew each day, mostly because she was fair. She opened my previously white, well-heeled mind to the painful awareness that people of color were only slightly better off than 100 years earlier.

Hard-working Minnie and her kin would spend their precious Saturday free time fishing in canals around our neighborhood. They invisibly stood with their bamboo cane poles on the rocky shores of waterways woven through affluent neighborhoods in our south Florida paradise. As a budding 12-year old do-gooder, I figured my friend-mentor, Minnie, and her kin would appreciate something cold to drink during their sun baked fishing expedition, so I would mix up a few cans of frozen lemonade, grab paper cups, load everything into my bike's basket and head off to find the fishing hole du jour.

Somehow, I managed to do this without my parents' knowledge, because I knew they'd stop my mission of mercy before I even opened the lemonade cans. My Dad wasn't racially tolerant, to say the least, and fraternizing with the dark-skinned help would doubtlessly be forbidden.

I usually managed to locate the fishing party and never returned home with a full jug of lemonade. I sat on the banks of south Florida canals surrounded by Minnie and others—her kids, neighbors and friends—thoroughly enjoying my time with them. Their cane poles stretched over dark waters of the canals, bread balls hanging on hooks, with great hopes of catching catfish.

I didn't realize then that this wasn't the sport of fishing—but rather the art of providing dinner for hungry families at no cost but time. Minnie earned a scant $8 a day for her Herculean parent-like efforts at our house. The lemonade and good will could hardly make up for the injustice my family—like so many others before and after—perpetuated. It is called slavery without the plantation.

Poverty was a new phenomenon for me to ponder from the comfort of my secure middle-income upbringing. Homelessness wasn't an issue then, or at least was significantly less than in the later part of the twentieth century. My first brush with homelessness came as I reached my teens. My parents recruited me to help my Dad prepare the Christmas gifts for my four younger siblings. They safely stored the gifts in their business warehouse, but they needed assembly and wrapping. I was proud my parents considered me worthy and mature enough to help.

On a cold (for South Florida) December evening, Dad and I went over to the warehouse on the edge of town. He offhandedly mentioned someone lived in the concrete block structure next to their unit and pointed it out to me. I vaguely recall a stark garage-like space, one light bulb hanging in the center of the room, with a cot as the only furnishing. I urged my Dad to let me return with some extra blankets—after we did the gift assembly.

I remember thinking often about the person in that cold, bleak warehouse, and how wrong it is for some to have so much when some had so little. My thought process was inevitably shaped by my Catholic upbringing and my voracious reading of biographies of saints like Francis, Clare and Martin de Porres. Perhaps my minor forays over "the line" as a teen made me more susceptible to taking what became a major leap into my 20+ years career of working with impoverished and homeless persons.

For me, seeing the barren concrete shacks horizontally stacked in the dusty neighborhood of our HeadStart kids assailed my naïve sense of justice for all. On the outskirts of relatively affluent Pompano Beach, these spartan huts provided the most basic of shelter but nothing more, with no playgrounds or ball fields—a stark contrast to life as I knew it, us with our 5 bedrooms and three bathrooms, screened-in pool and plentiful places to play.

My migrant experience left me conflicted—happy to think I could alleviate some suffering for the kids by working with them in the summer program, but I was deeply troubled by the disparities between my life and the pathetic existence of these kids. This episode was more worthwhile for me than for the kids, burning in my heart the painful knowledge of poverty and inequity as it affected kids I knew, and a patent disdain for the unfairness in how society valued people based on the color of their skin.

The relative bliss of my high school years was shattered by two key tragic events—the murders of Martin Luther King and Bobby Kennedy. I missed the true significance of John Kennedy's assassination, but Martin and Bobby's death rattled me in ways I couldn't process. Something was dreadfully wrong in our country, the wealth contrasted too painfully with abject poverty and racism. Little did I know how significantly this theme would recur in my adult life.

My mediocre grades and my parents' ultimatum—one year of non-nun college before they'd let me go to the College of St. Francis in Joliet—led me to a fascinating year of public school at St. Petersburg Junior College and apartment living in Clearwater, FL. Besides my scholastic and athletic endeavors there, I learned from a friend that parochial schools sometimes hired college students to teach PE part-time so I went to my parish priest with the inquiry—"Would you happen to be looking for a PE teacher?" Dumfounded, he asked who sent me. I simply replied that I was looking for a part-time teaching job, and he hired me. Classroom/basketball court management came easy to me thanks to my previous experiences, so I avidly pursued a semester of what I thought was going to be my career—teaching as a nun.

The freedom of life out of the house, on the other side of the state, 4 hours from parental supervision also gave me the "opportunity" to see what role alcohol would play in my life. For me college life was alcohol, not drugs. Alcohol was legal, at least for those over 21. My confidence and mature poise usually made up for the lack of years, so I was often the designated buyer of some nasty tasting cheap beer that provided the mood enhancement for our free time. Looking back, my awareness of the lure of alcohol also gave me the understanding of how easily some people slip into an addicted state, throwing their lives into a tailspin. I came close…could have easily trashed my life too. It's genetic—and a challenge faced by my kin present, past and probably future.

My first steps crossing the line as a teen undoubtedly prepared me for my adult encounters. And stumble though I may, I haven't gone back, though sometimes I wished I could...and yet I'm grateful for—and personally richer because of—the people I have met on the other side of the line.

2. Finding the Right Path

*M*y move to Joliet in the summer of 1969 marked a milestone in my life! This adventure far from south Florida held much promise, but the Joliet Franciscans, like most North American religious communities, were changing their admissions procedures, which meant that I'd have to finish college before being fully accepted into the convent. The College of St. Francis campus was adjacent to the motherhouse and us aspiring nun-wanna-bes participated in a variety of activities with the sisters.

Teaching was my profession, no doubt about it, so I pursued a part-time teaching assignment, ironically at St. John's School, where my former grade school principal and 8th grade teacher/nemesis, Sr. Thelma, was principal. She was desperate or I matured, but I managed to teach PE all year without incurring her wrath, a new occurrence for me!

Rebellion, my genetic response to things that didn't sit right with me, found me leading a protest of the reputably horrible food in our cafeteria. My comrades and I figured out how to bring the cafeteria manager to her knees by thwarting her orderly world and radically varying the number of people who showed up for meals. The thrill of victory came when we sat down with a college administrator and the food service supervisor to discuss the proposed improvements.

This advocacy didn't endear me to the administration and I proudly flaunted trouble throughout my college career. Other college activities, sanctioned and not, gave me plenty of time to discover and perfect my non-conformist side. Fascination for rooftop parties and venturing into forbidden parts of the college, e.g., the nun's quarters, spiced up a fairly normal college career. My junior year, when I didn't teach, I almost flunked out. That year I gained invaluable wisdom in community organizing as one of the leaders for the "Walk for Mankind," the precursor for today's walks and runs for every activity under the sun. I learned the value of hard work, the lesson of how many people say they'll help prior to disappearing, the humongous amount of effort to pull off a successful event, the incredible generosity of people and their businesses, the real meaning of what walking 30 miles means, the delight of a hot bath afterwards, and how grades drop when you ignore your class work. I also, for the first time, saw abject poverty in Joliet. It was there long before me, but I never ventured into "bad" neighborhoods because they were, well, bad. We survived our walk through these less affluent areas which burned images in my memory.

Thousands of miles away, American troops engaged in what became a world-changing war in Vietnam. My college classes, typical and mostly tedious, offered little challenge to my increasing dissatisfaction with status quo. One bright spot was a philosophy professor, Don Williams, who flagrantly defied stereotypical images of Catholic college instructors. Bearded, long black hair hanging down past his shoulders, garbed in tie-dye shirts, jeans and sandals, he exposed us to counter-thinking. Vietnam War— wrong! Nixon—worse than wrong! Military thinking that espoused killing the enemy—evil! And so a small band of "renegades" marched down the previously virgin Joliet streets, chanting, waving our radical messages scrawled on our signs.

This minority sect met regularly for Sunday night Mass, complete with folk songs reflecting the new guitar masses tolerated by the post-Vatican Council Catholic Church. My guitar hung from my neck, my untrained but strong voice led the band of rebels in songs reflecting our growing discontent with our nation's leadership. I devoured books speaking of modern heroes— Malcolm X, Martin Luther King, Gandhi, and others. I learned protest songs of Peter, Paul and Mary and others, music that reflected despair and hope during the ongoing turbulent times of the early '70s.

One summer, Pat, my college roomie and co-conspirator, and Rita, a like-minded rebel, and I grasped what seemed to be an opportunity to get out of Illinois, earn money, and have some fun. My family bought into a theme park in the mountains of North Carolina. They had the gift shop franchise and needed workers. We all were capable of hard work and my parents welcomed us. Suffice to say slavery had lots going for it compared to working for my Dad. His dictatorial ways made for tensions from the start. We resented the hours, his attitude, and the fact that we'd never had time to appreciate what was probably a beautiful area. Smoldering underneath was a resentment of taking money from families who probably didn't have enough for basics, much less to spend on helium balloons obscenely inflated in cost and popcorn that cost pennies to market but depleted the spending money of those succumbing to the tempting aroma.

A joint decision was made: we'd quit and go back to Illinois. For Pat and Rita it meant little more than a change of plans. For me it was a family-wrenching moment that found my Dad disowning me, or so he said. We drove off the mountain with $75 to my name and two friends to comfort me following the painful departure. (To his credit, my parents did pay for college, but for everything else I was on my own. I survived. Those were the days such survival was possible.)

It took me an extra year to finish college because of my teaching activities, but it was worth it. My last year I made deans' list despite teaching full-time! I had a resume filled with experiences, not that I needed it to get into the convent. For my last year of college I got to live "in community" with 4-5 nuns in nearby Rockdale. This eye-opening preparation didn't dissuade my fervor for religious life, and despite my unrefined community living skills, I was accepted as a novice in August 1973, the only one in my "class." This long sought milestone was finally reality. ***"Sister Diane" was my name, short-lived was my game…***

3. Who Knows Where Each Step Leads?

Maybe the undivided attention of my novice director was too much. Maybe I was too much for her, or them—the sisters of the community that I thought I'd spend my life with—but six weeks after I entered religious life I left, disenchanted.

Lots of things were wrong, but most profound to me seemed inconsistency—some people could do what they wanted and I couldn't do the same things I had been doing for years. Being a novice meant a very structured way of life—praying lots, cleaning areas that weren't even dirty, no extra curricular activities, etc. With much painful deliberation behind me, I met with the head nun and told her I was through. I left on the Feast of St. Francis, the nuns' biggest feast day. I headed home, but instead of staying in the warm south, Atlanta was now my family's home, I headed back to Illinois to continue my search for a meaningful life.

Though not insignificant, my Joliet years were relatively routine. I taught some more, including a couple of years in an all-black "inner city" Catholic school, by far my favorite teaching stint! I learned more about photography and public relations through various work activities, spent many years playing sports with a more senior group of fun-loving, beer drinking women, and bumped around looking for meaning. I spent a few summers umpiring and then running the Joliet Park District's busy women's and men's softball league. I finally left teaching, disenchanted because of what seemed to be a growing movement of parents not taking charge of their kids' discipline, and began exploring other careers. Tired of paltry Catholic school salaries, I wanted money. I turned my love for sports into income by officiating volleyball, basketball and softball. I got to know more and more people in Joliet, became active in a small racially diverse church on the "bad" side of town, and discovered poverty and housing injustice went hand in hand.

My search for money led me to a new profession that combined my innate sales ability with an entirely new field—lighting fixtures sales. I boldly approached the new owners of a lighting showroom that was in process of opening and asked if they had someone in mind to run it. I got the job based on being in the right place at the right time. I thought my greenback ship had come in! Finally, out of church work, into the world of sales, and selling items that actually had value to boot!

Three years later I found what betrayal meant. A woman I hired used my absence during my vacation to push me out and move herself into the boss' favor. Unemployment in Joliet in the early 1980s was depressing. Over 20% of the population was jobless and I was one of them. Standing in the unemployment line remains my most un-favorite memory, though one that later helped me understand alienation and failure. Because of my supplemental professions of officiating, substitute teaching and other dabbling I didn't become homeless, but I was devastated. I had no idea of what I wanted to pursue as my next profession.

One of my income-producing activities was doing inspections of homes in foreclosure. I'd often just have to drive by to verify the house was still standing, but sometimes I had to interview the owner to determine the probability of their repaying and to examine the inside of the house. I really became dismayed by multiple versions of "riches to rags" tales I heard from a variety of soon to be home-losers. They were real. Their stories usually chronicled a typical pattern—job loss, unfortunate circumstances, falling behind on payments, foreclosure notices and all the disastrous sideshows that accompany a loss of that magnitude. People just like me...

Seeing widespread suffering motivated me to get involved in various activities in our church aimed at addressing injustice and poverty. I began to learn about government policies that promoted suffering and community programs that alleviated pain. I eventually teamed up with a few like-minded individuals to explore housing issues affected by this explosion of poverty.

This led me down a path I would have never considered. I met a Catholic Charities' worker, Mary Ellen Durbin, who told me about a weekend social justice workshop she thought would be worthwhile and might lead to a job. What did I have to lose? I went, spending an inspiring time with lots of good people wanting to right some of the wrongs of poverty. Yes, this felt good.

In what is still a profound memory, I can remember staring at the orange carpet by the altar during a prayer service seeing a sparkly fleck on the rug. I recall thinking, "that little sparkle, probably only noticed by me, still shines, just like I can shine in this world, undiminished by the vastness of poverty." Shortly after the service Mary Ellen told me that a 6-month position was open at Catholic Charities, one that required no degree in social work (good for me and my philosophy degree). The person would need to lead the agency's self-study process for eventual accreditation. I could do that. I applied and got the job, not knowing what I needed to do or how to do it, but figuring I'd be able to do it somehow.

My ambition was fueled by more than the regular paycheck, but that sure helped. As I met with program staff and acquired the information needed for the accreditation process I became awed by the number of people needing help—counseling, emergency assistance, advocacy—and the few resources available to do so. Not being able to keep a narrow focus, I became more aware of people without homes—men, women, children—and realized that no options were available to them. When my curiosity became too much, I discussed the situation with my boss and co-workers. Sensing my willingness to help and the fact that my project was coming to an end, my boss tossed me the challenge—do something about homelessness. He said they'd be able to get a state grant to put people up in motels for short periods. I needed to administer the program. Hmmm.... didn't make any sense to me, but I pursued the challenge and devised a plan that sort of worked for a winter or so, but the shortcomings were obvious—where do people go when we pull the plug on their motel stay? My questioning inspired a small group of like-minded community leaders to explore how many people were staying in motels due to homelessness. The findings were astounding—and led us to extrapolate that Joliet needed a shelter.

The nice thing about small not-for-profit agencies—if you raise a concern or come up with an idea you get to do it. Knowing nothing about homelessness other than what I learned encountering some homeless people I assisted with motel rooms and other services, I was charged with the task of exploring a program called PADS, Public Action to Deliver Shelter, in nearby affluent DuPage County. Strangely enough, one of my most powerful teachers flitted into my life like a sparrow...

4. The Tiny Sparrow Flits Into My Life

*T*he young, blond, frail looking woman, always wearing faded bib overalls haunted me. I'd see her walking all over town, on the rough-and-tumble streets of Joliet, in poverty-ridden, gang infested neighborhoods unfit for human habitation, much less a defenseless, confused woman walking at all hours of the day and night.

I'd often see her gingerly stepping backwards, sometimes talking—to herself, I guessed, because no one else was around and cell phones with microphones and ear buds weren't invented yet. I eventually dubbed her "the Sparrow," this nameless creature as nondescript as a sparrow, flitting all over town, unnoticed by most, except thugs who tormented her, and me with my penchant for underdogs, or in this case, underbirds.

Not surprisingly, "the Sparrow" entered the picture early in my Catholic Charities days in Joliet, even before our shelter opened. People I knew asked me about her. Others had noticed her wandering our streets. A problem-solver by nature, I felt compelled to delve into this mystery. Who was she and what was her story?

Realizing nothing would happen until I found out more, I chanced it and finally stopped to talk to her. She didn't seem to register that I was a concerned human being. I felt like I invaded her world. I didn't learn much except that I had a lot to learn about mentally ill homeless persons.

Even to me, with no training as a mental health professional, she seemed out of touch, disconnected, and quite vulnerable. She obviously had no place to stay and possessed nothing except the clothes she wore. My inquiries to local mental health professionals yielded no useful information—some knew of her but cynically declared her hopeless. Their efforts to help her failed, and since she was "non-compliant," she couldn't get help. That's the way the mental health system at the time operated. You had to be lucid enough to ask for help and to cooperate with the providers. They pretty well told me it was futile to think I could help her—which has historically challenged me to try even harder.

My more prolonged contact with her occurred after I found her beaten, robbed of her disability money by someone who knew how easy of a mark she was. Her battered face, dark bruises contrasting with her fragile features, infuriated me. My underdog protector mode kicked in and I became determined to do something to help her. I refused to believe this was an impossible situation.

Even though she had no place to live, some people must have let her stay with them for reasons I didn't want to speculate. I astutely figured that her disability checks she received at the beginning of each month attracted predators, therefore my first order of business was to get her to let me hang onto the bulk of the $300-something she received. Over time, and with lots of patience (on both of our parts), we eventually got to the point where she trusted me and allowed me to hold her money (in the CC business office), giving her small amounts to spend as she wished.

I struggled with the reality that men of the lowest caliber were taking advantage of her, but she didn't seem too concerned about it. I couldn't lock her up. I couldn't follow her around every minute. I could just worry that these sexual escapades wouldn't leave her dead, pregnant, or infected with HIV/AIDS, the scourge *de jour*.

After my formidable efforts to get her some help, the Sparrow finally began working with the county mental health program, and was taking medications. She complained mightily about the meds because of side effects, especially bloating which became obvious even to me as she began to stretch the seams of her trademark baggy overalls. She also had frightening seizures, freezing up and becoming catatonic. She once had a spell while sitting in the CC kitchen waiting for me to come down to give her some money. When summoned downstairs, I was shocked to see what these meds did to her. I began to understand why people dependent on psychotropic medications were reluctant to take them despite the relief from their psych problems.

Eventually, once I started the Will County PADS homeless shelter (no longer called by that name), she stayed there off and on. By that time she would also be a common visitor in the CC office, stopping by for some money, chatting with the other staff who had gotten to notice and care about her by then. Her network of caring protectors grew as people learned not to fear her just because of her mental illness.

As I became more aware of her disability and the accompanying challenges, I inquired among other social service professionals as to the alternatives for housing and services. Dismayed, I found that because of her age, her mental illness (schizophrenia) and her track record, the Sparrow was out of luck, a determination I couldn't accept. So I looked further.

In the meantime, the Sparrow stayed at the shelter irregularly, and still kept in touch with me, allowing me to hold her money. She'd occasionally get jumped by punks wanting something from her. In one of our frequent visits, she referred to her father who she said lived in a small rural community about 75 miles from Joliet. He rarely saw her. Her mother lived out of state and they didn't seem to have any relationship. With her permission, I spoke with them by phone to no avail. They loved her in their own way but didn't know how to care for her. A sad declaration by parents, but understandable to some extent because her erratic behavior was frequently difficult to manage.

I was desperate for a solution to her homelessness. Despite her simplicity, she was more "high maintenance" than I could handle because my responsibilities were growing and seemingly countless homeless people needed my attention. I couldn't accept the idea of her wandering the streets with her untreated mental illness, but I was frustrated with her incompatibility with human service agencies. She wasn't as desperate as I was, but she was at the point that spending another winter wandering the streets was more than unappealing, so she somewhat cooperated with my inadequate efforts to find a solution to her homelessness.

A town about 70 miles from Joliet had a residential program for persons with mental illnesses. We went to check it out and I was unrealistically hopeful that the Sparrow would find it suitable and the operators would accept her—preferably on the spot, relieving my burden and meeting her every need. That wasn't to be, so we looked further. Another 20 miles away from there was a boarding house known to accept people with mental illnesses like the Sparrow, so I talked her into trying it, thinking it would be the solution if she'd just give it a chance.

Although she agreed to stay there and the owners seemed willing to work with her, I had an uneasy feeling about the solution. Sure enough, before I got back to Joliet they called my home to say she took off and they didn't know where to find her. I headed back, making the 70-mile drive perplexed as to the next option. I located her wandering the streets. We went back to her room in the boarding house. In order to get her to stay, I reluctantly agreed to sleep on her floor so she wouldn't be alone the first night. Ouch. Floors are hard.

She went AWOL again, and somehow managed to end up back in Joliet before I even knew she was missing from her program. She showed up at our office, disheveled, exhausted, saying she hitchhiked from her new town. She wanted some of her money so she could go stay in a motel. What was I going to do?

She returned to her new "home," which wasn't really a program, but more like a sanctioned dumping ground for unwanted people, and remained there for a short time, giving me short, but welcome respite from the heavy responsibilities of making sure the Sparrow was safe while I tended to my "real" responsibilities. I knew her solution was temporary, and she bounced between programs, housing, homelessness, and back again indefinitely.

Eventually she returned to Joliet to stay, cared for by an informal network of good people. By this time, volunteers from the shelter and others had become more aware of her, extending a newly-created support network. She seemed immensely happier than when I first reached out to her.

When I left Joliet in early 1990, I figured our paths would separate. My new job, running a shelter in Aurora, was pretty demanding and I hardly got back to Joliet, 30 miles away.

But the Sparrow found me, coming for a few short visits, once with her father. She seemed relaxed and coherent, having received intensive mental health services for a while, combined with a nurturing environment from countless people in the "City of Brotherly *(and Sisterly)* Love."

The Sparrow, in her trademark bib overalls walking by the side of the road, talking to herself, one of so many vulnerable and discarded souls wandering our streets...

People like the Sparrow fit the definition of "chronically homeless," a pseudonym for lost causes, not worthy of expending very limited resources on. Few options were available to keep homeless people like the Sparrow from freezing to death during winter months, a reality that deeply troubled me then as it still does now.

5. Lessons, Lessons and More Lessons…

Our cadre of shelter-starters drove up to Naperville one night to visit the PADS site, housed in a church hall. Despite my vast encounters with scary drunk softball players and other characters, I remember thinking, "We'll probably get killed tonight by some crack-crazed homeless guy."

No one uttered our common fears on the drive up, but we all felt the same: how could a few church volunteers safely handle a bunch of homeless people? Burdened by our apprehension we ventured into the hall. I was instantly disappointed—where were the homeless people? A handful of adults, with few kids, sat around eating, quietly talking, playing cards, but I didn't see any bedraggled folks. A guy came over towards us, introduced himself as a volunteer, and I proceeded to ask him a really dumb question. "Where are the homeless people?"

"Here," he nonchalantly replied. Here? You mean these quiet, normal-looking adults and children? I was dumbfounded. So were my colleagues. Invited to sit down, our host explained the basics of PADS—hospitality without lots of restrictions brings out the best of people. Make this hall seem like home for the homeless and they'll appreciate the effort, meager as it is. Hmmm…. I was beginning to catch on.

Following our enlightening episode, bolstered by the alarming numbers garnered by our survey of motels in the Joliet area, inspired by the very low start-up cost for the PADS model, we decided to start a shelter in Joliet. Our intense efforts to recruit volunteers and develop community acceptance eventually prevailed. Fighting what turns out to be textbook opposition to homeless shelters, Will County PADS opened in February 1988, housed not in a circuit of church halls but in one site generously provided by Second Baptist Church, right down the street from my parish church, on the "bad" side of town.

We never hurt for business, with blustery Illinois winters sending even the hardiest souls inside as temperatures dropped into the negative numbers. Nothing could have prepared me for the night when I was registering our "guests" and I looked up to see a former student standing in line. Ten years before, "Wanda" sat before me in our sixth grade homeroom. Her embarrassment and my disappointment collided. Her need for a place to stay brought home to me the reality of homelessness affecting those I know. It was just the first of many painful lessons in that subject.

My enthusiasm for this ministry lit my heart on fire. I finally found something that required every bit of my talent and then some. My work became my life. I dove into the deep and turbulent waters that encircled ministry to poor and homeless persons. I swirled around newly formed advocacy groups aimed at not letting homeless shelters and soup kitchens become permanent solutions. As President Reagan slashed housing assistance for the most needy, and as remnants of the brutal economic slump of the 1980s left a swath of homelessness, I began to learn how politics and poverty intertwined.

My first valuable lesson provided me the impetus to leave my adopted hometown of Joliet for nearby Aurora. Joliet, like several mid-sized cities in Illinois, decided that the salvation to their "inner city blues" would be to spruce up the downtown enough to attract one of the riverboat licenses being floated in the state legislature. Riverboats hold the illusory promise of riches for all but only deliver the big bucks to the lucky investors. Casinos are a highly competitive business and those wanting to be the big players will stop at nothing to attract the tugboat-shaped golden goose. As Joliet's dilapidated downtown received a facelift by ambitious developers, scores of small, affordable rooms and apartments were being torn down, casting their occupants either into the few available living quarters elsewhere or onto the streets. "Wrong, wrong, wrong!" my socially active heart screamed to my sometimes-impetuous brain that struggled to contain my flapping lips. At a meeting convened by my real big boss, Bishop Joseph Imesch, the development bigwigs stared down the do-gooders who were being too publicly dismayed about the loss of affordable housing. Those big-bucks developers were generous supporters of the Diocese of Joliet; included in the benefactors' largesse would be Catholic Charities. But, when the Bishop stood up and pledged support for the efforts to spruce up downtown I knew my Joliet days were over. I left shortly after, handing over the challenge of Will County PADS to my capable co-worker, Jill Skole.

In 1990 I took the job of PADS shelter director at Hesed House in Aurora, 30 miles away. The shelter was part of a multi-service approach, with "one-stop shopping" for people in poverty—food pantry, soup kitchen, clothing distribution and shelter—a unique and ambitious ministry not under the auspices of one body (or a bishop!), supported by dozens of faith communities and operated by thousands of volunteers.

My previous experiences barely prepared me for what would face me in this chapter of my life. For the next 13 years, I would dig deeper into myself than I thought possible. I'd learn to do more things—including becoming technically competent, a far sight from my anti-typewriter days of yore. I'd apply my unpolished writing fervor to newsletters designed to inspire support of this ministry. I'd refine my grant writing skills to help raise over a million dollars a year to operate and maintain this huge facility. I'd develop my public speaking expertise to recruit volunteers and encourage support. I'd apply my mechanical abilities to plumbing and electrical emergencies that plagued this facility. I'd discover how to climb on the roof of our former incinerator building to scare off anyone who thought it would make a safe haven for drinking and whatever. I'd advance my public policy advocacy to levels I wouldn't have imagined possible.

PART 2—

PRIME TIME DRAMA:
PEEK BEHIND SHELTER WALLS

Blessing of the Apaches

"Now you will feel no rain, for each of you will be shelter for the other. Now you will feel no cold, for each of you will be warmth to the other. Now there will be no loneliness, for each of you will be companion to the other..."

6. Lights (We Hope), Camera (With Surprising Results) and Plenty of Action!

My Hesed House colleagues and I often mused about a weekly TV series based on our adventures, but someone needed to write the script, produce it and cast it, all of which sounded like a lot of work.

We barely had time to tell each other essential things we needed to know—who had chickenpox (and where we put them), what toilet had overflowed (and if or when the plumber was expected) or whose mental state was deteriorating (and if it was feasible to think they'd be able to obtain help from the hospital). None of us had time to escape what one co-worker referred to as "the vortex" and write a short essay, much less a book. This non-stop human drama frequently occurred simultaneously on several stages. You could almost hear the director's cry, "Lights! Camera! Action!"

LIGHTS—we would on occasion find ourselves light-less in the City of Lights, Aurora. Power failures would be caused by an ice storm, high winds or similar phenomenon. Sometimes it would be caused by the unknown. Often it happened right at our peak time—dinnertime, which can make things quite interesting. Imagine having 100+ homeless persons under one roof, with a handful of volunteers and one staff person—and the lights flicker and fade. Very interesting...but never as disastrous as one might expect.

CAMERA—we would take pictures of each new person for our records and, eventually as equipment improved, for ID cards that helped us register and keep track of our 800-1,000 different individuals we'd serve each year, with the bonus of providing people with some form of (pre 9/11) identification. These IDs created a record of existence, and the photos often made me think of class pictures. I couldn't get over the number of people who smiled. I was dismayed at the rapid deterioration of most faces I saw year after year. But they still smiled...

ACTION—we had plenty of it! No day was the same as another. The unexpected was the only thing we expected. Mechanical drama, human drama, political drama. I learned that human theater was my choice—at least I could count on an element of goodness with humans, even those least likely to be expected to act decently. Machines and government policies—they represented headaches: expensive, frustrating, and ill timed. I preferred people to machines and government any day!

The Main Stage

I directed the largest emergency shelter in Illinois outside Chicago. PADS, as it was commonly called, is formally known as Public Action to Deliver Shelter, Inc., the original model of an emergency shelter program replicated in more than a dozen communities[2], mostly in Illinois. Our shelter was under the roof of a multi-service ministry known as Hesed House, ironically housed in Aurora's former municipal incinerator.

Aurora, Illinois' second largest city with a population of more than 157,000, reflects commonalities with dozens of mixed industrial cities in America's Rust Belt, including Joliet, my previous stomping grounds. On the fringe of Chicago's suburbs, Aurora's poverty rate hovers around 10%, comprised of an estimated 40% Hispanic, 10% African American, and the balance Caucasian. (2000 census figure for Hispanics is 32%, but a significant population of undocumented immigrants, mostly Hispanic, increase the actual number, to as high as 45%.)

Aurora's and Joliet's growth of homelessness in the 1980s parallels other communities across the country with similar conditions: insidious abject poverty, loss of quality jobs, sprawling high-end subdivisions, soaring rental housing costs, the demise of mental health residential programs and services, severe reduction of supportive services (health care, counseling, family support), violence (gang and domestic), increasingly harsh welfare cuts and a general denial of the existence of rampant socio-economic malaise.

Nationwide, the '80s set the stage for burgeoning homelessness that has continued into the 21st century. During this same period, incomes for the wealthiest Americans skyrocketed and health insurance coverage diminished[3]. As newly constructed mega-houses with their luxury floor plans became the rage, rundown homeless shelters sprouted up in church basements, abandoned storefronts and vacant municipal buildings. In 1982, Aurora's PADS shelter started out in a rotation of church sites, using basements, parish halls, gyms and kitchens to accommodate the, at first, small band of "street people," as the populace was commonly (and mistakenly) described. As I saw in Joliet, enlightened persons, mostly volunteers from local faith communities, recognized that those coming to the shelter had ties to the community. In fact, most (85% or more) either claimed Aurora as home or had relatives or employment in or around the city. Anecdotal evidence based on initial interviews with first-time guests disputed the shelter's critics who believed starting a homeless shelter would attract hordes of homeless nomads from Chicago. That same argument was the common objection in communities that followed Aurora's lead in starting a faith-based PADS program, including our Will County PADS shelter. I heard it religiously by people claiming to be religious but objecting to opening a shelter.

Summer Theater: Tent City—Desperate Solution for Desperate Times

The limitations and challenges of a winter emergency shelter are not obvious to the unaware, but to those who rely on this bandage-like "solution" to homelessness, and to those who work at them, some obvious shortfalls exist…

Most shelters in our area depend largely on volunteers from faith communities who make a huge commitment of time, people, resources and more in order to staff their congregation's monthly night at the shelter. They're it—with meager assistance from a staff person at the beginning and end of their twelve hour turn. Their volunteers do everything—bring food to feed 150+ men, women and children; sign in "guests" as they're called in the ministry of hospitality; bring and distribute toiletries and laundry soap; oversee the sleeping areas (imagine being one of the guys to supervise the men's area with 94 guys crammed in); clean up after meals; prepare sack lunches for workers and anyone else who needs one; and cook breakfast, serving it to the whole crowd who must leave by 7 a.m. due to lack of staff. Yikes! That's a lot to ask of any group.

During the summer months, our shelter operated in a much slimmer mode, again totally dependent on volunteers who are harder to recruit at that time of year for any number of reasons. The original theory, dating back to the early '80s when this model of shelter began, was that a time-limited season would encourage people to kick in gear and get their lives together. That theory has many flaws; it prevailed but worked less and less as time went on and previously limited resources—affordable housing and jobs paying living wages—became almost non-existent.

It's really ludicrous to think that homelessness is easier in the warmer months. Sweltering heat can be even more devastating than cold for people in frail health—as many homeless people are. Heat causes tensions to rise—documented by increased number of police calls in warmer weather. Landlords evict people easier, knowing someone won't freeze to death.

Utilities cut gas, water and electricity forcing delinquent families to suffer or move. People aren't as inclined to be nice and take someone in during warmer weather, maybe because they don't think being out in the heat is so bad. Mosquitoes, especially those carrying potentially fatal West Nile virus, pose increased danger. Non-homeless punks roam the streets looking for vulnerable victims—so not having a roof over your head and walls to protect you means you're out there with the crazies.

My first summer at the shelter caught me unaware. I never went out back to see what was going on in the space between our building and adjacent railroad embankment. Towards the end of summer, we found out that a few hardy souls were "camping" back there, in the rough, unfinished land behind our former incinerator. They scrounged building materials, carpet scraps and other items to protect them from the elements; fashioning primitive lean-tos that offered limited protection from inclement weather and hostile passersby.

Being a long-time tent camper myself, I got thinking…what if we set up a controlled campground for the folks who demonstrated the ability to behave themselves (within generous limits)? Hmmm…this idea had possibilities, and barriers, such as Aurora's no camping ordinance. I formulated my arguments and sold the concept. We set up parameters, strategized with the staff of the newly opened transitional shelter in the other part of the building, and solicited tents and other camping supplies.

I interviewed and selected dozens of candidates. Many were called, few were chosen. Well, maybe more than a few. Actually, we made some well-intentioned but naive choices of the charter "camper club." We learned! After a huge non-sanctioned bonfire/drinking (and whatever) party got way out of hand one night, we pared down the roster and learned that structure would probably be best for everyone.

One more comment about this unique Tent City (appendix vii). According to those who would know—Michael Stoops of the National Coalition for the Homeless among others—this was for a long time the only campground of its kind in the nation. The structure, a benevolent dictatorship with me as mayor and each tent having an elected/selected/default representative in a "city" council, allowed us to run things with relative success. I oversaw 13 seasons. My co-workers, some incredibly hard working and streetwise along with being compassionate, contributed significantly to the success of this unlikely venture. The 70+ bodies and souls in Tent City survived by generous donations of tents and other supplies, surprise visits by good Samaritans laden with home-cooked food and practical clothing, and occasional nights inside when the storms were too horrendous to remain outside.

Not to say Tent City was a vacation for the campers. It was grueling. Weather, bugs, critters large and small and gang-bangers kept life interesting. Personal hygiene (or lack of it), proclivity for the bottle or other enchanting substances, unauthorized and often unwanted guests, snoring and other bodily sounds, well, you get the idea....

Some tents were incredibly neat, often those occupied by former military personnel. People with mental illnesses either were amazingly neat (compulsively?) or astoundingly messy. These canvas (and later nylon) walls represented one thing to almost every camper—home. Be it ever so humble, it was their space. It also became a community—often with ties closer to persons than in ritzier neighborhoods. It was more often than not safe and peaceful. I, and other staff, would sneak by late at night, figuring our unannounced visit would catch someone doing something wrong. We often were disappointed—happily!

The Setting—Standing Room Only!

The only thing I saw skyrocketing during the last decade of the century was homelessness. Men, women and children—typically more than 120 a night—would come "home" to our pathetically over-crowded, under-staffed, inadequately-resourced emergency shelter.

A disgruntled guest, whom I had previously kicked out for disruptive behavior, was probably the cause of a surprise visit from the fire marshal in the early 1990s. When I was alerted to the marshal's presence, I gulped. We were at the craziest time of the year—right before Christmas. Our numbers were often dozens over-capacity. I met him and tried to nonchalantly chat. His brusque demeanor led me to believe that trouble was brewing. He asked to see where the men slept. I led him upstairs to the men's sleeping area. He asked me how many guys slept there. I became instantly ignorant, "I dunno, maybe about 70..." I half-heartedly mumbled, knowing that we figured out how to wedge 94 guys in if the sleeping pads were laid out properly. He whipped out his calculator, counted ceiling tiles, entered numbers and without another word, posted an official sign on the wall listing our occupancy limit as 64.

I went down to find our executive director, explained the situation, and commented that I would lead a parade comprised of the "overflow" to the fire station that night. A call to the mayor prompted the mayor to call the fire chief, who promptly called the fire marshal who grudgingly called me to rescind his order. We didn't like the overcrowding, but since we were the only shelter in the area, it was us or nothing for the displaced individuals and families seeking haven under our roof each winter evening.

We'd strive to create an atmosphere of mutual respect so peace would reign each night. We didn't frisk people. We didn't do police background checks. We admitted people under the influence of alcohol or drugs if their behavior was not disruptive. We often, despite the odds, managed to accomplish at least a minimal standard of respect and tranquility, sometimes in astounding proportions. We accomplished that remarkable goal, I believe, because we made every effort to get to know our "customers" and to acknowledge them as human beings—a rare occurrence for many homeless persons anywhere.

The PADS' model differed significantly with the few shelters in existence at the time. Most shelters were either domestic violence shelters or some form of rescue mission, run by evangelical religious groups, with many rules. Many places deny admittance to older boys (as young as 8); persons with active substance abuse problems; men, women, and intact families. Such restrictions, while on some level understandable, become barriers to the masses of un-housed adults and children. The allegedly oppressive atmosphere of some operations diminishes the already deteriorated self-worth of those forced to swallow their pride and accept Jesus in return for "two hots and a cot." Sinners deserve their fate tends to be the philosophy of some gospel mission-run shelters, at least that's the impression shared with me by those who stayed at missions.

Aurora's mission, Wayside Cross, stopped calling themselves a shelter, to their credit, and described their purpose as a religious residential program for men troubled by addictions. They have a separate program for women with children (boys have to be younger than 8-years old.) Their rules and expectations create a different kind of atmosphere than I am comfortable with, and yet I know it works for many persons who are ready for this intensely religion-based approach to sobriety.

My visits to Wayside and other missions left me with an uneasy feeling—that getting a roof over one's head depended on one's ability to accept Jesus—ready or not. For those not willing or able to make the leap of faith (assuming Christianity), they had to be actors/phonies or desperately cold. Feedback from guys I got to know who had stayed at missions in other parts of the country validated my impression. Sadly, exceptions, while I hope they exist, are probably rare.

Perhaps in response to the restrictive atmosphere predominant in some mission/shelters of the mid-20th century, another model evolved—hospitality-based, to embrace those rejected by other shelters and society in general. Fewer limitations, including on the population they were willing to serve, distinguished this "brand" from the gospel missions.

The PADS shelter uses what has become an "industry" model—volunteers from faith communities take turns during winter months providing staff, food, and supplies to augment the very inadequate government stipend to operate the shelter. Paid shelter staff, the ones who are theoretically supposed to know what is going on, are usually outnumbered a hundred to one by overnight guests. Not a good formula for success…but the tremendous contributions of volunteers combined with an incredibly dedicated staff, extraordinary cooperation from most of the guests, noteworthy effort from human service and medical personnel, and lots of help from above made doing the impossible at least somewhat possible.

Story Telling Opportunity Comes My Way

After years of seeking comprehensive, accurate portrayals about homelessness by credible journalists, I received a mixed blessing: time to write this book. For me, an unexpected separation in January 2003 from the job I loved gave me plenty of time to write and a strong reason to do so—I needed therapeutic activity and I also have a strong desire to clear up common misconceptions and myths about the people I have spent many years getting to know—homeless adults and children.

My Amazon.com research confirmed what I figured—no one from my standpoint, with close to 20 years of working with homeless people, had written a non-fiction book about homelessness. This book gave me something significant to sink my teeth into while waiting for my next career (Ch. 27) to get off the ground, and will hopefully serve to depict some misunderstood people—"the homeless"—as they really are, people like you and me who are now in a deep hole called homelessness. In talking with people of all walks of life about homelessness, one thing was perfectly clear to me: If you didn't have any reason to get to know people in homeless situations, you probably didn't begin to understand the breath and depth or the multitude of causes of homelessness. Even I, with years of experience running a shelter, found myself amazed, often pleasantly surprised, with the level of humanity I encountered.

Stories flowed, telling themselves—different but the same. Adults and children, lovable and unlovable people, tagged with the same label, "homeless." The stories, while powerful on their own, reflect some systemic realities common to homeless persons across the land. I am compelled to comment about these realities throughout this book. Interwoven between or added at the end of chapters are my observations, painfully passionate, that point out what I have come to believe are flaws in society, government and/or religious institutions that perpetuate or exacerbate homelessness.

My "Co-Stars"

In addition to my own observations and learning process that brought these shortcomings to light, I have spent immeasurable hours in conversations with a wide range of homeless men, women and children, some who felt free to share their painful episodes with me in great detail. I can't but speak out about injustices. I owe it to those I have met who are mostly denied a voice of their own. I've never been accused of being too subtle...

Of the thousands of homeless people I had the honor to get to know in my years "in the business," not one was the same as the other. I would constantly be surprised, sometimes shocked, often heart-warmed, at the person behind the label "homeless." Stereotypes I held flew out the window. As intriguing as I found the debunking of myths surrounding homeless persons, this book will hopefully begin to accomplish the same for others.

When I first started writing, my hopes were meager—seeking the healing benefit of sharing something important, in this case lives of people who have touched me deeply. Painfully dismissed from my longtime and all-engrossing job of shelter director, I struggled with remembering and wanting to forget the mosaic image imbedded in my head and heart. I found I could not forget the lives that were so much a part of my life.

As I pondered what to write and why I should write, I realized that no one could write a book as I could. At least no one had. No time, no energy left over after 12-hour days filled with drama and challenges. No perspective or ability to step outside the arena and look back in with a sense of perception that enables one to appreciate the goodness that threads through the lunacy. Most importantly, the story needs to be told in order to give voice to the voiceless. I am one of those ridiculous eternal optimists—I believe things can change for the better.

30

Government: Villain and Supporter

Hopefully I will be able to accurately depict the often-insane systemic causes of homelessness. People just like you[4] and I have found themselves in one of the most frustrating situations in American life—pushed off the table of prosperity like crumbs, with little hope at regaining the piece of the American dream central to our nation's legacy. Often, if not the direct cause of homelessness, government policies contribute significantly and/or perpetuate the situation.

Despite what may seem like my rantings at the "haves" of our country, I have had the benefit of getting to know many people of extreme wealth—and many are kind, well-intentioned citizens who contribute much to improving society, by donating sizable amounts of money and also giving of their time and talents. I have also come to know and respect politicians on both sides of the aisle who care deeply about the plight of the "have-nots," even though hampered by leadership's dismissal of this perceived insignificant, non-voting population. Modern presidents of both parties left this nation with a Civil War-sized division spread throughout every state of the Union— fatalities of poverty and homelessness on one side, those who still have resources on the other.

The Tragic Plot

A major disconnect exists—one which keeps us from developing the solutions needed to eradicate homelessness, a daunting, but doable, task. When pitted against government spending priorities, our nation's ability and/or willingness to systemically seek solutions to homelessness dwindles.

- Housing assistance programs with a successful track record are routinely decimated by budget cuts, forcing people to the streets.
- Funding reductions force drastic personnel cuts rendering meaningful social service programs ineffective.
- Government policies place harsh restrictions on access to support that could help vulnerable people, and create obstacles to make getting help difficult, if not impossible.
- State and local governments decry federal budget cuts as they slash human service spending, leaving beleaguered non-profit leaders few options but to pass the cuts on to their clients through service and staff cuts.
- Access to life-saving resources—health care, substance abuse treatment, counseling—gets harder for those who need it most.

The result is that during this year over 1% of this nation's population, 3.5 million individuals and family members, will find themselves homeless in this land of plenty. Millions more teeter at the edge of homelessness. It is inexcusable, in the richest country in the history of this world, especially as you get to know the human side of the suffering and the toll it takes on the individuals, their loved ones and their communities.

For those who wonder how homelessness happens to so many people, some commonalities exist. Becoming homeless takes many roads, often winding around and crossing over the same paths, including:

- Family loyalty, love and/or resources failed when a person's addictions, medical crises, mental illness and/or any combination of personal struggles become too overwhelming.
- Relationships, seemingly made in heaven, find their way to hell, either destroying those most vulnerable or shattering future dreams, thus creating painfully real nightmares.
- Job loss, which destroys the household income stream, upends the most-often fragile economic stability, adding emotional turmoil and all that accompanies that condition.
- Health problems, especially for the uninsured or underinsured, tend to be the fast track to homelessness.
- Poor health—caused by a combination of destructive choices, vulnerable genetics, limited healthy options, being in the wrong place at the wrong time, or a detrimental dose of all of the above—can hasten the trip to homelessness.
- For those lacking insurance, access to quality medical care has become rare at best, inadequate to non-existent at worst.
- A person's bad choices, mistakes, and/or criminal acts become permanently etched on one's record of life and haunt the wrongdoer at every turn, becoming significant barriers to attaining decent housing or sustainable employment.
- Systemic homelessness affects some people in foster home placements, group homes and correctional facilities. They leave a structured environment, often inadequately prepared for survival in a demanding society. When their meager life skills fail, they often hit the streets, often soon "recycled" to institutions.
- Credit problems, inopportune pregnancies, poor choices of business or marriage partners, ill-chosen words in an argument

with a boss or a police officer, all can swirl around into an eddy that sucks the possibilities of self-sufficiency from a person who may be prone to misguided behavior.

• Disasters—fire, floods, hurricanes and tornadoes—disrupt those fragilely housed, casting them into the storm of dependence on others until tensions unravel the temporary arrangements.

• Skewed economics—jobs paying less than a living wage, unaffordable and substandard housing, costly or non-existent transportation for impoverished workers—contribute significantly to root causes of homelessness.

• Unscrupulous employers, mortgage lenders, landlords and loan companies take unfair advantage of people with fragile financial resources.

• "Self-medicating," the abuse of alcohol and/or drugs, to numb physical and/or mental pain often is often the only "solution" to untreated physical or mental conditions.

• Addictions, in addition to the pain-killing craving of those self-medicating, spiral freely on the streets and in crack houses. Drugs and alcohol are readily available.

• To any or all of the above maladies, add pervasive poverty and a critical shortage of housing options for even those with moderate incomes, and homelessness lurks right around the corner.

The slide from self-sufficiency to homelessness is much more complex than the above reasons, but those elements commonly afflict most persons in homeless situations. Those unpleasant realities should not obscure the human worth of men, women and children without a place to call home, but they often do. Government policies, or lack thereof, often create a "slippery slope" for those most vulnerable. The "hand-up, not hand out" philosophy sounds good, but often keeps people in the vicious cycle of homelessness longer than necessary. Increasingly, government requirements for shelters and programs serving homeless persons force a "skim the cream from the top" mentality so the agency can meet tougher performance standards. Those who sink to the bottom—those with hard-to-treat mental illnesses, addictions, or combinations thereof—are shunned.

Fading Legacy of Inspiring Performers

Sadly, voices to speak out on behalf of those in need of help continue to fade—falling away to cynicism, death, or hopelessness. My mentor and hero, Mitch Snyder, died in 1990. Snyder made his mark on the federal government's policies for homelessness when it was still possible to shame the government into action. John Donahue, head of the Chicago Coalition for the Homeless, died in 2003, following a decade of significant presence in compassion-fatigued Chicago. His predecessor, Les Brown, whose decades long fight for justice for Chicago's mostly unloved homeless population despite a longtime struggle with life threatening diseases, died in 2005. Barb Brent, who dared to start the PADS program in affluent DuPage County (IL) before community leaders were ready to acknowledge homelessness, died in 2004, after suffering physical and economic pain for many years. Dr. Holly Kabakovich, a local doc and treasured friend, started an all-volunteer medical clinic at Hesed House in 1991, but died suddenly in 1995 at 36.

Thanks to inspiration from my friends and mentors, and most of all, from my homeless brothers and sisters, my voice, I hope, will continue resonating. My mission is to encourage and challenge those who care, those who think they'd like to care, those too afraid to care, and those who refuse to care. My challenge is simply to ask that you *cross the line* into the world of un-housed, unloved, unimportant persons. Experience, explore, and/or educate yourself about homelessness in your community. You will likely be richer because of it.

Front Row Seat

Come with me. Venture across the line that may be keeping you apart from guys like John…

Marines stand tall, proud of being in the Corps, until they fall like John did, from alcohol abuse. He slurred his words and snarled impatiently at others' stupidity. Usually a happy drunk, he rarely caused problems other than needing someone to carry him to his spot on the floor where he would sleep off his overindulgence. He was, at first glance to the unknowing volunteer or staff, the same as the other drunks who came through our shelter—staggering, reeking of booze and cigarettes, loud when regaling his tablemates with stories of his Marine days.

John's almost toothless smile, his boyish friendly face, belied the pain he carried and attempted to drown with copious amounts of the cheapest alcohol he could buy. A lifetime "Aurora-boy," John spent several years homeless following a divorce that was by his admission alcohol related. He, when not "enchanted" (my euphemism for drunk), would be helpful and even act as an unofficial host for new arrivals.

Because we opened at 7 p.m. and closed at 7 a.m. (due to our dependence on volunteers with demanding schedules), most guests had way too much free time and too little constructive opportunities for worthwhile activities. Weekends were particularly difficult because of a lack of places open to homeless persons. That combination of no place to go and too much time is lethal for addicts, as John proved one spring day…

My Saturday afternoons, when our offices were closed and I could justify putting my over-taxed phone on mute to get some paperwork done, were precious, and frequently quiet and productive. Not this one Saturday in March. I was disturbed by one of our regulars, Jim, who had raced up to my office after convincing the person who had answered the door that a life-threatening emergency occurred. He quickly described what happened: a group of our guys were sitting in a field adjacent to our property, drinking and smoking. The weeds caught fire, evidently from a cigarette or match, and John, who had passed out, was caught in the flames. I immediately called 9-1-1 and raced outside.

The fire trucks and ambulance arrived shortly after I came upon the grizzly scene—John lying on the ground, his jeans below his knees burned through to his flesh and bone. I could barely register the shocking scene. The fire extinguished, the paramedics sped to the hospital with this pathetic charred body. The rest of the guys stood silently until the sirens faded in the distance. They tried to piece together what happened to their friend. They offered lame excuses, "We were all drinking, we didn't notice John sleeping in the grass…" and we all tried to process this horror. Those of us who knew how to pray did so, hoping against hope that John would not die before reaching the hospital.

After extensive medical care, lengthy rehabilitation, and an unplanned alcohol treatment program consisting of months in a physical rehab facility, John miraculously walked again, albeit painfully. Recognizing his good fortune, he soon became a faithful volunteer in our daytime drop-in center. His scarred legs became his medal of honor—and his license to preach sobriety to anyone who he thought needed it. John, who managed to find a small affordable apartment, realized that he had been given a second chance for a reason. He works hard at sobriety, and is determined to support others in their quest for addiction-free living.

Throughout his lengthy rehab, John had scads of visitors and countless letters from guests, staff and volunteers to encourage him. Perhaps those supports, combined with a newly rediscovered spirituality, kept him strong during this arduous episode. Something did—beyond what he described as incredible medical care—and his gift of new life would allow him to be a beacon of hope to others in similarly hopeless situations.

Underlying Theme: Hope

John's story shows how homelessness, at best, is a convoluted situation that does not happen in a vacuum (Ch.26). Although causes of this socio-economic condition require attention by policy-makers, this book will not pretend to explore in depth the sociological and economic complexities of homelessness and poverty but rather to depict vignettes of people mired in these conditions. My forthright intent—motivate more individuals to see beyond the discouraging myths of "the homeless" by experiencing a more hopeful glimpse into the persons behind the label. This insight may possibly encourage more people to cross the line separating the domiciled "haves" and the undomiciled "have-nots."

Crossing the line is no easy task. Some persons avoid homeless people like the plague, fearing it as a contagious disease. Myths about homeless people abound—crack-crazed crazies wielding knives and other weapons, drunk and slobbering grizzled old men standing under bridges and in alleys huddled around warming barrels, babbling and erratically functioning men and women who don't know up from down, urchins who dart through city streets snatching wallets from unsuspecting shoppers…and while some of these images may reflect some reality somewhere, they are far from my perception of literally thousands of men, women and children who lack a place to call home who found their way to our shelters.

Other barriers are even tougher. I've found that for some with considerable wealth, homelessness is the extreme representation of poverty. Again, poverty and homelessness represent failures to be avoided and, for those with money, these conditions reflect the opposite of what they have been seeking—wealth, power, stature, and respect of those around them. Hanging around "losers" would be a waste of time. Writing a check might be the most to expect of some wealthy persons. Others scorn homelessness and those associated with this pathetic malady. Fortunately, just as with homeless persons, wealthy people don't fit the same stereotype. I have gotten to know and appreciate many people of means who literally gave the shirt and jacket off their back to their brother or sister in need.

My stories will hopefully depict men, women and children in homeless situations for who they are—at least who I got to know them to be. My eyes needed to be opened, which happened over time, despite my prejudices. I challenged thousands of ordinary, well-intentioned and fearful men and women to put their faith in action as volunteers. Often I used stories such as those in this book to build their awareness. Their heartwarming and life-sustaining response empowered them to cross that line separating them from the dispossessed in our towns. This book will hopefully inspire increased action such as:

- Accepting persons in homeless situations as human beings, deserving of respect, shelter and other assistance.
- Volunteering at or supporting a shelter or other program to assist homeless persons.
- Encouraging availability of local services (schools, health care, counseling) for homeless children and adults and/or
- Advocating for better governmental policies and priorities to reduce this solvable dilemma.

Plenty of opportunities exist to involve persons of all ages (Appendix 5) with alleviating this appalling condition that shows little sign of abating and is expending more human capital as each day passes.

Our nation is ripe for a widespread "compassion-epidemic." Resources exist. People of good will can be found in every town and city, in halls of government and in leadership positions of faith communities and corporations. Reclaiming human resources now strewn on streets of our cities and towns would restore hope, not only to those hopelessly ensconced on our streets, but more importantly to those of us fueled by a passion for peace and justice who need to see signs of hope.

Our country will benefit by a whole-hearted recommitment to millions of men, women and children who need both reasons to hope and means to reach their dreams. Their reasonable dreams include: a roof over their heads, medical care to keep them healthy, counseling and mental health services to ease their agonies, meaningful work opportunities for those capable, and respect for those who cannot be contributing members of society. Instead of angrily and grudgingly tossing crumbs of U.S. economic bounty in a less-than-half-hearted approach to ending homelessness, imagine the momentum that could be created with a holistic and well-funded commitment to putting a roof over everyone's head! The people on the streets are worth saving. Ask their loved ones. Ask those of us who have come to know them. They hang onto hope that one night they'll have a bed of their own to crawl into just like we do. We, those of us gifted with compassion, are that hope.

Stars of the "Show"

A post-shelter evening spent with former colleagues inspired me. When inquiring about some of the people I had come to know and love, I heard amazing stories about the least likely characters attaining independence. Some managed to land on their feet after incredible efforts becoming sober and/or drug-free. Some finally gained access to public housing after interminable waits on lists that held faint hope for thousands of income-challenged families and individuals. Some creatively linked up with other homeless persons to combine limited resources and avoid the life-destroying loneliness typical to shelter "alumni." Some died. Some disappeared. Some opted for the structure of institutional living found in state prisons. Some were imprisoned against their will, some unfairly. Some landed in nursing homes. For those who held on to hope and "graduated," I rejoice. For the rest, I hold them in my heart, hoping for whatever "the best" may mean.

I know that each graduate, as with those who have survived thus far, had at least one element in common—hope kept alive by someone loving and caring for him or her. Maybe someone was lucky enough to still have family or loved ones that maintained some contact. For those we saw nightly, that love came from devoted volunteers who bonded with different people staying at the shelter, spending time during the night or early morning sharing conversation and coffee. It came from dedicated staff that would go far out of their way to find resources, to offer encouragement, or to just convey care by a simple greeting. Often that love and care manifested itself in small things— a new pair of socks, a smile while serving salad, passing along a novel from one avid reader to another. The essential element of compassion—conveying care, validating one's existence—can only be done people-to-people, not mandated by government, and will foster human respect that makes life bearable. My years in this field blessed me with witnessing a rich, constant flow of hope-giving compassion.

Incredible as it may seem, courtesy and community, rarities outside shelter walls, were common inside this crowded and strange "house" where a menagerie of a hundred or more people came for safe haven each evening. Countless persons commented to me about how often they heard words like "please," "thank you" and "excuse me." Maintaining an atmosphere of respect seemed to accomplish many benefits—including a constant reminder of the worth of each person. That reminder, I believe, is essential to preserving hope in almost hopeless times and circumstances.

As wealthy gated enclaves spring up across this country, the inhabitants would do well to learn from those on our streets and in shelters who have honed the meaning of "community." When persons can live shoulder-to-shoulder, share scarce resources, offer encouraging words, extend a hand to help with matters big and small—that's community.

Paradoxically, the loss of community when a person leaves a shelter or other form of institutional living can be devastating. Although significant, moving out of the shelter means more than a loss of structure and free meals. People thrived on the quality of community living, albeit overcrowded, at our shelter. I struggled with my feelings of how we created a "good news-bad news" situation—the camaraderie common to our shelter environment restored a feeling of worthiness but probably kept people with us longer than necessary because they feared the loss of the supportive atmosphere.

The often-overlooked concept of community might explain why Ray (Ch. 25) was willing to splurge his Social Security check treating his cronies to too many rounds of beers at the local tavern instead of kicking back with a six-pack by himself under a bridge. He, as well as his drinking buddies, enjoyed spending time together, a concept not limited to the well heeled. Dennis, the hapless, lovable creature (Ch.18), despite his multiple mental and physical limitations, would tell me, "I like my place but I miss everyone here, and no one gives me chocolate chip cookies." It's a common lament among housed and homeless. We long for love, or at least involvement in a community that knows and cares whether we come home at night. The home can be a mansion, a shelter or something in-between.

My immeasurable treasure throughout this most challenging shelter director career will always be my memory of love shared by staff members, volunteers, with, by and from the shelter residents themselves. That love was shared in big and little ways. It always involved sacrifice. It required unimaginable patience. It came from the least-likely sources. Without that love, survival was impossible. With it, anything was possible.

That love was never one-sided. Whatever I managed to give to the masses of housing and hope-deprived individuals was only because I felt the love they had for me. It is a strange concept to try to describe in words. It defies the stereotypes prevalent in our egocentric material-driven society.

Giving and getting back, it's why some people are really happy and some are not. I know—I crossed that once-unimaginable line. The price of happiness is well worth it!

7. Going Over the Line—An Overture

OK, just to be clear—not everyone in a shelter has endearing qualities, just as not everyone in a neighborhood is likable.

Anyone stepping into a shelter would probably benefit by some introspection. My encounters working with homeless people has been a mixed bag—but not so much for qualities the homeless people have, but more because of my limitations. Ten very helpful lessons are offered for those thinking of volunteering at a shelter as well as for those with some experience who might want to tweak their understanding...

LESSON 1—PREJUDICES—know thyself!

It's hard for me to admit, as it is for most people, that I have my inexplicable prejudices, which often get in the way of getting to know someone in a positive way. It's been fascinating for me to see how I've dealt with that humbling reality during my years as a shelter director.

I'm prejudiced against anyone who says they're not prejudiced. I painfully became aware of my racial prejudices when I first encountered racially mixed couples and/or large black men who come out of prison. As I struggled with that shortcoming, I realized that my childhood was strewn with negative racial images—from all-too-common slurs from family members to the racially charged tumult of the '60s.

Add to my "prejudice list" was anyone who comes out of prison; mentally-ill drug addicts; sex offenders; slobbering drunks (men and women); clean-cut too-good-to-be-true looking men; and holy-rollers. I'm sure the list could be longer, but you get the idea—lots of people who came to our shelter annoyed me or frightened me, until I let myself get to know them. Being aware of what triggers your anxiety and why helps you balance your prejudices against unfairly discriminating against someone.

LESSON 2—RESPECT AND STREET-SMARTS

A handful of characters remained on my "I don't trust you as far as I can throw an elephant" list, some for good reason, but I struggled to treat everyone with respect. Respect can diffuse a lot of tension between staff/volunteers and the homeless clients, whom we referred to as guests.

41

Fortunately, I also have a healthy dose of street smarts augmented by a pretty good radar—handy when facing a large number of people every day and night. Sometimes my radar detected trouble before it started. My trick was to balance awareness of my prejudices with my innate sense of someone, which was even more of a trick when faced with not only a room full of homeless persons, but a crew of volunteers, and the inevitable unexpected crisis that kept things unpredictable. Most volunteers can prevail with more compassion than street smarts, but staff definitely needs that sixth sense to notice problems before they explode…

LESSON 3 – TROUBLE: OFTEN NOT WHERE YOU THINK

While unknowing spectators would automatically look to the throng coming in our door as trouble, wiser persons would be open to less obvious possibilities. Fortunately, I was blessed with staff that usually possessed an uncanny ability at spotting potential trouble…

My first full-time assistant, Harry was a large man, pleasantly disarming and not macho—good traits when dealing with people who feel threatened or vulnerable. We worked well together. I felt he caught on quickly to the tricks of keeping things smooth despite endless possibilities for disaster. He was good at being consistent with the guests and letting them know what the limits were. They tended to respect him.

One Saturday night while working together, Harry noticed a new guy come in and pulled him aside to register him. Since the man spoke no English and Harry spoke no Spanish, Harry inquired among the volunteers for someone bilingual. "Joe," a new volunteer, offered to translate, helping Harry obtain the minimal information needed (name, birth date, etc.) and began to go over the few rules we had with "Pedro."

When Harry got to the "no guns or knives" section, he picked up some tacit vibration between Pedro and Joe. Harry inquired of Joe as to the nature of the confusion and Joe said that since Pedro was only passing through, he told Pedro that it was okay to keep his gun. *Yikes!* Harry nicely, but firmly, indicated that this was not okay, but Joe seemed to side strongly with his new "keep the gun" policy.

Not wanting to create a scene in the middle of the dining room filled with 80 or so other people, needing some higher authority, and being appropriately frightened at the possibility of a total stranger having a gun, Harry sought me out. I was in the kitchen, blissfully chatting with volunteers.

A visibly nervous Harry brought Joe and Pedro in, asking me for a moment, and explained the situation. I probably gave one of my famous

"You've got to be kidding" looks to Joe and asked Pedro for the gun. Pedro gingerly pulled it out and I bravely but carefully took it—a .45. I've had limited contact with guns but I knew the basics—don't pull the trigger, or go anywhere near it.

I then clearly reiterated our long-standing and very wise policy—no weapons. Since Pedro wanted to keep his weapon, this unfortunately would not be the place for him. The kitchen door, right behind us, provided him a convenient place to depart. Joe strenuously objected, and I vehemently told him to shut his mouth. Pedro caught the drift and headed for the door. I used my very limited Spanish, "¡Adios, hasta pronto! Gracias..." and bid him farewell. As he was going out the door, I handed him his gun as I had promised, and again said adios.

He caught on way faster than Joe, this first-time volunteer here with his wife. I turned to Joe and said, "You're fired!" or something similar, then called 9-1-1. I alerted the police to Pedro's description, that he had a gun, and added that I had a potential problem with a volunteer I was kicking off the property.

Joe hollered in to his wife who was serving food in the dining room, "Honey, can you believe it? She's kicking me out!" The police arrived quickly and reinforced my authority with Clueless Joe. Harry breathed a sigh of relief when the police said they had picked up Pedro as he was walking down our driveway. Joe left, with his wife, and never came back. All goes to show that even volunteers can be a problem.

LESSON 4—FAITH-FILLED HUMAN TIES BIND US

In a program with more than 60 faith communities who all brought volunteers that they've organized for their monthly turn working at the shelter, you're bound to have some weirdoes like Joe. We estimated over 5,000 volunteers—a conservative calculation. Coordinators from each congregation were responsible for recruiting and supervising their crew. We were just happy for (almost) anyone who showed up to help.

Across the board, the volunteers were a wonderful group. Over the years, I came to know some of them well. They provided a huge job benefit; a constant reminder that some people "cared enough to send their very best"— themselves.

Inspiring reasons fueled their dedicated involvement. Practically all of them knew someone who is, was or could be homeless. The stories trickled out—painfully private tales of a loved one's alcoholism, drug addiction, mental illness, prison, domestic violence and more. Many expressed that at least they were doing something to help someone, and that maybe someone was doing the same for their loved one. Their passion made it possible for them to sacrifice far beyond even unreasonable expectations.

They faithfully show up, despite Illinois' horrendous winter weather or their painful personal storms. They prepare and serve nourishing and delicious food to a varying size crowd (60-150). They go out of their way to solicit new boots or gym shoes and lovingly distribute them to guys who couldn't remember having a new pair of shoes, much less a pair that fit. They shake down donors, docs, corporations and Santa Claus. They respond at a moment's notice to an urgent need for people, supplies, or money. And, perhaps most incredibly, they do all this and more with smiles and heartfelt love. Many have done this for 20 years or more.

LESSON 5 — EVERYONE CAN GIVE

Volunteers, both regulars and first-timers, would plunge in among 100-some strangers, offer loving hospitality in an endless variety of unique ways, prepare and serve gourmet meals with class and smiles, even for the most difficult to approach guest. They joke and sympathize. They overlook surliness, realizing that life on the streets doesn't create bliss. They relieve harried parents of crying babies or high-maintenance toddlers, giving a few moments of peace with someone reliable caring for their child.

Volunteers at our shelter tended to cross the range of investment banker and corporate lawyer to stay-at-home mom and crippled grandma. A few very special kids came with parents who had obviously prepared their offspring well—don't gawk, don't put yourself in compromising situations, offer your best no matter what.

LESSON 6 — SOME KIDS ARE AWESOME

Some kids could handle the place on their own. I had the pleasure of watching them from the first time they came and gauging their progress over my 13-year stint. I knew when my favorite kids came in, touring a group of new volunteers, I could depend on these "super" kids to properly orient the adults. They'd march them into the men's sleeping area, a huge room with a very specific order to laying out the pads (or mass confusion would result at the worst possible time), and the kid/crew chief would make sure things were done right.

LESSON 7 – KIDS OFFER US ALL HOPE

Kids provided me with immense hope. For the thousands of kids who came through as volunteers during my years at the shelter, I realized that as they got older, they would understand the absurdity of homelessness and poverty caused by injustice and economic inequity. Since kids would be the policy makers of tomorrow, I felt it a tremendous opportunity to help them comprehend these basic concepts.

An astute volunteer and friend, Jeff Leavey, also saw that potential. Jeff, a high school sociology teacher from up the river in posh St. Charles, contacted me in 1990 to inquire about the possibility of bringing a small group of his students down once a week to volunteer. He wanted to do it as part of their learning experience—he was teaching a unit on poverty and homelessness in his sociology class. Jeff got it—it was clear even before I met him in person.

Over my 13 years at the shelter, Jeff rarely missed a week with his class. Despite the excuses he could use, "I'm busy at home," "I'm coaching cross country so I'm too busy," "I've got to walk my crazy beagle," or any other plausible reason, Jeff would show up with his band of mostly affluent kids who had probably never seen a poor person, much less a room filled with homeless men, women and children. Jeff would tour the anxiety-filled kids, and then assign them to a post, taking care to switch them off so they could sample several jobs.

Jeff often laughed with me about the ride down to the shelter, as kids lost their ability to mask their fear of driving *into* Aurora, infamous for gang violence, not to mention heading to a homeless shelter. You could see it in their faces as they shuffled in the kitchen door, circled around Jeff like baby ducks. You could also see their faces as they became more relaxed. By their 8:30 departure time, they hid like fleas on a dog, having fun and hoping to avoid discovery.

As part of their class requirements, Jeff wanted them to make observations and to process those observations with knowledge. He left the "happening" up to individuals. Some kids would be engrossed in conversation with adults staying at the shelter. Others would have our kids involved in either homework or some quiet game. Even the introverts would have an opportunity to feel good about their experience by helping the volunteers clean up the kitchen.

One night, a particularly large group came with Jeff. He joked that no kids remained in St. Charles. He usually avoided bringing large groups because the shelter was always overcrowded—with guests and volunteers—and having kids stand around with nothing to do was not smart for many reasons. I cringed, but knew we could get creative.

I had just received my long-awaited copy of a poignant new book, *Where Can I Build My Volcano?*[5], written by a friend of mine, Pat Van Doren. This children's book, based on true encounters with a homeless girl and her mother, reflected stories Pat observed while covering the shelter as a photojournalist or later, while hanging around the shelter as my friend, concerned human being and board member.

After reading Pat's book, which features a kind artist's rendering of my office on the cover, I was anxious to share it with anyone, especially the kids staying with their families at our shelter. I asked Jeff's group if someone liked reading stories to kids, figuring a great after-dinner task would be to read to our burgeoning group of young ones.

"Jenny," a rather dumpy, lost-looking teen, raised her hand somewhat apprehensively. Her friend, "Tina," also volunteered, so I pulled them into my office, which didn't begin to match the neater version on the cover, and gave them a very brief "how-to" session, including how to come get me if any of the kids were acting up. I handed Jenny the book, snagged most of our kids, and got them settled in the family sleeping area, a cramped space about 12' x 16' filled with foam sleeping pads, bags of people's belongings, and tons of unidentified items typical of messy kids' bedrooms.

Since we were quite busy that night, I didn't get to think about the kids until Jeff was gathering his scattered flock to head north. Hmmm, yeah, I remember where Jenny and Tina are, I said after a brief near-panic pause. They're reading in the family room. I offered to go get them, which Jeff willingly let me do because it involved walking through the women's sleeping area, a stuff-strewn hazardous zone on a good night.

I could hear quiet emanating from the family area, a very rare sound at this time of night. Jenny and Tina took turns reading. I subtly snuck in, sitting down behind the group of normally hyperactive kids. When Jenny's turn to read came, I was awed by her poise, her expression, and her innate ability to touch the kids with her words. Tina did fine, but Jenny was awesome!

Since they were near the end of the story and all the audience would have protested mightily if I interrupted, I figured I'd do the right thing and wait. The story obviously moved our kids—a tale similar to their lives with characters they could recognize, including me as the benevolent shelter director who allowed the girl in the story to use her office to safely store her science fair project, a volcano. The story over, I suggested the kids get ready for bed and I would send their moms down.

As we were heading up to Jeff and the rest of the group, I asked the girls how it went. Jenny, almost blissful, exclaimed, "I loved it!" Tina echoed the sentiment. I had the presence of mind to express my thanks, and to remark on how well they did reading to this oft-challenging audience. They soaked up the compliment and headed out.

Next week, I remembered to comment to Jeff about how well the girls did. He confirmed my observation about Jenny's reserved disposition, an "under-achiever" by nature. Tina was in a different category—successful at most of what she attempted. I told him about Jenny's skill in relating to the group. He later told me how much it meant to Jenny to feel a sense of accomplishment, and that it gave her courage to pursue some extra-curricular activities in drama.

LESSON 8 – HOSPITALITY HEALS WOUNDS

I don't want to accuse Jeff of picking Wednesday nights because of the likelihood of getting outstanding chocolate chip cookies, but the thought did enter my mind. Each congregation tended to bring the same menu each month, so you looked forward to different groups because of, among other things, the food. My favorite item was homemade chocolate chip cookies, and Wednesday night groups tended to all bring superb chocolate chip cookies. Jeff figured out where the volunteers "hid" my favorites and tried to deplete my stash.

Amazing to me was the quality (and quantity) of food every night. I loved hearing the stories behind the wonderfully prepared offerings: the special batch of chocolate chip cookies, made by a disabled woman who wanted to do something nice for people (besides me!); the bountiful beef stew, a special recipe devised by a now-deceased local restaurateur; or the elderly woman's holiday-of-the-month individually decorated cupcakes. It touched my heart to watch the group of volunteers who came early to make a fresh fruit salad—a rarity and favorite dish.

The volunteers, through their hospitality, conveyed more than they could realize to the "throw-aways" of today's society. Whether it was a friendly personal greeting by the registration crew, "Hi, Tony, how are you doing this month?" to "Can I refill your coffee?" to the bedraggled, worn-out elderly man quietly sitting anonymously among the crowd, the volunteers restored humanity one smile at a time.

LESSON 9 – 'DO-GOODERS' DON'T CUT IT

Helping volunteers realize that as we strive to revitalize humanity we become more human was a constant joyful challenge for my staff and me. The sanctimonious "do-gooder" attitude doesn't work. A volunteer who exudes "I'm here to take care of you, you pathetic creature, because I want to do good," sticks out like a sore thumb. They usually don't return after their first turn, if they make it through it, because some of the ugly reality—someone vomiting, bleeding, or urinating—or because it is too discomforting to know homelessness exists in this land of plenty. Ordinary "do-gooders" fit in just fine.

No one formula exists for successful volunteers—it has to be unique to each person and must be real. The kicker was when I'd hear from one of the volunteers how a guest touched their hearts by being present to them in a time of need, "Allen sat with me and picked up that I was sad. He asked what was wrong. I told him my father died last week." Actually, overcoming our need to erect barriers every time we encountered someone different could help us realize our similarities as humans.

I think that realization simmered in the back of many volunteers' (and staff, myself included) minds. One thing that either propels people into crossing the line and trying this ministry or repels them far from it is our willingness to see people without homes as humans, with baggage as we all have, maybe victims of bad luck or choices, but humans nonetheless. Some people can allow that process, sometimes painful, to happen. Some can't.

LESSON 10 – JUST DO IT!

One of my favorite post-shelter colleagues, Deb Dempsey, homeless student liaison from the Elgin U-46 School District, shares her poignant "cross the line" analogy: Crossing the line into the unknown can be a scary thing. Even scarier is when we realize the darkness may reflect our own lack of enlightenment. Some people run the other way, some stumble around knowing that the light switch is out there somewhere.

The light in my darkness still shines brightly because of the people on the other side of the line—the one I dared to cross. Their trust, their smiles, their helpfulness, their shared secrets all reinforce my belief that we are here for each other. I'm so glad I crossed the line. I'm inviting others to do likewise.

Crossing the Proverbial Line Takes Practice — and Courage

As I frequently strain to figure out why some people don't seem to get—or seem to want to understand—the realities of homelessness, I try to recall that this is an invisible but very pronounced line divides people—on one side are those who find out (painfully) that the wealth, religion and government in our country can't protect people from poverty and homelessness. They, or people they know and love, have experienced poverty and/or homelessness. For those willing to cross the line, it means inviting, or at least allowing, uneasiness that comes from acknowledging the unjust difference between the "haves" and the "have-nots."

On the other side are those who feel that their entitled lifestyle will insulate them from whatever ails the rest of the world, who may have written off a loved one who stumbled into poverty and/or homelessness, or who scorn those with no money or home. They may fear that these social and economic conditions are contagious, and that staying far away from "those people" will prevent a spread of the "destitution disease." Being aware of people suffering from too little food, no place to live, etc., also impedes one's ability to enjoy such abundance without guilt.

That line, one we all probably resisted at some point in our lives, once crossed, means we can't ignore homelessness and/or poverty any more. We would like to jump safely back into oblivion—because it's quite impossible to erase suffering faces belonging to the people you know—but the images stay with you as you enjoy a bountiful meal or comfy bed or countless other relative luxuries that typically require money to buy. For some, these distressing images can fuel not only the immediate efforts of alleviating hunger or homelessness, but propel one into advocating for systemic change.

And the unenlightened others? Many people run the other way to avoid the line. Some don't even want to know what lies on the other side, much less be involved in seeking solutions. Some fight attempts to drag them over the line. Some blissfully ignore it. Some put blinders of hatred and apathy over their myopic eyes.

Some, though, find themselves—either by fate or by unavoidable circumstances—stumbling over the line. Some long not to stay, their contentment with life as they knew it shattered. Some delude themselves with the thought that going home, back to opulence as they knew it, will cleanse their minds of the disturbing encounter. Some find themselves forever moved—and they join the not-so-silent minority in declaring homelessness and poverty "crazy." Once you have crossed the line, you don't get to go back, at least not unscathed.

Crossing the line to an awareness of homelessness puts us in painful proximity with almost 16 million people (I fear this is a conservative estimate) in this country, 12.5%, who live in an extremely vulnerable economic state, teetering frighteningly closer to the abyss of homelessness. The official category "Risk of homelessness" is an ugly place to be, especially in the 21st century. It's so easy to fall over the edge—and increasingly difficult to return to normal.

In spite of the probably eternal existence of homelessness in this country, the last 15 years of the 20th century saw a massive eradication of the oft-flimsy government safety net—programs and policies designed (theoretically) to protect vulnerable men, women and children from hunger, homelessness and/or sickness. This swerve of national priorities literally shredded any security, albeit fragile, that the economically challenged 12.5% of our country thought existed, making it even easier for some in that 12.5% to fall into the 1% category who end up homeless.

What was behind the shift of this nation's priorities? My observations, based on my experience, studies[6] and confirmed by analysis of government policies by the Office of Management and Budget (OMB) point to the time of beloved Ronald Reagan as a key factor kicking off this new approach to ending poverty as we knew it by ending poverty assistance. Reagan called it "New Federalism" and hailed it as a move to smaller government. As I review now-historic books and publications I saved from my beginning days of social service, I am astonished, yet not surprised, that the doomsday cries of advocates like my mentor Mitch Snyder and others were way more truthful than President Reagan, "With his (Reagan's) very candidacy, war was declared on the poor."

Mitch Snyder was no social scientist. He was a voice in the wilderness, especially in the inhospitable region of Washington DC. His oft' reviled activist ways were dismissed as liberal rantings. However, his sounding the alarm about pending dramatic increases to homelessness and poverty proved to be truer than even he would have believed. For those curious about past trends in government budget priorities, I recommend the book, ***Homelessness In America: A Forced March to Nowhere,*** by Mary Ellen Hombs and Mitch Snyder, Community for Creative Non-Violence, 1983. It's a scary foretelling of what we see today.

A few good, balanced modern accountings of these seismic policy shifts can be found in books by respected authors and social scientists: ***Nickel and Dimed: On (Not) Getting By in America*** by Barbara Ehrenreich, and ***The Working Poor*** by David Shipler are among my favorite recommendations.

Ehrenreich weaves fascinating yet depressing stories of her deliberate plunge into poverty with enough documentation to accurately portray lives of persons working in poverty-level jobs. She worked alongside homeless workers. Shipler clearly portrays people's experience coping with poverty, with more data, and he manages to do so comprehensively. Homelessness and working often go hand-in-hand.

What Got Me to Cross the Line?

This book only grazes over theories of social policy. Qualified, compassionate writers such as Ehrenreich and Shipler spent many years of research to document the demise of the American Way of Life. Snyder, Dorothy Day, St. Francis, and nameless others provided inspiration for me as I first ventured into the world of poverty and homelessness.

I also found myself studying and observing at the compelling academy known as UHS, Urban Homeless Shelter. My years of running obscenely massive emergency shelters—night-by-night and day-by-day listening to and observing the greatest teachers of all—women, children and men who desperately sought not just a place to sleep but also a way to hold on—gave me more than knowledge, and permanently dragged me over the proverbial line of cluelessness into painfully enlightened.

Lest readers think I'm above the rest, a disclaimer. More often than not, I'd like to forget that even those of us who think we're enlightened often contribute to the broad and narrow causes of injustice. Despite my values, I buy sweatshop clothing. I vote for the politician who turns out to be draconian in nature (and don't actively campaign against him—usually a male—or her). I support businesses known to exploit women and children. I use products manufactured by companies infamous for hazardous waste production in our country or abroad. I ignore calls for increased involvement in social justice campaigns to improve living conditions for people in other countries. I respond impatiently or imprudently to someone in my path. Despite my shortcomings, I am on the side of the line that knows better. That doesn't make me better. It makes me more responsible to do better.

PART 3—

CAPITAL STRIDES: LOTS OF SMALL STEPS MAKE THE DIFFERENCE

"Never doubt that a small, group of thoughtful, committed citizens can change the world. Indeed, it is the only thing that ever has."

Margaret Mead

8. Simon Says

*F*or someone who spent years running homeless shelters, I always maintained it was ridiculous to have them. Of course, I am enough of a realist to know that, as bizarre as it is to jam people into these inadequate, almost inhumane, places, until something eliminates the need for the sardine-like flophouses, people need somewhere to sleep.

In the mid 1980s, homelessness had become this nation's growth industry, spawning a need for emergency shelters. For someone facing the prospect of having nowhere to lay one's head, shelters are better than nothing, but in our typical American tradition we've gone overboard. To securely-housed developers and municipal planners, shelters seemed to be the economical solution to replacing affordable housing demolished in bedraggled downtowns and scruffy communities across the country. Tear 'em down and put up a parking lot, casino, strip mall...

Incredibly, shelters don't even exist in some areas. In northern Illinois, many places don't have any human shelters—homeless, domestic violence or otherwise. Many communities don't hesitate to build animal shelters but growl vociferously at the prospect of providing a safe place to sleep for two-legged creatures. Most rural and small town areas across Illinois have no emergency shelters. Chicago has 2-3 people needing a bed for every spot available. For those who have adopted the NIMBY (Not in My Back Yard) attitude, bed shortages mean nothing. For those needing a safe place to get out of the weather or to put kids to sleep, it makes for horrible choices.

How did homelessness get to be so extensive? People elect lawmakers to make things happen in local, state and federal governments. When developers and planners get ideas of spiffing up a certain area, they need to get plans approved. If they need to clear out parts of town, tearing down old buildings to put up new ones, they get it approved by lawmakers. Money talks to legislators, and in much of the development going on across the country, money is central to success. So, if some "shanty" houses and apartments over storefronts are in the way of a shiny new development project, guess who loses? Rarely is the issue of where do displaced people go even get mentioned.

Early on I figured that legislators had a lot to do with how things worked or didn't work on the streets of cities and towns across the country. I plunged into learning about political advocacy and policy making. How does it work, I anguished, and how can we make it work better for those who need it most—my homeless brothers and sisters?

I prefer to avoid reinventing the wheel—so I talk to experts. In the early '80s I began seeking out people who knew more than I about poverty and housing. I didn't like what I was learning—that government resources were being used for lots of priorities besides taking care of poor and disabled adults and children. The trend in government programs was, as I saw it, less for those who need more and more for those who could get by on their own.

That angered me enough to force me into action, so I got involved with a few organizations, including Mitch Snyder and the Community for Creative Non Violence, CCNV. I liked the idea of creative and non-violent. The first time I heard Mitch speak was at a national homebuilder's conference in DC. I invited him to come to Illinois as a part of the Statewide Housing Action Coalition's Affordable Housing week in 1988. I was chair of the event and decided Illinois could use a serious dose of passionate radical activism that made a whole lot of sense.

Mitch changed my life and my thinking about our obligations to homeless persons. It was not only inadequate to "just" provide food and shelter, the "hots and a cot" mentality, it was unjust and disrespectful. Snyder's approach to homeless people was light-years beyond where I was, but I heeded his message and example of the need for creative systemic advocacy. I deeply respected his complete commitment to his (and my) brothers and sisters on the streets. I knew I couldn't join him sleeping on heating grates but I vowed to put my considerable creative energy into advocacy projects.

One national activity that grew into fruition in the late 1980s was the "Housing NOW!" movement, which culminated in a march in Washington, DC. I became the IL chair of Housing NOW! We sent hundreds of people from IL, including a busload from Aurora and Joliet, to the October 1989 march. I went to Washington to lobby—something I never really did before. It made sense to talk to IL legislators and let them know what we wanted—housing—when do you want it? NOW!

So a delegation of a half-dozen of us met with Illinois Senator Paul Simon. Hopefully I will never forget standing there, being awed by being in the presence of this great man. I figured our troubles were soon to be over as soon as we explained what we wanted. His response to us was deeply disturbing. He said, "Until we in Washington start hearing about problems, nothing will happen. And, I have to tell you, I haven't been hearing from constituents about homelessness and affordable housing."

Argh! He of all people would be sympathetic. But there he was saying that we hadn't made a blip on the radar screen much less created enough attention to motivate our seemingly inert government into action. My resolve boiled to the top of my psyche—I vowed to do everything possible to bring these issues to everyone I can.

I used that momentum to fuel my creative juices. Some of my cohorts had no problem conspiring with me. Others thought we were nuts and drifted away. But I knew that with our shelter volunteer base of thousands of voters, mostly from Christian congregations that espouse a commitment to social justice, it would be immoral for me not to try to use our shared concern—homelessness, and myriad causes related to this issue—to challenge lawmakers to help. That common sense focus was what I liked the best about the PADS' strategy: not only do we want people to volunteer at the shelter but we also expect them to advocate ending homelessness.

My sense was that the traditional Chicago-style of marches and picketing to protest something wouldn't work outside the Windy City. Suburbanites tended to discount "big city" tactics. So I put my brain cells together with a few other creative advocates and we came up with some inspirations...

In 1991 we formed the Midwest Coalition to End Homelessness, the cumulative outgrowth of some passionate activists from Wisconsin, Ohio, Illinois, Indiana and Michigan. The group sent written pleas to foreign embassies for foreign aid. We identified about a dozen embassies, wrote letters on behalf of poor and homeless persons in the "Rust Belt" and held a well-attended press conference. The uniqueness of the event and the valid point we conveyed gained us some good headlines, but even more satisfying was the response from the Swiss embassy that indicated what a sad state of affairs when this wealthy country couldn't take care of its own:

> *"Homelessness is a tragic and enduring reality of American life, as its roots and reasons lie deep in this country's social and economic structure. However, contrary to less developed parts of the world, the United States should have the means, moral and financial, to face its problems and imbalances without resorting to financial assistance."* Jean-Jacques de Dardel, Political Counsellor, Embassy of Switzerland, 1992, (Letter to Bill Faith, Midwest Coalition Chair)

We went into the newspaper business in 1995 creating The "Chicago Sum-Times," an authentic-looking parody of the popular Chicago paper, which we distributed to hundreds of commuters and to all 455 offices of Members of Congress in DC. Our headlines, stories and pictures proclaimed the pending doom of proposed welfare and housing assistance cuts. Lest someone think this was a flimsy attempt to attract attention, the Sun-Times lawyers called us to tell us "cease and desist" representing their paper. We did, proudly.

In the midst of these demanding activities, a shelter needed to run, including raising about a million dollars a year to keep the facility operational. I knew I couldn't slack on my responsibilities and somehow I managed, overwhelming as it often seemed. But just when things couldn't get more intense, something usually did, and in August of 1993 we found ourselves seemingly over our heads in a fight for justice that wouldn't go away.

9. 'Charlie" Opens School Doors for Homeless Kids

O
ne family at our transitional shelter had come from the far eastern part of Aurora, in DuPage County, one of the wealthiest counties in the nation. The family had been doubled-up with friends, their home lost because of a divorce. They had lived that way for about 2 years, but finally the landlord caught up with them and ousted the mom and her three kids. They landed on our doorsteps because we were the only nearby shelter.

Their plight was like so many other families we saw: divorce, domestic violence, economic crisis, no credit record, no safety net from relatives, and no options but homelessness. The mom and her three school-age kids adapted to their communal living environment. As summer ended, I was deeply impressed with the kids telling me, a former teacher, how excited they were to go back to their former schools.

I knew very little about what school the kids had a right to attend, so I looked into existing laws governing educational rights of homeless students. I found the federal McKinney Act seemed to vaguely cover the topic by saying the kids could go back to their original school if feasible and if the parent requested it. This mom wanted her kids to go back to their schools because they were doing well there, the stability would help them through this difficult time, and they intended to move back there once they got their own place.

I gave the mother the Illinois State Board of Education flyer, *Lost In the Shuffle,* and she called the Indian Prairie School District 204 administrators to inform them of her desires and to make arrangements for transportation. Shortly after, she sought me out, dismayed, reporting that the school district turned her down. They referred her to the local district, Aurora West District 129. She had no objection to District 129's schools except that she wanted her kids to experience stability, not mobility. I called, but I too was firmly rebuffed.

I sought advice from other advocates I knew. Their interpretation was the kids *should* have a right, but the consensus was that this right was not clearly stated in the law. The mom told the district she had the right to send her kids there according to McKinney. They drew the line in the sand by saying they'd sue to keep her kids out. *Yikes! This was getting nasty.* We found a *pro bono* attorney to represent the family. The attorney filed a counter-suit, and the whole mess went to court.

All of this "extracurricular" activity was brewing just as I was supposed to be getting ready for the October 1st opening of our emergency shelter and the wrap-up of the always-draining Tent City season, a combination that was a full-time job and then some. This school issue forced us all to go beyond what we thought possible. Suffice it to say that the ensuing two-month legal battle was draining.

After a few days of "home-schooling" at our homeless shelter, the judge at least ruled that the district must enroll the kids and transport them to their old schools pending the outcome of the legal challenge. We garnered tons of sympathetic press and public attention. I spent my days writing press releases, making media calls, plotting activities, and, oh yeah, ordering blankets and supplies for the shelters, hiring staff, supervising our campers, and recruiting volunteers. I will never forget my capable co-workers (Ch. 31) who pitched in spectacularly to make all this possible.

In the midst of this frenetic activity, we invoked assistance from our member of Congress, Denny Hastert, (prior to his Speaker of the House days) and Denny's Chief of Staff, Scott Palmer. They didn't offer any miracles as far as the legal struggle, but they found a landlord willing to rent to the family—in the same district—which provided the salvation in this case. The judge ruled against the family on a technicality: the kids finished the school year the previous year as homeless students (by a couple days), therefore the law only provided that they could complete the year in their original schools, requiring new schools for the new year based on where they were staying.

We received the judge's ruling on Halloween. Although crestfallen, we could at least, thanks to Denny and Scott and the understanding landlord, move the family into their new apartment in that school district so their stability was maintained. *Phew!*

Standing back from the insanity, we had a revolutionary thought. This was so crazy that the best interest of children was not considered in the existing federal law. Even the school superintendent, Tom Scullen, thought the law needed revising. Kids need stability, especially when their families were undergoing the trauma of homelessness. Why not get a state law passed that improved upon the federal law?!

My familiarity with legislative advocacy was extremely minimal as was that of the rest of our group of advocates. That didn't stop us and we moved forward in our quest, gathering a legislative wish list from associates across the state, consulting with people who were trying to improve access to school for homeless students in Chicago, most notably Rene Heybach, then an attorney with the Legal Assistance Foundation's Law Project. Rene and others helped us shape the foundation for a bill by the following March. We called our newly elected Republican state representative, Tom Cross, and asked if he would be willing to sponsor this bill. His willingness was impressive, and probably bespoke his naiveté—or his complete confidence in us to pull off this impossible task.

Many people had a role in the journey of getting this bill passed. We had amazing bipartisan support in the House from the bill's sponsors, including Representatives Mary Lou Cowlishaw and Tom Cross, true compassionate Republicans from our area; along with Chicago Democrats Tom Dart, Judy Irwin and Art Turner. Despite our seemingly impossible goal, they fought hard for us and gave us advice on how to move forward.

Our small group of advocates made weekly treks three hours south to Springfield for legislative hearings, lobbying and meetings with educational staff of both parties. We relentlessly pursued legislators along the "rail" (lobbyist parlance for the area outside the house and senate chambers), restaurants, and softball fields.

Our rag-tag band of do-gooders needed to convince the members of the Statehouse that our bill was worth considering. Undoubtedly the most significant element of our unsophisticated campaign was "Charlie," the poignant image of a homeless boy, his belly hanging out, his shoes on the wrong feet, cuddling a homeless cat, with the most enchanting look on his young face. Charlie, whose mother gave unconditional blessing and permission for her child's picture to be used by us, adorned every single piece of literature we put out about the bill. We called it "Charlie's Bill" and amazingly enough, legislators referred to "Charlie's Bill," instead of HB 3244.

My esteemed friend Pat Van Doren, photojournalist responsible for capturing Charlie's image, recognized the key role Charlie could play, offering an identity to emphasize one bill among thousands considered during a legislative session. In addition to creating and producing Charlie's image for our campaign, in the midst of her busy life as a photojournalist, she recruited two other photographers, James Svehla and Karen Kerckhove, who also sympathetically covered events at Hesed House. Pat persuaded them to partner with her on a photo exhibit, *Spirit On the Streets*, in October 1993. We also created a special *1994 Spirit on the Streets* calendar (and a '95 calendar), which included the best of the exhibit photos and the legislators' birth dates, with a message encouraging calendar purchasers to send their legislators birthday cards reminding them to care about homeless people.

Throughout the often blustery early months of 1994, we would journey to Springfield, three hours south if the State Troopers, road construction and fickle Illinois weather didn't slow us down, lobby—in its various forms, drive back and run the shelter, and repeat the same activities again week after week. Grueling didn't begin to describe the ordeal, but we had to be there—trouble was we had to be there—at the shelter, too.

"Charlie's Bill" made it through the House, thanks to some steadfast support from our amazed cadre of legislators who witnessed us navigating the confusing maze of policy making. Pat optimistically figured we'd be celebrating passage of Charlie's Bill through the Senate at the same time she and her photo-buddies would be displaying their impressive *Spirit On the Streets* exhibit at the Capitol. Her optimism aside, we dug into what would be an arduous battle getting the bill even considered in the Senate.

Thanks to the political savvy and connections of our group we were able to land some key Senate sponsors, including the lovable Aldo DeAngelis, a Republican Assistant Majority leader from the south Chicagoland suburbs. Aldo must have promised his first-born, his golf clubs or to cook one of his famous gourmet Italian dinners to get the bill through the renowned bottleneck of legislative doom controlled by Senator "Pate" Philip, an immensely powerful DuPage County Republican who was close friends with the Regional Superintendent of Schools whose territory included Indian Prairie School District 204, our battleground.

How Pate ever agreed to let our bill be heard, much less even be thought about, is a story I hope I hear in whatever version of life-after-death I make it to. Again, the story has so many ups and downs, crises and miracles, and surprise twists that it could make its own thick tome. So, as our photo-friends were hanging their poignant portraits of our homeless friends in the hallowed halls of the IL Statehouse, the Senate voted unanimously to approve Charlie's Bill in May 1994. We did it! Or so we thought...

The legislative process is never over, but we didn't know that then. We basked in victory, stunned that this fairly revolutionary piece of legislation made it through, much less in the first try. It would be impossible to cite the legislators whose significant efforts made this bill reality. Thousands of volunteers, homeless persons and ordinary citizens also called, wrote and otherwise offered support throughout this endeavor.

10. Illinois' Seeds Yield Bountiful Harvest

Shortly after Charlie's bill was signed, some people in Washington we had consulted, including coordinators from across the country responsible for their states' efforts to educate homeless students, invited us East. "How did you get that bill passed?" they asked with no small bit of jealous astonishment echoing in their voices. They listened to the tale of Charlie's role, improbable legislative support, and seemingly miraculous occurrences.

Their wise consensus was that their legislators were not as "crazy" as Illinois lawmakers, nor did anyone think they'd succeed in the labor-intensive process of getting massive support for homeless kids to get into school. Eventually, the hope of the state coordinators, who comprised a fairly low profile organization called the National Association for the Education of Homeless Children and Youth, was to include some provisions of the Illinois bill the next time the McKinney Education for Homeless Children bill came up for reauthorization in Congress, scheduled for 1998.

The year following passage of Charlie's Bill offered some alarming diversions from the never-quiet life at the shelter. As we geared up for the reauthorization push, Congress' devised a plan to eliminate all funding for McKinney programs in 1995, including the education component, at the time a paltry $28.8 million for the entire nation. My respected colleague in DC, Barbara Duffield, called me with this news. I knew I needed to pull out all stops. That potential disaster (which would have yanked Charlie's Bill back in the statehouse for revocation faster than I can type) threatened everything we worked for and everything we hoped for in the future reauthorization of McKinney. I placed a desperate call to Rep. Mary Lou Cowlishaw at home, something I never did before, to ask her help.

I explained the situation to which she immediately reacted like a mother bear watching her cub Charlie under attack! She promised to call me right back after she called "Harris," none other than the esteemed Harris Fawell, Congressman representing Mary Lou's home district Naperville. This Republican legislator evidently responded favorably, calling in some favor or something, because very soon after that the threat was removed.

In the meantime we had been encouraging our thousands of volunteers to fax messages to their Members of Congress, so much so that Denny Hastert sent one of his staff to ask us to STOP! UNCLE! You won. OK, that's more like it...homeless kids should count in Congress. Many people across the nation added their voices to this campaign, an effort capably headed by my friend Barbara, then with the National Coalition for the Homeless, an advocacy group in DC.

The two of us had the pleasure of working together over those exciting years, both of us passionate about true solutions to homelessness and both of us feeling a desperate need to do something to get the attention of Congress on behalf of homeless kids and their families. Our challenge: how to do it without endangering the small progress we had made on issues, without appearing to be wild-eyed radicals, without causing a seismic and tragic shift in Congress to further reduce the inadequate but life-sustaining housing and assistance for homeless adults and kids.

Barbara and I shared the same frustration—how to get Congress aware of homelessness and poverty when they seemed consumed by myriad issues, including what turned out to be the nastiest phase of politics in history, President Clinton's sex scandal. The political arena provided stiff competition, but *"Never doubt that a small, group of thoughtful, committed citizens can change the world. Indeed, it is the only thing that ever has,"* a humbling, but inspiring reminder from Margaret Mead, an enlightened 20th Century anthropologist. Sadly, our efforts to get Congress to improve the McKinney Education for Homeless Children and Youth program were faltering, for one main reason, Congress was preoccupied with other activities and shelved the reauthorization process.

Seemingly out of the blue, Rep. Mary Lou Cowlishaw called me to offer some help getting "a champion for homeless children in Washington DC." Her proposal was for us to jointly invite newly elected Congresswoman Judy Biggert, who took the place of retired Harris Fawell, to visit Hesed House and to ask her to help homeless kids from her position in DC. Wow! Mary Lou arranged for me to meet Judy at her office, drive the Congresswoman to Hesed House, and let us do our magic. We did a major sprucing up at Hesed House. I even cleaned up my Saturn wagon! I headed over to Naperville, not wanting to hope that this encounter could be the breakthrough we needed.

Mrs. Biggert was as gracious as can be. Her chief of staff, Kathleen Lydon, followed in her car. As I drove toward my home-away-from home, Hesed House, I began explaining homelessness, answering questions and offering stories. Judy and Kathy toured the entire facility, even venturing out to the mid-July steamy Tent City in our back yard. When we concluded the tour, we sat down and Judy asked, "So, what can I do to help?"

I knew she wasn't asking a rhetorical question, so I simply replied, "Get a version of the Illinois Education for Homeless Children Act, Charlie's Bill, passed on the national level." Might as well go for broke! I assuredly offered national support from people who felt as strongly as we did about this issue, knowing my buddy Barbara would be able to deliver that essential element. Judy agreed to lead the charge, and offered to send her legislative director, Jim Brown, to tour Hesed and talk over details as soon as he could come out.

Jim, from all appearances was a very young conservative Republican, with no prior experience touring homeless shelters, much less discussing issues pertaining to homeless students' educational needs. He was so affected by his tour and visit that he fervently apologized for the limousine that was waiting to return him to the airport. We assured him that limousines often parked in our lot—because guys who lived here drove them!

Shortly after that landmark visit, Barbara and I germinated an idea to generate visibility for our ambitious campaign. We devised a plan to use packets of forget-me-not flower seeds to call attention to the needs of homeless kids. We confidently figured that we could get someone to donate thousands of packets of forget-me-not seeds; we'd specially mark them with a message "Forget-Me-Not, Help Homeless Kids Blossom." Our thousands of allies across the country could enclose the packets with their letter to their Congressperson, and we'd have a lobby day, with homeless kids and their supporters talking face to face. Thus was born the "Forget Me Not, Help Homeless Kids Blossom" campaign.

The nice thing about working with Barbara is that she not only does what she says she'll do, she always does more. It keeps me hopping! We strategized: our timeframe—TOO SHORT—our resources—TOO SCARCE—our constituents—TOO BUSY WITH HOMELESSNESS IN FRONT OF THEM—our legislative supporters—TOO FEW—so we figured we better get going.

I was confident I could get seed packets because my good friends Gary and Donna Hartman of Geneva Flower Farm always could be counted on to help. I quickly called Gary and asked if he knew whom we could go to for our mission. He offered horticultural reality to say that it was getting beyond seed-planting time but he'd call Anna Ball, of Ball Seed Company fame. Yeah, that will do!

Gary called back to give me George Ball's number. He was president of Burpee Seeds. I got through to him, explained what we were doing, and he asked, "How many packs?" Well, that was something Barbara and I never discussed, so I grabbed the number 5,000 and he said it would take awhile, a few days, but he'd do it. He wanted me to send the proposed design for the label and he'd see to it that the seeds would be sent out as soon as possible. Wow! That worked.

Other pieces of our plan had similar success, relatively speaking. I called Denny Hastert's office to see what we needed to do to get a room in one of the House Office Buildings in mid-September. Barbara used her contacts to line up speakers, food, and other essentials. She put the word out to DC area shelters and programs for homeless kids, asking them to participate in this event. We worked with other advocates and steadfast supporters who contributed key elements to our plan.

We invited legislators who had seemed supportive of our relatively minor issue in the past. Republicans, Democrats. Scheduling, a logistical nightmare, but we lined up a few brave souls willing to participate. Reps. Biggert and Louise Slaughter (D-NY) committed to participate. Barbara used and abused her agency's interns, her spouse, her friends, and anyone she could think of to pull this impossible event off. I did what I could from the middle of the country.

With several calls and faxes between Barbara, Jim and me, the crux of a bill was crafted. On September 21, the day before our event, our champion, Congresswoman Judy Biggert, introduced the Stewart B. McKinney Homeless Education Assistance Improvements Act of 1999 in Congress. I couldn't believe it! Even though we had much ground to cover, we had made it this far, significant progress in my mind.

Soon it was September 22, the date of our event. Kids from shelters and schools piled off buses and filled our 200 seats in the huge event room in the Cannon Office Building. Some media coverage was present. Representatives Biggert and Slaughter and advocates spoke of the importance of remembering homeless families and the need to improve access to education for the estimated 1 million homeless kids in the nation. (We later figured too many adult "talking heads," an adjustment we made for subsequent events.) Following the rousing gathering, kids and their chaperones roamed halls of Congress, delivering packets of seeds, urging support of our meager "flower roots" campaign.

Our ferocious momentum was momentarily derailed when the legislative clock ran out on the reauthorization process. Undeterred, we planned a bigger and better "Forget-Me-Not" event for 2000. Mrs. Biggert remained committed and our unlikely enthusiast was none other than Jim Brown who developed the unfathomable alliance with his polar opposite, Barbara Duffield. Whatever works was my thinking...In the meantime, forget-me-not seed packets by the thousands made their way to the desks of congressional representatives, bearing heartfelt messages about the need to remember homeless families. I ordered another 6,000 packets which Burpee Seeds graciously and expeditiously provided.

Now that we established the framework of a national campaign, complete with an ideal piece of legislation to inspire our multitude of homeless kids' crusaders across the country, we focused all energies on creating a blockbuster Forget-Me-Not (FMN) event for May 2000. Our alliance expanded to include the Better Homes Fund and MASS Interaction, enabling us to broadcast our Kids' Day by satellite to thousands of students across the country. The FMN 2000 event focused on stories of homeless kids, poignantly related in front of an audience of 250 homeless and non-homeless kids and adults assembled in the impressive Hart Building Senate chambers, with student-viewers from across the country calling in with questions and comments for both legislators and homeless panelists. We brought a busload of kids and their families from Hesed House for this unique event. Congresspersons Judy Biggert (IL) and William Coyne (PA) participated at the Hart Building and Reps. Sheila Jackson Lee (TX), and Brian Baird (WA) by satellite/telephone connections from their states.

Nancy, a student from Aurora who had stayed with her family at our transitional shelter, was one of the panelists who shared some of her experiences, "Even doing schoolwork was hard because of the noise from all the other people in the shelter. But, even though my life was hard, I have done pretty well in school. I am on the honor roll and am studying hard so I can go to medical school and become a doctor. I want to help people. Our family became very close because of our experiences. As we were getting ready to go to sleep, we would talk about what happened to us that day. We dreamed of times that we would be back on our feet. We were at least happy to be together and to be safe." The icing on the cake for all of us was when the video of this event received an Emmy nomination!

While in DC, we took our IL contingent to visit their congressman, Speaker of the House Dennis Hastert. We were graciously received in the Speaker's chambers, in a room that has probably never been visited by homeless children and adults. I can't help but believe that our face-to-face encounters with Denny combined with the relentless efforts of Judy Biggert and the behind-the-scenes pushing by Mary Lou Cowlishaw paved the way for the eventual successful passage of the McKinney-Vento Homeless Education Assistance Act of 2001.

The inconceivable success of FMN 2000 floored us. The student panelists had far exceeded our wildest dreams in their ability to convey the painful realities of homelessness. FMN 2001 became a reality before the last extension cord was put away following the 2000 event.

FMN 2001, held April 23 at the Hart Building, attended by homeless youth from across the nation, including a busload from IL, assembled a powerful set of student panelists and Congresspersons Martin Frost (TX), Betty McCollum (MN), Eleanor Holmes Norton (DC) and Jan Schakowsky (IL) to round out the panel. Many tears were shed as each of these courageous teens shared stories about their families' journey to and through homelessness.

Thirteen year-old Alicia related, "My father tumbled down a flight of stairs carrying an old refrigerator, breaking his back in three places...Not only did we lose almost everything we owned, but we were looked at and treated like garbage. We were almost thrown out of school. Some of the kids who lived near the shelter told us their parents didn't want them near us."
Spunky Leah from Wheaton, IL, shared, "When we (Leah and her mom) became homeless we freaked out...The worst part of being homeless was my dog, Breezy, couldn't stay with us...We had always been together during our trying times..."

Rejection and deprivation permeated the other kids' stories: Living in an abandoned apartment with no heat, electricity or water; being forced to wash in dirty restrooms, knowing that dirty clothes would stay dirty indefinitely; inability to concentrate on schoolwork because they had no quiet space to study in noisy shelters; and the inability to form friendships because of their homelessness—and the stigmas it created—caused Congressional staffers and media representatives in the audience to become knowledgeable about how homelessness hurts kids the most.

Their growing concern about homelessness, especially as it affected families, was evident. The cumulative effect of over 11,000 forget-me-not seed packets spilling out on the desks of lawmakers began to get their attention. Finally...

Jim Brown and Barbara Duffield continued to hammer away at legislative language for the bill that shaped the McKinney reauthorization, now called McKinney-Vento, adding the name of Bruce Vento, compassionate Congressman from Minnesota who died in October 2000. The bill contained almost all aspects from the Illinois Education for Homeless Children Act plus some bonuses harvested from other states. Funding for this national program even started creeping upward at a time of widespread budget cuts.

In the last weeks before what became passage of this bill, issues kept exploding that threatened to destroy all of the work that so many people had invested in the legislation. Language needed to be compromised between House and Senate versions of the bill.

The most controversial matter was "separate schools." The current law allowed for schools to be set up to serve only homeless students. While some people figured it was beneficial for the students and educators, it segregated homeless students from mainstream classrooms. The potential for disaster if this element was kept in the bill was monumental. Barbara and others fought like banshee hens to prevent separate schools from being allowed. In the end a grandfather clause was inserted to allow existing programs to continue.

The final days found Barbara, Jim Brown and a few other dedicated souls working 80-hours a week or more to finalize language for the bill. So much invested, so much to gain, and finally, on December 18, 2001, Congress passed the final version of the McKinney-Vento Homeless Education Assistance Act as part of the all-encompassing No Child Left Behind Act.

Ironically, passage of this bill that had consumed so much of my life for the past 8 years was fairly anticlimactic. It came at a time when I was immersed in the stress caused by the growing numbers of families and single persons seeking shelter, our ambitious expansion of our sleeping spaces for women families, simultaneously struggling with trying to get our board to address what I saw to be a serious collapse in leadership.

A few of my trusted co-workers "celebrated" this victory by presenting me with a commemorative plaque. The fact that this celebration occurred privately in my office bespoke the strained work environment. This humongous victory for the "little people," powerless homeless kids just seeking an education, swirled into the vortex of organizational crisis, staff discord and holiday insanity.

The actual bill, which Congresswoman Judy Biggert had introduced in September 1999, became reality as part of the broad No Child Left Behind Act of 2001, signed into law by President George Bush in January 2002. Illinois activists celebrated passage of this bill in March, bringing together legislators, advocates, McKinney-Vento program representatives, and friends who contributed extensively to this success. Based on language in the McKinney-Vento law, Gary Dickirson, Illinois State Board of Education's homeless student coordinator, decided to strengthen the enforcement of this

law throughout the 900 school districts across Illinois. This restructuring led to my employment as Lead Liaison for ISBE in May 2003 (Ch. 25).
Little did I know how passage of that bill would change my life…

PART 4—

FAMILY VALUES FACE BLEAK REALITIES

"I have felt that people were 'mean-mad' at times and wondered if life were not treating them so harshly that they were unable to retain any of the qualities which make people lovable and that make life worth living."

Eleanor Roosevelt

11. A Crushing Sense of Powerlessness — And Heartbreak

Kids were the hardest to cope with at the shelter— heartbreaking for volunteers to see that kids needed to live there, challenging for staff to make sure kids were getting proper supervision from parents, and painful for the guests to see that even kids had to endure this wretched situation.

Amazingly, most kids who stayed at our shelter were fairly well behaved. Some had conscientious parents who kept them in line despite this abnormal setting they called "home." You could see the loving care that would hopefully compensate for the parents' failure to provide a place to live for their family. Other parents ranged from pretty good to pretty awful, much like parents in homes across this country. We insisted that parents keep a close eye on their kids for obvious reasons.

I'll never forget the image of a two-year old waddling confidently across the dining room late at night. "Why are you up here, Danielle?" I asked. "Where's your mommy?"

"I want a drink of water," she simply replied. "Mommy's sleeping." What struck me was that this little tyke was comfortable getting up in the middle of the night, stepping through a jam-packed room full of sleeping bodies of mostly strangers, climbing upstairs into a huge room with a handful of volunteers, and requesting a drink of water. What has this world come to that this would be a natural sight?

Perhaps what was most amazing was that many of these kids had miserable lives that none of us even wanted to know about, and yet they could adapt to living in this wacky community. In their short lives they've somehow survived harrowing abuse, abject poverty, neglected health care, nomadic and dysfunctional homes. Often, the crazy shelter environment was an improvement over their previous havoc-filled living situations. Most families were single parents (usually moms), although, occasionally, we had two-parent families and, on occasion, single male parents.

Every once in awhile, fortunately not often, we found ourselves stymied by someone's problems. A family who stayed at both the emergency shelter and the transitional shelter had a cute little 7-year old girl, "Maggie," with such deep psychological disturbances that I'm not sure she could ever get straightened out.

We expedited their move into the adjacent transitional shelter because Maggie disrupted the sleep time of all our families and single women by her uncontrolled behavior. She would spin out of control in a space literally covered with tired bodies trying to sleep on their pads on the floor. Her mother, understandably helpless, strained to also care for her other two children. I often intervened, removing the girl from the sleeping area, doing a gentle but firm time-out away from all the stimulation. It wore me out, but I had no other choice but to deal with her uncontrollable behavior.

One night, in the midst of the typical hectic pace of the emergency shelter, I got an urgent request for assistance from the woman working at the transitional shelter. Little Maggie, who with her family had just moved into their room earlier that day, was out of control. The worker knew I'd have the best chance to get the situation under control so she frantically called me.

Yup, Maggie was out of control, so I carefully restrained her and we went to the hall outside my office, which could be secured and was away from sleeping areas. I had the staff explain to Maggie's forlorn mother where we would go and what I'd do, giving mom the option of watching without her daughter knowing through the small glass panels in the hallway doors.

As strong as I thought I was, petite Maggie gave me a workout. For what seemed like hours, she screamed as I held her, trying to keep her from hurting herself and me. Her non-stop, shrill screeches and curses bounced off the concrete block walls, penetrating my head like a drill. She writhed, twisted, kicked and tried to scratch her way free. Eventually she settled down, worn out. Me too. We contacted some agencies the next day and tried to arrange help. The overburdened service providers could not help soon enough.

The next night pushed the situation over the edge—Maggie somehow managed to get a large, sharp kitchen knife and hid it under her pillow. Fortunately, someone discovered it before anyone got hurt. The crisis worker was called in and the family moved out, to where we don't know.

Hurricane TJ

One mom who had stayed at the shelter several years earlier returned, this time with her little boy, "TJ." Pathetic but endearing, "Terri" had encountered some alcohol-related difficulties, endured some horrendous relationships in her thirty years of life, and now was back in the place she least wanted to be again—a homeless shelter, this time with a child. TJ was a small kid for a seven-year-old, and he seemed adorable…until that evening.

My friend and lobbyist for homelessness issues, Barbara Duffield, was visiting for a few days, getting some "shelter time" to restore passion to fuel her advocacy efforts in Washington. She hung around, talking to folks, and was there when TJ and his mom arrived, so she chatted with them as well as many others. We let families stay inside during the non-shelter hours if parents carefully watched their children. So far so good. Terri seemed on the job with TJ.

The eye of the hurricane, from my Florida childhood memories, was an apt comparison to the calm before the shelter opened. Before our 7:00 p.m. start time, volunteers efficiently put finishing touches on meal preparations and went about the rest of the pre-opening preparations, even occasionally getting the "luxury" of visiting with each other and a brief moment of group prayer. We never knew when or if the tempest would hit, but if it did, it would guarantee to be at the busiest, most challenging time, when something horrible happened.

This time, "Hurricane TJ" erupted like a powerful storm in the women and family sleeping area. One of the women raced to get me and I rushed to find TJ literally bouncing off the walls of both rooms, springing onto and off the stacks of pads, upending plastic bags filled with belongings of the women and families, screaming adult-sized swearwords and just going nuts. Terri was standing, crying, and trying futilely to stop him. I grabbed him on the way by, quickly realizing that he was going to be a match for my strength.

I cleared everyone out of the room and used a pile of mats to sit on, holding him in a straitjacket hold, while talking calmly and soothingly to him. He cursed, screamed, and berated me and anyone he could think of with language I rarely heard even from angry, intoxicated adults. His tirade seethed with hatred and threats to his mother, himself, and me. All of this occurred as he thrashed about with all his strength and that of the demons inside him. I hung on for my life and his.

After what seemed to be an eternity, he seemed to calm down and we mutually agreed that I'd release him. Sucker! He sprang into action again, and I corralled him to repeat the entire process. Eventually, he wore down enough to convince me that a breather was possible. I tentatively released him, talking gently to him and getting lucid replies. We got up and went to the hall where his mother anxiously awaited. The situation seemed to be temporarily under control.

During this whole time, Barbara was aware of what was going on—as was everyone in the dining room. Her heart was breaking, for both TJ and his mom. I wasted no time going upstairs; instead, I headed straight to my office to call the Crisis Line. I explained to the mental health worker what had happened and asked what the options were. Unbelievably, they rarely dealt with kids, so she couldn't fathom the level of chaos that TJ just caused. I found out that the mother had to be the one to request psychiatric services, so I went to talk to her about it.

I strongly believed that TJ was a "danger to himself or others," criteria for involuntary hospitalization if the psychiatrist at the hospital agreed. I got Terri out of TJ's hearing and quickly explained the options. I had to tell her that staying at the shelter wasn't possible because of the level of his outburst. She reluctantly agreed to let the ambulance transport him to the hospital and I rushed to make the call. I hurriedly gave Barbara a heads-up on what was happening, which distressed her immensely because she had earlier spent some enjoyable moments talking with TJ and his mom.

Procedure was to call 9-1-1 and explain the need for transport to the emergency room because we had a person who was a "danger to himself or others." When I mentioned that it was a 7-year-old boy, the dispatcher was audibly taken aback. Somehow, that shock must have translated to the police who responded because when I met them at the door, one of the officers practically berated me for not being able to handle a 7-year-old. I tried to explain TJ's behavior and the officer scoffed at me saying, "I have a 7-year-old. He acts wild too, but that doesn't make him dangerous." *Grrrr...*

Just then, TJ raced through the crowded dining room toward the stairwell where we were talking. I knew he was winding up again and figured it was going to be trouble. "Officer Friendly" barely got a chance to register when TJ made a serious grab for his gun. As I used a split second to think of where to dive to protect my life, the officer prevented the unauthorized use of his weapon by pulling TJ's hand off it. In a flash, TJ bolted up to the third floor landing above our heads. He climbed up to the highest spot possible, screaming at the top of his lungs, "I'm gonna jump! I'm gonna kill myself!" The officer finally got it. This kid was a "danger to himself or others."

Mom and TJ went to the hospital, and TJ was admitted—itself a rare occasion as I felt they tried to keep people from being admitted just to save money. Unfortunately, but to no surprise, Mom signed TJ out the next day, thinking they could return to the shelter. This was the part of my job I hated worst—to tell someone they couldn't come back. It was excruciating when it was a family. However, I could not risk this type of behavior in the midst of the unstable environment we had on a regular basis. Sadly, their options were extremely limited, but Terri was creative and they found someone to take them in for a while.

How did this episode look to Barbara, the "outsider" who sympathized with both shelter staff and the homeless people who had no option but the shelter's inhumane communal living environment? Later that night we rehashed the painful events. She said TJ and this tragic incident would be forever seared in her heart and mind.

Her first thought was "what on earth could have happened in a mere 7 years on earth to make this child want to kill himself?" She wondered what kind of events would lead someone that young to want to end it all, and so publicly? Barbara later described the scene from her perspective of sitting at a table in the dining room:

> *"I remember the guy, maybe Harold was his name, who didn't see that I was sitting at the same table as him, and who, as we all sat in stunned and horrified silence, watching TJ's little body at the top of the stairs, said 'That person... from Washington.... where are they now?' To me, it was as if he were saying that THIS was homelessness— THIS was the reality of it— and someone needed to bear witness, to truly know what it was. I remember feebly saying something dumb like 'I'm here' and then feeling a crushing sense of powerlessness..."*

Barbara described witnessing my "crushing sense of powerlessness," something she was not used to seeing from me. "...you, usually the tireless crusader for justice and systemic solutions, were understandably tired and jaded. We talked about the need for wholesale change in social policies, housing and income especially, and I remember you saying something like 'I wonder—even if we got all that—someone would find a way to screw it all up.' It was, for me, evidence of what messed up systems do to people—the people who suffer the problems, and the people who try to help them. I knew you'd bounce back—and you did—but it was so hard to see your pain that night."

TJ was imprinted in my heart and mind, too. Above my desk I taped up a reminder of TJ—a valentine card he had given me the day before his outburst. *Fortunately, kids like TJ and Maggie rarely came our way, but that didn't stop us from knowing that youngsters just as deeply troubled were out there and hurting with very few resources to help them. Having children in a shelter environment was hard enough...but knowing some couldn't be helped in today's social service scene infuriates me. Logic, fairly rare in government policies, dictates more resources are needed to assist families with kids like TJ and Maggie. Even if kids like these manage to grow up into adulthood, they will likely have little chance of a productive life. They will most likely be a danger to themselves and others until our nation is ready to truly prioritize the value of each family...*

12. Parent Trap

*O*ne phenomenon I struggle with is when the parent is almost totally incompetent and the kids seem highly functional. I'm sure psychologists can explain it theoretically, but witnessing it is something else.

"Anne," the Midwestern-like wholesome looking mother of "Lynn" and "Cindy," appeared "normal" at first glance, but she was totally incapable of rational thinking. To make things worse, "Jack," her "significant other" was a person high on my list of people I could not tolerate. He spent most of his life in jail and prison, which to me seemed the best place for him. Problem was—the state kept releasing him.

Anne, a military veteran, had some functional sides—she worked regularly at temp jobs[7], didn't seem to drink or drug, and she seemed normal when you first talk to her. She appeared to take care of her girls, as well as could be expected, but didn't ever seem interested in breaking the pattern causing them to be homeless.

Her delightful girls, Lynn and Cindy, are a year apart, Lynn, with a reservoir of enthusiasm for life, at the time in 8th grade. Cindy tended to be extremely reserved, but we became "buds" as time went on. I admired how they looked out for each other and how they were always willing to help around "home."

The family's been homeless most of the past 7 or 8 years. They'd drift to the shelter, leave when it got warmer to live in their beater-van, move in with family, wear out their welcome and repeat the pattern.

When they were gone, I'd wistfully think maybe they got their act together, and then they'd show up again. Jack, if he was out of prison, assured me that he'd behave, but he was incapable of it. I knew he'd physically abused Anne, for she showed up with bruises, or wearing sunglasses to cover her battered eyes. He was smart enough to never try it while at the shelter. I tried discreetly talking with her about it several times. Anne might be mentally ill, but has staunchly refused any attempt we made to offer her services. A brother lived in town, so he helped her out on occasion, especially in the summer.

I always tried to seem impartial, but with Lynn and Cindy it was rough. They are cool kids. They're bright, polite, curious and funny. One of my favorite memories was a few years back, when they were about 9 and 10, and I asked them to join me in some gardening. It was a beautiful spring day after a grueling winter and I needed to do something—anything—outside. We checked with Mom, who said OK, and off we went.

I'm not a master gardener, and they had never gardened, so I could share my rudimentary knowledge with them. That's a weed. That's a flower. When we began weeding the flowerbed, worms clung to the clods of dirt we pulled up with the weeds. "What's that?" inquired Cindy. "EEEW!" chimed in Lynn. "Don't be afraid of the worms," I said in my confident botanist tone. "They do good things, like make the dirt even richer." (I didn't go into the poop part.) Both girls trusted my explanation and undertook a serious worm-protection strategy. Lynn pulled up the weed, exposing the frightened worm. Cindy, with her Mona Lisa smile, gently removed the worm and transferred it into some fresh dirt. Then she tossed the weeds in a pile.

Over the years I've watched my little buddies grow up into pretty decent kids. They've always been well-behaved and usually take the new kids under their wings to help them adjust, sharing pointers on how to get along with staff or their newfound "roommates," all 20 of them. They'd help volunteers set up for meals and relentlessly pursued my permission to help distribute toiletries or serve food.

Recently, when Cindy seemed more impassive than usual for a long period, I became concerned that something horrible was going on in her life. Or, I wondered if something horrible that had happened to her in her past was rearing its ugly head inside her head. Experts believe, and I have witnessed, that childhood sexual abuse is a prime factor in adult dysfunctional behavior—homeless or not—and knowing the man in Anne's life, I wouldn't be surprised if this could be the cause of Cindy's aloofness.

Because Cindy's teacher was a volunteer and a friend of mine, I felt comfortable sounding her out about my concern. She noticed a difference in behavior too, and felt the same apprehension. She alerted the school social worker, an over-burdened but kind woman who tried talking to Cindy about what was bothering her. Nothing of consequence ever developed, but we tried to leave the door open for Cindy to approach caring adults when she was ready.

Cindy's teacher made sure this youngster was able to realize a dream—joining the school band. The teacher got her a clarinet. Playing in the band with her classmates offered an opportunity for normal activity—and time away from the shelter. Cindy also joined her school's basketball team. After going to one of her games, I offered to find a gym to let Lynn practice basketball. She needed it! I held an unrealistic hope that I'd be able to join her to offer her some pointers from my previous basketball playing and coaching days. That never happened.

They'd show me their report cards—pretty decent grades considering their inconceivable distractions. If they, or other kids staying with us, needed school supplies or something special for class—cupcakes, valentines, etc., they'd ask. I comforted myself thinking at least they knew someone cared about them, even if we couldn't protect them from the worst of life's evils.

Appearances Can Be Deceiving

Families, homeless or not, face immeasurable challenges. Often what they face—alcoholism, drug addiction, domestic violence—doesn't become apparent for a long time. In social work jargon, "they present well."

"Frank," "Mollie" and their kids didn't seem atypical—poverty, rough breaks—but for this somewhat rare two-parent homeless family, the red flags didn't appear till later.

The family had lived in a modest rental house in a nearby neighborhood until job loss caused them to lose housing. They had been at the shelter for a short time previously, and managed to seemingly get back on their feet. Dad had that tough biker look; tattooed arms, beer gut, long wild hair and an intense anger in his eyes. Mom, pleasant and nondescript, took good care of their three energetic and enjoyable young kids. They seemed as normal of a family as we've seen.

My capable co-worker, Jesse Hernandez, and I were cruising through the beginning of a warm, seemingly peaceful, fall evening—a seasoned volunteer crew, tasty pot roast meal, balmy weather that made it possible to keep doors open. Jesse was in the kitchen when he heard shouting outside. He quickly alerted me to a potential crisis and we both raced out to the darkened driveway area to track down the source of the disturbance.

A car, stopped on the hill, with Mollie and kids inside. Frank was on the outside, beating on the windshield, shouting death threats to Mollie. He was obviously drunk and very aggressive. With not much thought other than fear for what would happen if he broke the window, I snapped and raced up behind him, grabbed him by the collar and flung him to the ground. The battle was on—his intoxication vs. my fury. He staggered up, seemingly unaware of me and focused on pounding on the window, with Mollie and the kids cowering inside. I repeated my furious hurling a few more times.

This type of "combat" defied our policies and procedures for guest interaction, but I couldn't avoid the intervention. In the meantime, Jesse, who is no wimp, but is limited in his ability to grapple with angry drunk men because of his crutches and amputated leg, scrambled inside to get help. He called the police and then went into the dining room and shouted, "Diane needs some strong guys to help her NOW!" When I looked up the hill from my battle, it looked like the cavalry racing down the hill towards us. Some of our biggest, strongest, meanest guys arrived just in time to subdue Frank who, by this point, figured out it was "just a woman" who had been flinging him to the ground. With Frank on the ground, restrained by my tag-team, a terrified Mollie drove the still intact car up the driveway safely away from the turmoil.

"What do you want us to do with him?" asked my rescuers, obviously eager to rip off Frank's limbs. Don't hurt him, just keep him from moving was my reply. The police arrived quickly, but Frank's drunken fury stymied them. It took four cops to get him into the paddy wagon. Mollie and the kids were unhurt but traumatized. I was physically and mentally spent, but relieved to stop what would have been catastrophic for Molly and her kids.

Mollie and I both signed complaints and we mutually vowed to show up for the court date to make sure Frank would get what he had coming to him. He was originally charged with attempted murder and domestic violence, so we figured he'd be locked up for a long time. Mollie appeared courageous and steadfast in her desire to have him locked up, unusual for most women in similar situations. She never appeared to waver in her determination to keep Frank away from her family by making sure his charges stuck.

We touched base before the court date; she was still steadfast in her determination. We went together and sat patiently through hours of judicial activity. We watched the legendary bailiff intimidate anyone daring to disturb the court's order. When no one else remained, I went up to the state's attorney and asked what was happening with Frank. In what seemed to be an afterthought, they finally brought Frank—dressed in an orange jumpsuit and bound in chains—before the judge, giving us our long awaited opportunity to see him put behind bars for eternity.

In case I needed a reality check, I got it. Justice, when it comes to domestic violence, often fails. The clueless judge admonished Frank for his behavior, ordered him to "stay away from Hesed House and his family, and to get anger management counseling." When the judge asked Frank where he'd go, he said he could stay with his mother in a nearby small town. I groaned inwardly so as not to provoke the bailiff or judge.

The impossibility of this unemployed and unemployable man getting anger management counseling in a town so small it does not even have counselors didn't seem to faze the dispenser of "justice." The impractical expectation of him staying away from Hesed House and/or his family would be impossible to enforce in a way to make any of us feel safe. *Don't do it again. Get a grip. Stay away.* Yeah, right...

We were incensed, but it made no difference. Mollie and her kids soon left the shelter, and family members rallied around them the best they could. I saw them occasionally at our soup kitchen or food pantry and they seemed to be doing OK—at least Frank had stayed away. Mollie did express concerns about her health, but she focused on her kids, ignoring her unattainable need for medical care.

I never saw Frank again. The last I heard, Mollie died of heart-related problems. Her terrifying life with Frank, the lifelong hardships of poverty, the indescribable ordeal of single parenthood and long-term lack of even a minimal life-sustaining health care combined to take this mom from her kids. I wondered what the judge would say about that.

Reducing the trauma of violence for kids...isn't that a worthy goal? When families have limited options and find themselves choosing between bad and worse, or when they slip between the cracks—or in some cases abysses—of our tattered safety net, they often tumble into the streets like garbage. What we need is a good recycling program, and to commit to improving protections for families in crisis.

13. Basketball and Bootstraps

*B*ootstraps get worn with use, finally failing, usually at the worst possible moment. "Naomi's" did—when she was 18. With her 3-year old toddler and her soon-to-be-born baby, she hit the streets. Sullen, hostile, homeless and pregnant single parent with child—what a combination!

Naomi moved into our transitional shelter, referred by a local agency when they ran out of options for her. Her attitude reeked—or so it seemed to staff who expected cooperation or at least a hint of sociable behavior. They were ready to kick her out when I asked if I could intervene.

I don't recall what made me think I could do anything. I didn't work directly with the transitional program and I didn't know Naomi except to see her in passing. Yet, something told me to try...

She came up to my cramped office. This attractive, stocky girl-woman sat belligerently on the swivel chair, twisting and turning in constant motion, motion that effectively prevented eye contact. I tried the normal, direct approach, "So, what's keeping you from cooperating down there?" She glared at me, silent. Hmmm...that worked well. "Do you have another place to stay?" Silence again. Knowing that she and her adorable baby were going to be kicked out if something didn't change for the better, I was desperate to salvage the situation. "Where did you go to high school?" I nonchalantly inquired. She looked at me like I was crazy, so I followed up with, "Did you play sports in school?"

Now she knew I was crazy, but a flicker of something registered in her eyes. "West High. Yeah, I played basketball," she hesitatingly replied. "Why?"

Okay, now we're getting somewhere. "I thought you looked like you could be a 'jockette,'" I replied. That elicited an even stranger look, but she had at least engaged in conversation and we began to have eye contact. "I played lots of basketball when I was in school, many years ago, and you just reminded me of kids I've coached and refereed," I offered.

"You played basketball?! You coached and reffed?" she asked incredulously. Ah, the ice, it cracked, I thought.

Once she started talking, my gut instinct was confirmed. What she was holding inside was going to be painful to share. Naomi, a scared teenager with no apparent options, didn't want to trust anyone, but she realized that she was backed against the wall and I offered the only hope she had.

84

Unfortunately for me, that meant her burdens were going to, at least in part, become mine. Incredibly, she unloaded them on me, starting with her memories of her mother's boyfriend repeatedly sexually abusing her. Sensing where this was going I stopped her and said, "I am not a counselor. I don't want you to think I'm doing any therapy with you."

"You seem like you care," she responded with a wisp of life in her eyes. "No one else does." She continued to tell me that she became pregnant at 15. Her baby, "Neecie," was all she had. Her mother kicked her out when she became pregnant again, this time by a boy in school. She quit school a few months shy of graduation, and has lived with friends since then. The teen pregnancy agency she turned to had no viable options, probably in part because she was not easy to work with, so they referred her to our shelter.

This young, black mom and her daughter shared a college dorm-style room with "Jackie," a white single mom who didn't have custody of her kids at the moment. They didn't get along, due in large part to Naomi's nasty attitude. Racial problems were brewing between them, and that ugliness could spread throughout the household of 38 homeless men, women and children staying at the transitional shelter. I just *hate* racial troubles.

So, as Naomi unloaded her pent-up anger, despair, and frustrations, I sat there thinking, "No wonder she was so bitchy. This is a horrible load to carry all alone." Beyond that I had no clue as to what solutions may exist, but I felt buying time was a worthwhile result of our talk. We agreed to touch base frequently and I offered to be a sounding board if she needed to explode at someone. I offered to try to find counseling resources, which I knew were scarce for uninsured, impoverished women.

She nodded and said OK; her ever-so-slight smile gave me a flicker of hope that we had averted a disaster, at least for the time being. Few options exist for impoverished pregnant teens. Even if a residential program had an opening, the young woman must be willing to cooperate. That appeared unlikely with Naomi.

Her stay at the transitional program included giving birth to her second baby, "Tasha." During her 9-month pregnancy, Naomi struggled to live "in community." For her, as well as anyone who has been abused, living in a mixed household sets off untold internal alarms. Her people skills lacked polish to say the least. I intervened several times as she spouted off at someone. Once she cooled down, she seemed to understand where she went wrong.

I asked Naomi if she felt she wanted counseling to help her process the abuse. I explained what I knew and what I've seen—many homeless women suffer from substance abuse and mental illness, often a result of unaddressed issues related to abuse. She agreed and I gave her the name and number of the domestic violence shelter to call and ask for help. They offered counseling at no cost and agreed to work with our residents. She went to a few sessions, probably not enough to "fix" things, but at least enough to give her some coping skills.

For about 18 months, Naomi and her family stayed in this temporary haven, designed to give a family or individual time to gather resources, develop life skills, and to regain independence. Those worthy goals may be attainable for some, but for others, like Naomi, it's like trying to do rock climbing with her hands tied. She needed to finish her high school education, which meant GED (General Educational Development) classes. She was quite smart so she accomplished that without too much difficulty.

Since she had two small children and no job, she qualified for welfare. That pittance, $223 a month cash assistance[8], plus the invaluable medical card, gave her the beginnings of a nest egg. One-third of her income went to room and board, one-third went to savings, and she could use the rest for personal needs. She began the journey to independent living by looking for subsidized housing. That was quite discouraging for her and a good reality check for me.

I knew the theory—for every one person looking for subsidized housing, three or four need it but can't get it. The housing authority had a years-long waiting list (which is the same, if not worse, today). Back then, candidates for housing didn't need to crawl through the proverbial eye of a needle like they now do. Current HUD (U.S. Department of Housing and Urban Development) policy now allows housing authorities to adopt a "zero tolerance" policy, so if Naomi had a criminal record from her earlier "stupid" teenage days, being caught with pot or some typical "crime," they could deny her housing. Fortunately, she didn't have a record, but she still had to cope with the long waiting list.

After what seemed to be interminable waiting, Naomi persisted and eventually received a Section 8 certificate. That meant she could approach qualified landlords and assure them that the federal government would pay two-thirds of her rent, based on market-rate. She eventually found a landlord willing to rent to her. Her apartment, for which the government paid $420 and Naomi paid $80, was a dumpy tiny place on the edge of a crime-infested neighborhood.

She embraced her newly acquired home like a palace, and we helped her get gently-used furnishings and household items. Naomi and her babies moved into their new home thinking they had the world and all. That feeling was short-lived.

Living on almost no income, she had $143 a month left after paying rent. Naomi learned how economically vulnerable she was. Getting a phone was impossible without help. I got someone to donate money for utilities' deposits—she had no credit history. Heat was included, a good thing since she couldn't have afforded it anyhow.

She struggled to feed her family with WIC (Women, Infants, and Children) coupons and food stamps. She was able to get some food from the local food pantry, but since she didn't drive, she had to depend on friends for a ride—after she arranged for childcare.

An obnoxious welfare worker pressured Naomi to get a job. (I gauged the obnoxiousness by a conversation I had with her about Naomi.) This caseworker exhibited no awareness of the realities facing this struggling mom. Naomi's utmost concern was for the well-being of her children. Any job she got would require her to find quality childcare, a rarity in our area. She'd be lucky to find a job paying minimum wage, not enough to support a family. She needed job training before she'd have a chance to truly support her family. She had no transportation and couldn't rely on our area's erratic public buses. It was a disaster waiting to happen. The caseworker was not offering any help for Naomi to bridge the gap between welfare and self-sufficiency.

Welfare "reform" was being formulated in both Springfield and Washington, DC. Legislators, unaware and/or insensitive to myriad obstacles facing moms like Naomi, were poised to "end welfare as we know it," as if what existed was a picnic. For heads-of-households like Naomi, yanking the rug out from under them would inevitably lead to an immense feeling of failure and the likelihood of homelessness. I knew Naomi's fragile mental state could not take a return to a shelter.

Truth be told, Naomi wouldn't have survived "independently" without some covert help from people I recruited. She "cheated" in order to make sure her babies had a roof over their heads, food, heat and electricity. The income funneled to her "off the record" enabled her to bridge the gap between welfare and reality in order to stay out of a homeless shelter.

I monitored her spending. I had been led to believe in my pre-social service days that all welfare mothers were drinking and drugging. In reality, welfare "cheats" were typically desperate moms trying to survive impossible situations. President Reagan's "Welfare Queen" image was far from the truth.

87

Her kids had typical sicknesses, including asthma. Naomi underwent a serious bout of gynecological problems, which her medical card covered. But her medical coverage did not include specialists that her condition warranted, so she continued to suffer immense pain and fear. She regularly suffered migraines and had high blood pressure.

If life didn't hold enough challenges, in between everything else, she had an unplanned pregnancy, not unusual for many teens, especially those with a history of sexual abuse. The brief counseling she had didn't repair the major trauma that she had experienced in her formative years. Yikes! I cringed with what I imagined her future to be.

It was at this point things were reaching a major crisis. Naomi called me often and I could tell she was losing her precarious grip. She walked the edge of suicidal, understandable for the anxiety she was trying to endure.

When Naomi's baby was born, the crisis floodgate burst. Her son, "Jacob," was premature—by two months. Naomi's health problems worsened, including her blood pressure. She had required complete bed rest for the last half of her pregnancy. After his birth, Jacob was hospitalized for two months until his weight and vital signs stabilized. Naomi was beside herself trying to figure out how she and her family could survive this next challenge. She made the wise decision to have her tubes tied to prevent any future unplanned pregnancies.

Jacob also had a hiatal hernia that caused life-threatening symptoms—he couldn't breathe because his esophagus closed—when he had his frequent seizures. Naomi would tell me about these crises after she managed to get through them, "I called 9-1-1 and the ambulance took us to the hospital," she matter-of-factly reported to me. Jacob was often hospitalized for a few days and then returned to her. She needed to beg a ride or take a cab to and from the hospital, quickly using up her meager resources.

It seemed to me that her life was one crisis after another. I couldn't fathom living with these ordeals, but I had to encourage her to keep trying. Her blood pressure caused additional ordeals. Medical care for her and her babies was so sporadic and inadequate, I felt my blood pressure rising.

Doctors could choose to accept patients with medical cards or not. They were often reluctant because the state's reimbursement rate was so low—one-third of what they normally charged—and extremely slow—often six months or more overdue. Frequently, doctors scheduled "non-emergency" appointments for months after patients called. Naomi, with her medically challenged family, could have kept a medical staff busy full-time.

About this time, the federal government's much-touted welfare changes were enacted. Illinois quickly adopted the "5-year and you're off" plan. Naomi's days on welfare were numbered. Administrators pressured caseworkers to kick people off for the least (often imagined) infraction. Fear and ignorance made welfare policies even worse than they were. Naomi, along with countless other mothers, found herself in crises beyond description. Caseworkers, rewarded for reductions in welfare rates, were ill informed about new policies and frequently misstated regulations to terrified parents who were often ill equipped to survive even in a friendlier environment.

Naomi had been filling me in on what her caseworker was telling her. "Get a job. You're not gonna stay on aid forever," was the condensed version. It was at this point I snapped. Naomi, already overstressed by the hand life had dealt her, felt the threats were real and that sanction was imminent. She knew if that happened it was back to the shelter, for her a fate worse than death. I knew this worker was pushing too hard and was wrong to tell Naomi she had to get a job. I did some research on what correct policy was and called the welfare office supervisor. He tossed me to the caseworker, a fruitless and anger-producing experience.

Naomi's "refusal to work" was based on an awful reality. Her son, Jacob, needed a trained childcare worker capable of performing life-sustaining medical procedures. Unfortunately, such childcare is rare. Actually, affordable, qualified childcare is hard to find, even for middle-class parents, so expecting Naomi to locate someone who could adequately handle life-threatening seizures was unlikely at best.

Now I was in the fight for blood. I contacted an organization, the National Poverty Law Project[9], and spoke to their welfare expert, an attorney with little tolerance for this type of abusive behavior. I described the situation and she asked to speak with Naomi, who had already given me permission to discuss this case. She and Naomi spoke, then they called the welfare worker, a good use of three-way calling. The lawyer laid down the proper policy to the worker and informed her boss of the problem. The caseworker backed off, but it didn't improve their relationship. Naomi's case made the Poverty Law Project's newsletter as a sad example of welfare policy gone awry.

Naomi felt the pride of standing up for what was right. I was delighted she was empowered by this agency to achieve the impossible. She soon began computer classes to prepare for the day she could finally go to work.

Her crises ebbed and flowed. Just when I was in crisis mode for myriad other job-related reasons, I'd pause and think, "I haven't heard from Naomi in a while. I wonder how she's doing." Inevitably, the phone would ring and it would be Naomi with another catastrophe. For me, the helper-agent, I couldn't imagine the scope of what these situations really meant. I didn't have time or mental resources to let my mind wrap around Naomi's struggle to survive. I just did what I could do to help her through whatever I could help with, and prayed.

Fortunately, the family helping Naomi with financial problems continued to be her salvation. She tried to budget and be the skilled household manager she needed to be. Trouble was, no one could budget with less than half the money she needed for the most basic expenses. This family rose to the occasion at holiday time, back-to-school time, and eventually all the time. They helped her take Jacob to his doctor, a specialist whose office was 30 miles away. They drove her to welfare appointments because the logistics of childcare and transportation were impossible.

Her pride in providing for her family motivated her to seek another apartment. Heat problems, roaches and mice, and a rising crime rate gave her even more worries. She researched the market and found an ideal place. I needed to wrangle with the landlord to get him to lower the security deposit, $1,500, based on the apartment's market rent of $750 a month. Her rent would be adjusted because of her Section 8 certificate, but he wanted two months' rent up front. I vouched for Naomi's character and her responsibility as a tenant. He relented, lowering it to a measly $1,000. The family from heaven helped again. God bless them!

Eventually, Naomi did what she really wanted to do. She was offered and took an entry-level job at a federal agency in town. She was ecstatic! I tried to hide my big picture concerns—was this job realistic in light of her family's massive health problems? She assured me the woman providing childcare was able to handle Jacob's emergencies, which had fortunately abated somewhat as he got older. Her girls were doing well in school and when I stopped over at their apartment, I marveled at how clean it was. Her job meant a significant rise in her income-based rent, but she felt it was worth it.

Shortly after moving into this dream home, working at a job she loved, her kids well cared for, the roof caved in. In a classic "Murphy's Law" situation, Naomi was horrified and shocked to find she was pregnant. It couldn't be! She had her tubes tied. Medical tests confirmed her pregnancy and her doctor ordered bed rest because her health was so fragile.

Sadly, when women suffer sexual abuse as children, as Naomi had, it can cause a dysfunction in their own sexual activities as adults. Such may have been the case with Naomi, as I slowly came to understand. Complicating matters further, birth control devices were not available to women with little or no income, giving them the unrealistic option of abstinence as the only way to avoid pregnancy. In a perfect world, that may work, but this world is far from perfect.

Naomi decided to get an abortion—a decision I respected although it troubled me tremendously. She actually thought it out quite thoroughly, factoring in her health, her track record for giving birth to sickly babies, and the devastating economics of another mouth to feed. She reasoned that if she went back on welfare, an option she didn't want to face, her clock was ticking to the end of the five-year period she'd be eligible for benefits.

The family helping her also respected her decision, though like me, they were deeply troubled by it. Naomi's surrogate mom gave her a ride to the doctor who was to perform the abortion.

Much to everyone's surprise, and to Naomi's dismay, she was too far along to have the abortion, so she endured the extreme discomfort of the pregnancy, taking off time from work to have the baby. Her baby was born, fairly healthy, and the doctor made sure her tubes were tied.

The logistical challenges of caring for a vibrant family under ideal circumstances overwhelm me. I couldn't imagine how she coped. Her friends and her angel-family were there for her in ways I couldn't fathom.

She juggled home responsibilities, went back to work and is today doing her best to struggle with the multitude of tribulations that will always face her. The angel-family continues to be her lifeline, and they have received a wealth of knowledge from this single mom who has continued to stare down life when it gets too ugly.

According to popular belief, welfare reform was a resounding success. I'd like to think it was too, but it's hard to justify that stance when one sees the insidious effects of poverty that encumber so many families. Homelessness doesn't often happen instantly when poverty is the cause. It erodes a person, a family, destroying the underpinnings of stability. Bad credit, limited options for job advancement, strained family relations, shaky child care arrangements, unsafe neighborhoods, and the stress that is the by-product of this unstable life…these painful realities are the norm for those struggling to stay on their feet after the welfare rug was pulled away. So many families (and individuals) are one crisis away from homelessness, and it doesn't even need to be a big disaster…

14. Amazing Survival Story

Despite popular belief, imprisoning the perpetrator doesn't always eliminate the devastation of domestic violence on families. The violence, if left to run its course, destroys peace of mind, trust in the legal system, financial well-being, fragile family relationships and more.

"Beth," a seemingly self-assured woman, and her six All-American kids showed up one nasty February night. They lived nearby and the older kids attended the Catholic school down the street. The three younger ones kept her busy during the day while the older kids were in school. No one knew the trauma occurring behind the walls of their modest home.

"Brian," Beth's ex-husband and childhood sweetheart, had recently received a long prison sentence for a drug-related crime and for weapons violations. One of his buddies followed him to prison for sexually abusing two of her kids. Their marriage, long ago shattered, lasted as long as it had because of religious beliefs, despite violent abuse that became the norm. Mom and kids endured beatings and berating on a painfully increasing basis. Their divorce—and his subsequent long overdue trip to prison—gave the family a slight respite, quickly destroyed by a downfall into homelessness, hastened by severe financial problems.

An only child, Beth's parents lived in town, but her abusive and alcoholic father made getting help from them out of the question, so she tried her best to take care of the kids by herself. Her welfare check didn't come close to covering their minimal essentials, and soon they were evicted for failure to pay rent. Somehow, the kids seemed to take this change of housing in stride. The turmoil experienced in their short lives fostered a resilience that allowed them to appear unfazed by this new episode. They knew some people at the shelter from their neighborhood, which made it easier for them to adapt to this bizarre new household.

Good parenting can make a huge difference in how kids adapt to this alien way of life—sharing their "home" with more than a hundred other strangers. Beth struggled to minimize the negative and tried to keep things "normal." One of the most memorable sights I've ever seen at the shelter was her two oldest girls coming back from school dressed in their sweaty basketball uniforms and as they walked through the crowded dining room, many of the guests inquired "Who won?" as the homeless players headed down to change their uniforms.

This family quickly earned their way into the hearts of staff members, which benefited them. Late one evening, when our impossibly overcrowded family room needed to accommodate yet another family, I was forced to come up with a solution—fast. Bypassing normal admissions procedures, I asked Beth if she wanted to move her family into the transitional shelter and she hastily agreed. The two of us literally moved the kids in their sleep; the older ones practically sleepwalked, while Beth and I carried the babies from one crib to another.

Despite the unorthodox entry into transitional housing, the family adapted quickly. The local newspaper covered their plight and a landlord surfaced, offering them a Section-8[10] house on the other side of town. Beth hid the good news from her kids and used every possible moment to scrounge furnishings and household items, decorating bedrooms to match her kids' personalities and reflect their favorite pop celebrities.

The long-awaited moving day was momentous, with the paper's photographer covering the kids' arrival into their new home. Some of us went for the occasion, a rare opportunity to see a happy ending to homelessness. The kids were ecstatic and Beth got the ultimate parent's payback—big hugs and heart-felt thanks from all her kids.

We kept in contact—unusual for me. I usually didn't have the luxury of "extra" time or energy to assist families once they left, but Beth needed help in so many ways. Still locked up, her ex found out where they were living from some of his buddies and was threatening Beth. Although she thought he was behind bars for a long time, his deteriorating health made him a candidate for early release because the state didn't want to get stuck with medical bills with someone they considered less of a threat. This scared her and the kids to death. I made several desperate calls to police and corrections officials and tried to alert them to this crisis-in-the-making. Even though he didn't get released (a bureaucratic anomaly), the fright that Beth and the family endured was devastating.

This incredibly steadfast Beth and her family faced multiple challenges—of the sorts that would derail even a stronger person—but they amazingly continued to make progress, albeit with difficulties. Her oldest kids, now teens, gave her a run for the money, with all-too-normal problems facing teens today. She tried her best to keep a grip, but almost lost it with her middle son, "Josh."

Scrawny Josh had some understandable "issues" and was acting out in school and home. His acting out was severe—and Beth worried about the younger kids getting hurt. She wasn't working at the time so she could take care of her youngest kids (child care was too expensive and almost impossible to find). So, other than a measly monthly $485 public assistance check and occasional bags of food from our pantry, she had no resources. Getting psychological help for Josh was out of the question. I offered to look into places to get help for her and her out-of-control son, but even I, with my extensive connections, came up empty handed.

Desperate, we even approached the Department of Children and Family Services, a beleaguered agency charged with preventing child abuse and neglect. Trouble was that Beth wasn't abusing or neglecting her kids, so they couldn't help. We looked into boarding schools and she pursued every possible lead with all the persistence of a determined mother, but no luck.

Things got so bad that Beth eventually managed to get Josh hospitalized in a nearby psych hospital where they drugged him into submission. Beth was horrified with their idea of "treatment" and even more distressed dealing with the DCFS worker now assigned to the case who informed her that the hospital was going to release Josh to her. She maintained, rightfully so, that he wasn't any better—just sedated—and that his problem behavior would continue once the sedative wore off. Because she rebuffed their attempt to have him released to her in his zombied state, DCFS charged her with neglect, a bogus charge that would show up on her record if she ever applied for a child-related job.

Her stress was incredible—just dealing with this one kid—and she had 5 others who had their own problems. Despite these ordeals, Beth knew she needed to start working on her college degree if she ever hoped to be employable at a decent wage. She started taking courses at the community college. Beth would come over to the shelter late at night, while her mother watched the kids, so she could use the computer and access the Internet to do her course work. Beth's academic progress bespoke her intelligence and determination.

In the meantime, Beth's mom, an intelligent Hungarian immigrant chained to an abusive, alcoholic man, finally was mercifully released from this relationship when he died. Beth, an only child, knew how bad things were for her mom. Now freed from this cruel condition, the two of them formed a team to help each other survive. Her mom had access to some financial resources that her husband had kept from her, so she was determined to do what it took to help her grandkids. One of their most interesting tactics was buying a horse!

They kept this horse—which they saved from the glue factory—at a stable in a nearby rural community. Beth took the kids out to visit the horse every chance they could get. She didn't know anything about training a horse, but they learned by doing. Josh's interest in the horse flourished and Beth figured it was a "carrot" to help him improve his behavior. It worked! Josh soon straightened out enough to eventually become an honor student and a star basketball player in his grade school.

Once things got back to "normal" for her family, I knew she could use some extra money, and I was looking for someone to work part-time at the shelter. We briefly discussed it and she eagerly embraced the opportunity. We both knew she had the street smarts, compassion, and energy for the job. She saw it as a welcome break from kid care (while Grandma babysat), and I was pleased to give her an opportunity to give back. Many of the volunteers remembered her from her stay at the shelter and welcomed her progress as a sign that some families could traverse myriad problems and return to normalcy. Few knew of the level of those problems.

Life wasn't all well; especially when she got word that her ex was near death and was transferred to a prison closer to home. She was distressed to find out her oldest kids sneaked down to the prison hospital to see their dad. Some of that trauma eased when their dad died, removing this abusive figure from their lives.

Beth, her younger kids and her mom still come to the soup kitchen and shelter for holidays. They deeply appreciate the help given to get their all-too-typical family back on their feet, and they sympathize with other families in similar situations, often extending much needed help and encouragement to families in similar straits.

One recent Christmas, her youngest daughter, "Jenny," called with an offer to play Christmas carols for the people staying at the shelter. Her 9-year old innocence and compassion touched my heart deeply and I enthusiastically responded "yes," scheduling this budding Beethoven to play at a time when a few folks would be around who would be an encouraging audience. She capably played an array of tunes, joined at our broken-down piano by a host of kids staying at the shelter and a few music-loving adults. They didn't know this performer had once been homeless and that her mother sacrificed greatly to make sure her daughter had the opportunity to learn to play the piano.

The joy on Jenny's face brightened the room and somewhat soothed my tired heart. *Don't give up, don't give up, don't give up...*

It awes me how the resilient thread of survival and vitality can weave through families who have experienced so much turmoil. It saddens me how difficult it is for them to get the help they need to improve their situation. Their often-unnoticed fiber fills our communities with an unappreciated strength. Their tried-and-tested filament attests to the reality that not all families that have been tattered and torn will be irreparably shredded. We can learn lots from them…

15. Never Give Up!

D ivorce and family break-ups contribute significantly to the ranks of homeless families. Rarely are the problems simple, as was the case of "Lynda" and her four kids. As bad as things are leading up to the divorce, often circumstances worsen immeasurably, with women and children suffering the most.

Although Aurora was their home, Lynda took her family to Chicago after her divorce, and they struggled to survive by staying with friends and relatives. With a family of five, they understandably quickly wore out their welcome at one place and moved on. When they had money, they stayed in motels. Eventually, the family ran out of options, so they "lived" in the family's compact car, a challenge made more difficult by the fact that this was a large family—physically speaking.

For three months during the fall, the family struggled to survive, sleeping in the car, washing up in fast food restaurants, and, because they lacked a permanent address, not attending school. They finally returned to Aurora and to our emergency shelter, fearing overcrowded and scary Chicago shelters.

We fought to get them back into their schools of origin, as specified in our newly passed state law[11] governing the rights of homeless children to education. The school district, on the east side of town, had a hard time believing that these kids had been out of school for three months and they directed the family to enroll in west side schools near the shelter. No, they get to go to the last school they attended, we reminded the administrators, who relented.

Eventually, the kids settled into a routine of sorts and mom tried to find work in order to get off welfare.

The saga of Lynda trying to get back on her feet became one of incredible proportion. Lynda would get hired, be excited about her job, usually a nursing home happy to hire a certified nurses' assistant, and she'd go to work. Shortly after beginning the job, she'd get sick—endometriosis, related to her menstrual period. She'd miss several days of work due to what appeared to be legitimate sickness, and would lose her job.

Relentlessly, she'd pursue her goal of employment, and repeatedly the pattern of work, sickness, and firing would occur. She used her medical card to go to the doctors who prescribed medications that failed to help. Her relentless pursuit of employment was both admirable and insane. I can't imagine how a person tries, fails, and tries again as many times as she did. She knew recent changes in welfare laws made it imperative to work, and she wanted to, but she couldn't get past the very painful condition that knocked her off her feet each month.

Her kids, though basically good, struggled with this crazy life of sleeping on pads on the floor of a very crowded family sleeping area. Neither they nor any of our kids had privacy, a basic need, especially for teens and preteens. They had no quiet place to do homework or to just chill. Their personal belongings were crammed into two lockers and garbage bags they had to store in the car due to the severe overcrowding in the family area. They lost their personal lives, as dismal as they were, and became enmeshed in shelter life.

Soon after the family entered our emergency shelter, we explored the next step of transitional housing. Although Lynda had a spotty work history, she seemed to effectively care for her kids and showed no signs of drug or alcohol abuse. We discussed the demands of our transitional housing program—hard work to get back on your feet, a maximum two-year stay, paying room and board (based on income), helping out with chores, keeping a close eye on your kids and getting along with others. She agreed, and the family moved into two dorm-style rooms, a palace compared to the emergency shelter's family area.

Lynda's oldest daughter, "Liz," really fought this unnatural communal lifestyle. She was 17, a senior in high school, and struggled mightily with her family's troubles. She was happy to move in with her boyfriend once she graduated. Although she had typical teen-parent conflicts, she managed not to burn bridges with her mom or with shelter staff, so she was welcomed for future visits. She got a job and helped her mom with taking care of the kids, especially when her mom was infirm.

The other kids weren't perfect—report cards not as good as they should be, behavior issues at school—but Lynda managed to keep a grip on her kids despite her concerns about her health. Her second oldest, "Meg," a sophomore, faced major problems at school. Because the kids missed three months of school, she was behind in her studies. The district eventually placed her in an alternative program which Meg and her mom fought because Meg had dreams of going to medical school and she rightly felt this could impede her plans.

The kids soon adapted to the relatively less hectic living in the transitional program. They were enjoyable kids, helpful, well-behaved, and funny. They got involved in school activities—sports, band, and clubs. The school bus would pick them up in front of the shelter, a traumatic thing because their schoolmates would know where they lived and tended to make fun of them.

Lynda, in the meantime, was raising staff's suspicions about her irregular work. Does she want to work? Are these frequent debilitating attacks real? Why doesn't the doctor do something? Is she on drugs? Those questions and more began to undermine the family's stay in the shelter. Her staff contact person became antagonistic and things were starting to get ugly.

Sadly, it's easy to misjudge a person's chronic sickness, especially when you think they're getting medical care. Doctors, however, frequently treat women, especially those reliant on the medical card, with less care than women who have adequate insurance. Unfortunately, economics and prejudice play a significant role in the quality of medical care.

Meg, who fought being in the alternative program, finally settled down to put her intelligence to work. She began excelling in school and entered the regular class as a junior at the beginning of the next school year. Her brother, "Eddie," ambled along through school, succeeding at sports because of his size, doing passable work in his classes. Meg's other sister, "Lisa," meandered through classes, uninterested in much of anything, but not causing any problems.

Eventually, Lynda underwent a series of progressive medical treatments which finally led to her being properly treated for her frequently misdiagnosed, extremely debilitating ailment. She regained her strength, got a job and kept it—a noteworthy accomplishment! The family was on track for moving out of the shelter, but they had already exceeded the time limit set by HUD regulations. The director decided to ignore the limit, a rarely used option. It bought time for the family as they eagerly looked forward to moving into their own place. Despite the best intentions, living in the shelter got very old for all involved.

Barbara Duffield, my friend from Washington, DC, who worked for the National Coalition for the Homeless, contacted me. She had received an inquiry from a producer of a national TV kids' news program who wanted to include homeless kids in a show on the presidential election. Barbara asked me if I knew of anyone who would be good and I immediately thought of Meg.

Many people don't think of the traumatic effect of a homeless kid "coming out" to classmates. Among the things you wouldn't want your schoolmates to know, homelessness is top on the list. Meg had struggled with wanting to let her friends know of her plight, but she feared their rejection, so she kept a low profile. She couldn't ask them to come to her "house" because of where she lived. She carefully and painfully balanced conversations to keep them away from home topics.

My experience with other kids, who, with their parents' consent, went public with their homelessness in media stories, was positive. I worked with them and the media to keep things real, to avoid unnecessary sensationalism, and to respect areas of the young person's life that didn't need to be part of the story. In every instance, the young person felt a sense of empowerment that opened other doors for them. Often, they became able to educate classmates and teachers as to the harsh realities of homelessness.

After giving it considerable thought, Meg agreed. The TV people flew her and her mom to New York and treated them like celebrities. Both Meg and her mom loved the experience and it gave Meg the opportunity to express some long-held feelings about homelessness to a nationwide audience. This was a turning point for her as she then sought opportunities to advocate for homeless issues. She became an ardent, effective spokesperson.

Meg's senior year brought an outstanding accomplishment. I was aware of the LeTendre Scholarship[12], given to outstanding students who were currently or formerly homeless. Since Meg had been doing so well in school, I suggested to her and her mom that she apply. She got word that she won, which meant a trip to North Carolina and an appearance in front of an admiring gathering of hundreds of educators who worked with homeless kids. To this encouraging audience, she shared her dream of being a pediatrician— a dream formulated after she received and witnessed loving care from our volunteer medical professionals at Rainbow Clinic.

When we returned from that event, I received a call from a Chicago radio personality who invited us to be guests on her talk show. The ride into Chicago proved to be an enriching event for Meg and an enlightening opportunity for me. Meg shared more intimate details about her months living in a car with her family. Although I thought I knew what an impact that had on them, it turns out I had no idea. She was so devastated by this unwelcome isolation that she felt suicidal. Meg worked through it with her mom's help and a reservoir of inner strength that she found when she realized she had a lot to offer.

You could tell that Lynda and her family were fast heading for the moment that they'd be able to move out with pride. Lynda, who became an unofficial mentor to new families moving into the shelter, had been working hard, saving her paychecks and searching for a suitable home. Her kids were on track in school, well-behaved, and we all knew we'd miss them, despite the four years they stayed at our shelters.

Lynda's job became a lifeline for her and she thrived doing what she does best—helping others in a treatment program. Even though she wasn't an addict, she possessed lots of street smarts and compassion to guide people who have lost their way due to addictions. Meg also began working there as receptionist, taking classes at the community college while putting her dream of college on hold until she had adequate resources saved. Their home, a modest dwelling not far from the shelter, became the symbol of success for some of the other families who were friends with Lynda and her clan.

About a year after the family got back on its feet, I was desperate for a part-time assistant in the morning to help volunteers get folks moving out of the emergency shelter by the 7 a.m. closing. Lynda came to mind and happened to be in our lobby as I walked through. I asked her and she enthusiastically replied, "Yes! I'd love to be a part of the staff of this place that helped me so much." We arranged her schedule to accommodate her obligations to her family and to her full-time job. She performed her responsibilities admirably—as a benevolent drill sergeant.

Her kids stop by often and help with large and small projects. They don't know many of the residents at the transitional shelter, but they freely offer suggestions for survival and success as they get to know the kids staying with their families. They had the equivalency of a four-year education program during their stay with us, and chances are that they'll be able to turn their knowledge into valuable lessons to help others in the same situation.

Families struggling for help often find themselves scorned by the helpers, me included. Skepticism, when it gets beyond the healthy level, becomes a barrier, often impenetrable, denying the consideration that we would hope for if we were in that same position. That's probably a good time to use the "Do unto others…" approach.

16. Terrible Teen Years

Sitting at the dining room table, Chris played with a "Hot Wheels" car, zooming it over the yellow-laminate road, oblivious to the multi-level drama playing out around him.

Besides acne, fickle friends, and searching for one's identity, teen challenges include homelessness for some unlucky kids. With or without parents, the lack of a place to live makes life hell for kids in their formative years.

This chunky bespeckled boy-teen, had a mom to speak of, but she had her own problems, including homelessness on a fairly regular basis. "Wanda" had been married to a tow truck driver with a reputation for alcohol-fueled fury. She grabbed her own bottle and hung onto it for her own diminishing sanity. Chris came along at some inconvenient point in this marriage destined for failure.

Watching kids grow up in a shelter is not a pretty sight. Those who experience multiple stays illustrate the vulnerability of a society that cuts back services, giving up on the hard to help, leaving the most-troubled to fend for themselves. Chris, with his mental limitations and his man-boy physique, was ripe for a life filled with bad choices.

"Hey, where's Chris? I haven't seen him for a while…" I'd comment to his mom. Wanda mumbled something about he was in "juvie" and let it go until I'd press further. Seems like he got locked up in the juvenile justice center for joy riding. At first I was taken aback but, after several repeat performances, I too became blasé about his hobby of car snatching.

While Chris was generally well liked by most staff and regulars at the shelter, he was even more appreciated by bullies who needed a dupe for their capers. They'd talk Chris into helping them, sometimes bribing him with a toy car, and got him to help with petty crimes—breaking into vehicles, shoplifting, etc. If Chris got caught, well, he was a juvie and wouldn't have to do hard time.

In his spare time, Chris developed a love for other people's cars. He must have learned valuable skills from his "friends" about how to steal them, and he practiced his trade diligently, getting caught time after time.

His powerless mom was ill equipped to do anything meaningful to intervene. Her alcohol-impaired thought process didn't allow her to figure out that she needed to get a place of her own so she and Chris could focus on his future—however bleak that would be. Or maybe she was astute enough to figure out that she didn't have enough money to get and maintain her own place, nor could she earn enough if she got a job, and besides, who would watch Chris if she was at work…

So, as with many families, they tried as hard as they could to survive. They became resigned to the pattern of moving in and out of homelessness. Chris missed more days of school than he attended because he had more fun hanging out with his buddies, stealing cars, and driving through the streets of Aurora late at night. He was busted, busted again, and busted again, until he reached the ripe age of 17 when his repeat offenses made him "an adult" in law enforcement terms.

He had a few stints in the county jail, the overcrowded facility on the edge of tony Geneva, up river from Hesed House. Although he never talked about it, his sullen behavior when he returned from one of those "vacations" as many guys referred to their time in county, gave me reason to believe he had been sexually assaulted. So goes a hapless teen's foray into adulthood.

I can only speculate that his traumatic sexual incidents, coupled with his dysfunctional birth-to-teen years, swirled around to create an emotional collapse that needed the anesthetic effect of alcohol and drugs to help him cope. We tried getting help for him and his mom, but what was available, meager as it was, required a lot more cooperation on their part than either was capable of, so they hopelessly staggered through their days and nights.

Chris' burly size belied his child-like thinking. See car, want car, get car…First it was toy cars, but he became obsessed with real ones. Steal car, get caught, go to jail, get out, come to shelter, steal car. What a pattern for disaster. It didn't take long. His 17th year was his last joy ride. His high-speed crash into a telephone pole gave him the only relief he could imagine.

'Textbook' Case

"Sarge," the substantially built woman with fiery red hair, demonstrated repeatedly that she was on the road to recovery—from her life of crime and her addictions. Her three girls lived with family who figured they'd have the girls forever because Sarge's life patterns seemed permanently etched—drugs, poor choices in mates, crime to support her crack habit, prison to keep society protected from the likes of her.

No one, me included, would have taken odds on Sarge getting her kids back, but she did. This arduous process took a long time, rightfully so, because she had convinced authorities and anyone who knew her that motherhood wasn't her best trait. First to return to mom was her 12-year old, "Mandy," who proved to be more of a challenge than her foster mother could handle. Mandy wanted to come to live with Mom, even if it meant in a shelter. Not so fast, I responded, not eager to add a volatile pre-teen to our overcrowded mix of functional and dysfunctional women and kids.

Sarge and I spent much time discussing what she wanted. Yes, I had to admit that in the time she spent with us Sarge was showing positive traits, including using peer pressure on her roommates to keep things neater and quieter in the women-family sleeping area. To me that spoke volumes for her leadership ability! That place was a nightmare to govern. Her moniker, Sarge, reflected the role she took with her self-assigned responsibility. The women and kids listened to her.

Eventually, Mandy came to test out what might become permanent. I made no promises, but from what I found out from a variety of sources, our hellhole of a shelter would be better for her than where she was. I probably knew it was inevitable, but I gave appearances of resistance. Short stays became longer. Finally, with many misgivings, I capitulated, and Mandy became official.

At first it was as promised, Sarge kept a short leash on her feisty daughter. They eventually moved to a crappy motel on the outskirts of the border of Oswego and Aurora, one of countless "no tell motels" that no one wants to talk about because of their seedy character. Their "residence" gave Mandy access to the Oswego school system, a fairly lily-white community priding itself on small town quality of life.

This mixed-race mixed up child was enrolled in school but found that the regular classroom environment was too much to handle. The school tried kicking her out, but Sarge asked me to intervene, which resulted in her getting into their alternative program, one designed for challenging kids. That she was...

Many adventures comprised this ill-fated family's attempt to get back on its feet. Hormones raged, with a love affair between Mandy and "Jimmy," an equally matched lovable homeless dysfunctional kid with disaster written all over him. Teen love can drive responsible adults crazy. This relationship had all the ingredients of insanity for Sarge and me. It eventually ended when Jimmy was arrested for sexually and physically abusing a child at a friend's house. In the process, he fled to Mississippi to stay with family. Mandy followed, but Sarge went down to get her, practically dragging her back.

Too many pieces of this story must go untold because I cannot begin to recall, much less retell, this saga in family reunification. It could be its own book. Somewhere along the way Sarge was granted custody of her girls, which actually—and amazingly—seemed to be a good thing at the time. They got their own house in a nearby small town, with Mom working at a gas station and the girls trying to plug into the quiet life of this farm community.

Disaster was not far from the picture, and when Sarge met the man of her dreams, a strapping black man who recently came out of prison, I inwardly groaned, my fragilely restrained prejudices fueled by my radar for potential disasters on the horizon. Her inability to sort out her emotional needs from what is good for her and her family was a lifelong disability. His inability to live in this dysfunctional family was predictable. So was the outcome...he sexually molested Mandy, impregnating her.

This caused an inevitable crisis too big for this family to handle. Mom snapped, and her agony cried out for relief only available through the euphoric high of crack cocaine. Her income couldn't support her habit, so she resorted to her previous trade of petty theft, which still didn't produce enough cash, so she started selling drugs.

She lost her job, her kids scattered, her significant other went back in prison, and she bolted to Tennessee, taking her pregnant daughter with her. The plan, ill fated as it was, was to move in with a relative who promised that jobs were a plenty and life was good. I reluctantly helped them move by giving them bus tickets. For my part, it was getting rid of a problem that was too big to handle...a coward's way out.

Mandy wanted no part of the move. She had several "friends" of dubious quality that she didn't want to leave. This teenage nightmare had an active drug habit, a destroyed sense of sexual parameters, a shattered sense of self-worth, no educational skills other than her street-wise senses that have been honed by her many years of exposure to this worst kind of learning, no family to lean on, and now she was being ordered to go to Tennessee by her mother who had lost all sense of being a mom, much less a grandmother to a baby who would soon have no mother and not a lot of hope.

I knew what was going to happen—Mandy was going to run away, joining the ranks of thousands of unaccompanied homeless youth on our nation's streets. Surprise—she returned to Aurora, got arrested for prostitution, and began cycling in and out of the shelter.

Better Off Alone?

"Ricky's" forlorn face spoke volumes. His hopelessness oozed out like acne, his slumped shoulders shouting, "I'm a mess!" He wasn't kidding.

He showed up one night, desperate for a place to stay. Ricky was 16 at the time, unaccompanied by a parent, so we couldn't keep him for more than a night because of laws that prohibited sheltering unaccompanied teens for more than overnight in emergency shelters. (Something must have gotten lost in this legislative process. They forgot to appropriate sufficient resources to even begin to address the exploding homeless youth population.)

Since I couldn't see casting him aside after the magical overnight time period, I figured I needed to find out more about this scrawny boy to see if some solution could be created. I knew from vast experience that the state agency responsible for children, the Department of Children and Family Services, wouldn't want to deal with him. They had their hands full with too many cases of abuse and neglect. They'd tell me, as they had so many times, that since we had the kid, we could deal with the situation.

Oddly enough, I found Ricky endearing. He was so pathetic, filled with a sullen resignation befitting his circumstances. His mom and his two sisters were staying with an aunt in Aurora. He didn't get along with any of them. "They don't understand me," he rightly proclaimed. He reeked of anger. He wasn't going to be happy to hear what I was about to tell him—that he couldn't stay here without some responsible adult with him. I marveled at the absurdity of my position and this situation.

Knowing I had nothing but bad news to tell him, I figured I'd at least try to extend a life preserver to him—I told him things would be even rougher than what he had encountered thus far but I'd try to help him connect with some help. Since I at least didn't reject him outright he sensed that I was probably his only hope. We sort of bonded, fragile though his trust was, and he understood that I was at least sincere about wanting to help him.

He told me I could call his mother and find out what was going on for her. Some things I'd rather avoid, especially finding out that this was another family destined for disaster. She told me that they couldn't stay where they were any longer, so that ended Ricky's unaccompanied homeless youth status. His mom and two sisters moved into our overcrowded shelter. Oh great…

This family's saga defies telling. With all that was going wrong I could see that they tried their hardest, but the pervasive strain of mental illness kept Ricky and his mom from being able to get along. His angry outbursts challenged us because of our need to keep some semblance of order in the shelter. This high maintenance family would prove to be one of our most challenging—trying to find help; to guide them to solutions to their homelessness defied our best efforts. Our efforts were in part motivated by the realization that we wouldn't be able to handle this family much longer. We just didn't have the capacity to offer the kind of help needed for this multi-challenged family.

Mom wanted better for herself and her family. She was severely impaired by depression and could only get minimal help from local mental health agencies because they had limited resources and too many needing help. She was willing to work, but her despondent nature held her back. They eventually moved out, but just like other families beset with multiple problems, they moved in and out of homelessness. She worked, struggling with issues like transportation, childcare, and rising utility bills and rent. Ricky eventually set off on his own, choosing to move to Wisconsin with a friend of questionable nature.

All of these kids, and many more like them that passed through our shelter, have minimal chances for ending up as successful, productive adults. They often didn't finish school, in part because their multiple needs made education too challenging for both the schools and the kids. They had fractured relationships with their families, often because of myriad reasons— sexual abuse, drug and alcohol problems, mental illness on the part of a parent and the teen, high mobility, few options for gaining help to get out of the deep hole of homelessness and hopelessness.

Will they become anything besides homeless adults? I hardly think so. Can I blame them? No. They are forever etched in my mind as poster children for "the terrible teen years." Instead of blaming them, the rest of us need to accept the reprimand for letting families fall into the abyss of family dysfunction.

Massive changes are needed to the way we systematically abandon people, especially parents with kids and/or teens without parents, in need at their most vulnerable moments. Societal expectations of these beleaguered families and unaccompanied youth far exceed their ability to cope with day-to-day challenges, much less if homelessness is part of the equation. We non-homeless adults should try to imagine what it would be like to manage our family, with multiple issues screaming in our faces, with no place to call home and no way to get the help needed to get out of the situation. What can we expect?

How can we salvage teens before they face adulthood saddled with irrepressible feelings of rejection and hopelessness? How can we ease them back into a world that takes into account their life experiences, good and bad, and encourages them to strive for success?

PART 5—

THE BIGGER THEY ARE
THE HARDER THEY FALL

"Sometime in your life,
Hope that you might see one
starved man,
the look on his face
when the bread finally arrives.
Hope that you might have baked it or
bought it or even needed for yourself.
For that look on his face, for your
hands meeting his across a piece of
bread, you might be willing to lose a lot,
or suffer a lot, or die a little, even."
Daniel Berrigan, S.J.

17. Big Bill

*B*ig, gruff-looking Bill died last month at the early age *of 48. Formerly homeless, Bill pulled himself up by his (well-worn) bootstraps—and got a job, a life, and a wife. This lovable and loving man died while working at a job he loved doing—driving his cab in affluent Naperville. Cause of death? Most likely heart related—a broken heart and a sick heart.*

Bill belonged to the untold masses of "PWHI" or persons without health insurance. His cab-driving career offered him dignity and a small income, but no benefits. He trained as a truck driver but that career ended before it began because of heart-related health problems and no health insurance.

Bill and his deceased wife, Eileen (who had died of a heart attack the previous winter), both suffered from untreated heart problems. These ordinary working stiffs struggled to keep the roof over their heads but had no insurance and no health care provider willing or able to serve their life-threatening diseased hearts. (from a letter to the editor I wrote, published 7/1/99, Copley Newspapers)

Bill and Eileen tried to take care of themselves and would have seen a doctor had one been willing to see them. Too many PWHIs and too few docs. Sounds like an easy equation to solve, but it's cheaper to let people drop like flies.

Bill was one guy who defied stereotypes—he was pretty scary looking, a large biker-type, with a wild Fu Manchu mustache, deep piercing eyes—but he was delightful. He landed at PADS sometime in '98, and he blended into the crowd.

One night, someone in "the crowd" got a little rowdy and I intervened. The rowdy guy got a little more than rowdy, threatening my well-being, a fairly unusual happening. I was making my way to the phone to call the police when Bill stood up, got in the face of the drunk, rowdy guy, and told him to sit down and shut up. "Who do you think you are telling me what to do?" asked the troublemaker.

"I'm Father Bill," asserted Bill, fraudulently representing himself to the significantly intoxicated guy. At the time, we had "Pastor Jose" working as my assistant. Father, Pastor, the guy wasn't going to know the difference. It worked, and amazingly, he settled down without further problems. We joked about Father Bill for years after.

Bill, intent on getting back on his feet, eventually earned a spot in the transitional shelter and soon moved out to his own apartment, supporting himself by driving a cab, a job he loved.

He stopped by once in awhile, one time proudly telling me about the love of his life, Eileen. He brought her by to introduce her and show her his "roots." It was obviously love, despite the challenge that their pending marriage brought—her teen-age daughter. Eileen and Bill and I visited a few times, still joking about "Father Bill."

The joking stopped when he and Eileen faced the insurmountable challenge of attaining life-sustaining health care without either of them having insurance. I made a few calls, and arranged for her to be seen by our Rainbow Clinic, an all volunteer-run medical clinic at Hesed House. But Eileen's heart was too damaged and she soon died, leaving Bill and his stepdaughter to cope with this massive void in their lives.

A few months later I read a news story about a cab driver in Naperville, the affluent community to the east of Aurora, who died a few blocks from his home when he crashed into a tree from an apparent heart attack. Somehow I knew it was Bill. It was.

A few weeks after Bill's death, one of his friends—a big biker-type guy with tattoos, long hair and a ferocious appearance— came to the door asking for me. He, too, had stayed at the shelter a few years earlier. Although I didn't recognize him, he knew me.

We reminisced fondly about Bill. He told me Bill's stepdaughter was now staying with a relative. He brought some of Bill's clothing—the practical kind that served the cab driver well—and said Bill would want me to give it to someone who needed it. I took the bag of clean, neatly folded pants and shirts.

Stereotypes—we all rely on them to give us prominence in a world filled with "different" people...people not like me. Allowing the person to share their worth rather than me determining whether or not they are worth anything—what a novel approach to uncovering the wealth of people all around me! What tragedy occurs when preventable health care issues snuff out lives that have so much value...

18. Dennis the Menace

S ome people made it easier than others to figure out why they were homeless. Dennis made it extremely easy. His scrawny face with a sharply pointed nose combined with an unforgettable toothless smile. He seemed very simple minded, and his major speech defect made communication difficult when he was sober, impossible when he was drunk. His tall body seemed connected scarecrow-like and his every movement was jerky. His eyes, however, reflected his childlike happiness, and Dennis, besides being a real friendly, lovable guy, was one of the most appreciative people I've ever known.

At first, it seemed that Dennis' real problem was alcohol. He'd drink often, and many times I had to ask him to leave the shelter because he was too disruptive. He'd get real mean with anyone who teased him, and lots of guys thought it was funny to see him get mean because he was pretty harmless. Still, rules were rules and disorder couldn't be tolerated, so out he'd go, sometimes with great difficulty.

The next day, Dennis would return and in his inimitable way, he'd say, "I'm sorry Diane. OK?" I'd go through the routine of trying to make him understand what a pain in the butt he was when he was drinking, that he was so mean, and he'd cock his head and say with all innocence, "Really?"

Dennis, vulnerable and pathetic, was loved by just about everyone. His innocence, combined with his physical and mental disabilities, made him special. His sincerity and his goofy laugh warmed more hearts than we'll ever know. But he had a few detractors, sadly those who pledge to serve and protect—law enforcement officers and some guys on the ambulance crews. Understandably, Dennis was a real pain when drinking and he tested patience like no one I've ever seen. His encounters with them often ended with a ride to jail or to the hospital.

Because he was developmentally delayed, he qualified for extra help from an agency that worked with developmentally disabled people. We encouraged Dennis to cooperate, holding our breaths that he would make his appointments and not get sidetracked by his drinking buddies. Fortunately, the caseworker saw Dennis' lovability and went the extra mile for him several times.

He finally got his own room in one of the few local boarding houses, where he received the all-essential supportive services to keep him on the right track—at least most of the time—and all seemed well. Since he had no cooking facilities, nor could I ever imagine him cooking, we agreed to let him come for dinner if he was sober, and that arrangement seemed successful for a while.

Dennis is one person that benefited from the community atmosphere at the shelter. He loved people and they loved him. So, the pattern of getting him housed was a double-edged sword. Having his own room had an obvious appeal, at least for those of us who thought people should move out of homelessness. The trouble was, Dennis, like so many who move out of a crowded shelter, endured excruciating loneliness. We knew he would return, and after awhile, I became resigned to the fact that the only benefit of getting him housed was that it temporarily freed up a valuable bed space for someone else.

Dennis had his literal ups and downs when it came to alcohol. He was incapable of walking steadily when sober, so the alcohol made his gangly limbs even more ungainly. He fell often, and one incident found him walking by the local newspaper office, just a few blocks north of the shelter, when he just kerplunked his butt on the curb and couldn't get up. Someone called the police and they came, impatiently yelling at Dennis to get up.

He was so clumsy that it could be considered perverted entertainment to watch him try to stand. I can imagine that he was getting belligerent, as I have often observed, so the combination of ingredients became volatile. A friendly reporter who knew that Dennis was one of my buddies called me, reporting the dehumanizing scene as it was unfolding. Incensed, I was getting ready to head down the street to rescue Dennis, but he was tossed into the paddy wagon and hauled to jail, only to be released hours later, hungry and without means to eat.

His most recent room—a "hotel" which catered to the hard-to-serve population—was less than 2 miles up the road from the shelter, close enough for Dennis to walk, which made it easier for him to eat regular meals. He was losing weight due to a chronic health problem, so his doctor and his caseworker were encouraging him to eat a lot and gain weight. "See Diane, I gained 2 pounds!" he proudly boasted in his mumbly voice. I tried to keep him stocked with easy-to-fix food, including his favorite and mine—chocolate chip cookies.

Since he lived just up the road, I often offered to give him a ride home at night on my way home in part because no one should be out in the bitter cold, but mostly to make sure he got home safely. He'd patiently wait, thanking me profusely, and we'd chat as we headed to his boarding house. Although I couldn't understand 90% of what he said, we'd have a great conversation on the ride home. I'd pull in his driveway and he'd get out, thanking me over and over. Then he'd awkwardly walk toward the steps, stop, turn and wave with his gawky motion that I grew to love. People like Dennis were the reason for my existence.

Our unspoken agreement about the ride home, and his being able to come to the shelter for meals, depended on his sobriety. Dennis did fairly well, but once in awhile, the staff, already entrenched in a busy night would get a surprise: a dripping-wet Dennis staggering in after an unplanned encounter with the shallow Fox River that paralleled his route. Fortunately, some of our guys would find him, looking like a nearly drowned shivering cat, and make sure he made it the rest of the way to the shelter. "I'm sorry, Diane," he'd repeat over and over again as I firmly directed him downstairs to the men's shower area.

Fortunately, the guys knew the routine—they'd gently but firmly take him down to the shower, strip him, run warm water on him while one of us went hunting for Dennis' new outfit—head to toes. We'd toss the dry clothes at one of the helpers who would help him get dressed and they'd get him up to the dining room for a hot meal. "I'm sorry, Diane. I won't do it again," he repeatedly and sincerely promised to my unspoken "Yeah, right."

Over the years, I tried my share of tough love with Dennis with mixed results. If he came to the shelter intoxicated (but dry) I'd have him leave unless the weather was too nasty. He'd usually go without much more than a grumble, often with an, "Oh, OK, Diane. I'm sorry."

One spring night he came right at our busy opening time, his intoxication noticed by my staff during a "preventative maintenance" check outside before 7 p.m. Determined to be quite intoxicated, Dennis got the boot before even getting inside. He may have sat around outside the door for a while, then gotten up to leave. A little while later, one of the guys came in all upset, summoning the nearest staff person outside adjacent to the building. Dennis had apparently tumbled down the outside stairs, and was lying motionless with head on the ground and his tall body stretched over the stairs, his feet still six feet up on the stairs. When I came out, I remember standing there with tears of frustration, thinking, "Damn it, Dennis, now look at you…"

We called an ambulance. In the meantime, we tried to make sure he didn't move, covering him with a blanket that held our hopes that our meager efforts would keep him alive. The steep concrete steps were unforgiving and lethal. The ambulance crew did their best to gently move him, strapping him onto a board to minimize chances of further spinal cord damage. My heart sunk, because I figured this was the end of Dennis, and that we would all feel bad that we sent him away, in essence leading to this tragedy.

The next day I went to visit him in the intensive care unit of the local hospital. The head nurse realistically, but kindly, gave me no reason to hope that he'd survive. Despite tubes in and out of his body, his childlike innocence radiated, contrasted by a few sprouting strands of beard. That he had to suffer so much pain so needlessly tore at my heart.

I returned to the shelter to call his sister who lived in a nearby town. She and I had a heartfelt conversation, expressing our mutual love and frustration with Dennis. His sister came and we kept what we all thought was the deathwatch. He was unconscious for several days and I figured the worse.

After several days of bleak reports from the hospital, we were all still amazed that Dennis was still alive, albeit in critical condition. They transferred him to another hospital that handled spinal injuries. When I visited him there, he was immobilized but semi-conscious. His expressive eyes let me know he was as happy to see me as I was to see him.

I hardly knew what to say because I still figured he was not long for the world and it was my last chance to say goodbye. Trying not to cry, I told him we missed him and that everyone was praying for him. He smiled, at least registering the sentiment I was sharing. I had to leave before I totally lost it, so I just squeezed his hand and said I loved him and left, figuring it was the final goodbye.

Before my next visit, I called the hospital and spoke with one of his nurses. I thought she'd just say he had gotten worse, but she gave a guardedly optimistic report. She said he was even eating, a good thing because he had no extra body fat to begin with. I bought him a few candy bars, figuring they could at least melt in his mouth, and drove back to visit him.

"Amazing" hardly expresses his progress! He lit up and spoke animatedly with me, and my translation rate was still about 90% unclear. He kept saying, "I'll bet you thought I was a goner," which I could not deny. He repeated sounds that I took for "Thanks for the candy," and "thanks for coming to see me." His deep eyes spoke even more of gratitude and love.

Dennis' injuries, combined with his previous condition, limited the hope for much quality of life *if* he survived, which was still questionable. His sister informed the hospital that her brother might have Huntington's disease, which would eventually immobilize him, even without this latest fall. Incredibly, he made sufficient progress, enough for the hospital to transfer him to a special nursing home where he would probably spend the rest of his life.

I visited him a few times there, stopping to get chocolate chip cookies on the way. "Thanks for the chocolate chip cookies!" he enthusiastically responded. The last time I saw him he was walking—stiffly, but walking. "It was a really bad fall, huh, Diane?" he kept repeating and I kept agreeing with him. "I'm really lucky to be alive, huh, Diane?" to which I could only shake my head yes.

Dennis, like so many other homeless people I knew, could have benefited from a community-style supportive living environment. It would have been cheaper in the long run, especially with the medical care he now needed. However, he, like so many others, must teeter on the edge of life before they get any real help, and some never make it.

Letting a goofy, gangly guy like Dennis enter my life has enriched me immeasurably. How easy it is to scorn, to spurn, to deny help to guys like him…How often we judge a person on appearances… How many guys like Dennis are out there? Instead of turning them away, I will try to grasp their beauty before it's too late…

19. An Angry 'Buddha'

*E*d, a Buddha-bellied, mixed race thirty-something guy right out of prison, tested our open-door policy at the shelter. We tried to accept all persons in our program, despite what could be legitimate preconceived notions about potential behavior issues. That's how Ed got in. Ed looked like he could qualify for the top of the "most-likely-to-not-succeed list," but he got his chance to make or break it. I held my breath.

"Snarly" doesn't begin to describe his demeanor. He grumbled at people, and due to his size and appearance, Ed was menacing even when he was sleeping. I chatted with him about his attitude a few times, boiling the message down to "be nice." "I'll try to be nice, Ms. Diane, I'm really trying," he promised, but he needed plenty of reminders.

Ed was doing laundry one day in "laundry lane" when I stopped to chat with him. We began talking about his progress. My attempt to give him some positive affirmation was unexpectedly met by him sharing how his "anger management" therapy—mandated by the Illinois Department of Corrections upon his release from prison—was progressing. He proudly, but cautiously, reported that his counselor told him he was improving too.

Ed's first stay with us must have been nondescript because I don't remember any major problems. My memory, while shaky when I walk into the grocery store without a list, astounds me when I needed to put past events (of a negative sort) and faces (perpetrators) together. Ed's successful completion of his first season at the shelter qualified him to be considered for Tent City, our very strange and unique "solution" to summer homelessness— the time the shelter closes down for the warmer weather. Amazingly enough, Ed behaved throughout the grueling summer as one of our "campers."

Toward the end of a long Tent City season, as I was preparing to meet the volunteer coordinators for our annual orientation, Jesse, my assistant, indicated that I was needed out back. He seemed quite concerned and he updated me as we moved quickly to the campground. It appeared that Harold and Ed were about to engage in World War III, an uneven match between Harold (Ch. 22), a tall but mentally inept guy, and Buddha-Ed.

As I stepped outside with Jesse, I heard angry shouting. Ed and Harold were about to kill each other, an assessment confirmed by the fact that Ed was holding an aluminum bat in a menacing sort of way. Jesse and I moved quickly toward them.

"Ed, No!" I kept repeating, "Ed, No!" I hated to think that his progress of the past year was going to be destroyed by a swing of the bat towards Harold's already damaged head. I walked closer; looking at his rage-filled eyes, and hoped my scared-to-death feeling wasn't showing.

Our time-tested method of handling this type of crisis: Jesse, the faster of us two, bolted to the phone to call the police. (Cell phones were too expensive, especially if they "disappeared" during a predictable mental lapse of a beleaguered staff member. Our cordless phone was typically useless outside our fortress-like building, making them less likely to be stolen.) Jesse was able to accurately describe the emergency to the dispatcher. I, with my physical presence and poise in tough situations, was still considered "mother" by even the most-dysfunctional person. You don't fight "Mom."

With memories of my men's softball umpiring days probably swirling in my subconscious, I walked fearlessly (yeah, right) up to Ed and placed my hand on his shoulder, talking to him quietly, urging him to give up the bat. His anger seethed, nostrils flared, sweat pouring, eyes glaring at poor Harold, who was boldly but foolishly threatening to harm Ed. Somehow, Buddha decided to respond by harmlessly releasing the bat, and then he compliantly walked with me. I assured him that it would be a good idea to wash off the pepper spray that Harold had sprayed at him.

It was a conflict over food. The leftover prime rib donated and served as dinner to the campers had been set outside for the guys coming "home" late from work. Ed came home from work and he was HUNGRY! He proceeded to snatch a generous portion of beef, much to Harold's disgust. They angrily exchanged words—no love lost between these two—and Harold figured this was a great time to use his pepper spray (a weapon he had unbeknownst to us), so he aimed at Ed and *pssssttt* right in Ed's eyes.

Now, I've never experienced pepper spray, so I had no idea how painful it was. Ed was being an extremely good sport and went with me into the restroom to wash his eyes. I semi-mothered him through this process. (I've since heard that washing the stuff out wasn't such a good idea.) Then we went to find an ample amount of food (my idea was reward Ed for not knocking Harold into the next county). Ed was happy, relatively speaking, things had settled down out back, so I went to join the meeting in progress.

Jesse had things moving nicely. So I stepped in and laughed, explaining the "little" conflict away with a few words. Then I inadvertently touched my finger to the corner of my eye ever so slightly and YEOW! I had a trace of pepper spray residue on my fingers, and it really burned my eye. I excused myself and quickly went to wash my eye, gaining a new appreciation—and amazement—of Ed's discomfort. Remarkably for anyone who knew Ed and Harold, no further retaliation occurred.

Ed and I got along just fine for several months. He really tried to be respectful and control his anger. He frequently got impatient with others— sometimes understandably, but he managed to control his volatile temper. He was understandably discouraged about his possibilities for escaping homelessness because his prison record kept him from getting good jobs and housing. Most employers or landlords want nothing to do with ex-cons. But he kept trying…

Then, one Friday night in October, after the shelter had been open for the season for about three weeks, I was the only staff on duty—not a big deal for me. Actually I enjoyed the quicker pace. It was an atypically quiet night and the dining room was half empty, a mere 60 or so people, which seemed deserted to me. I was in the adjacent office registering a new guest when my "teacher ears" picked up the sound of trouble in the room. I quickly ended the registration, ushering the new person out, and I stuck my head around the corner toward the noise and saw tables and chairs flying, with a circle of guys forming around Ed and an unknown person who was at the moment sprawled out on the floor.

Just as I was assessing the situation—a fight, Ed and someone—I happened to see Ed reach for his sock and pull out a steak knife. Yikes! That changed things drastically. Some unknown force propelled me in the direction of the action and I found myself instinctively using the once-tested formula, "Ed, NO!" as I moved in his direction. I said it a whole bunch of times. The crowd parted. I moved toward Ed, chanting my mantra, "Ed, NO!"

Fortunately, the guy on the floor was in no condition to continue the fight, so it was just Ed and me. The guys who regularly stayed at the shelter were in a respectful space—far enough to stay out of my way, near enough to help if needed. But these situations, rare as they were, were best handled by me. The guys knew it and respected the procedure.

Somehow, I backed Ed out across the room toward the dining room door that led to the parking lot. He still had the knife and he was obviously real pissed. He began stomping around like a mad bull as he got outside.

Now, by this time, I would have thought (and hoped) the volunteers would have called the police, but I had no way of knowing, so I started pushing the buttons on the cordless phone I was carrying (hoping I was in range) to make sure the police would get there pretty darn quick. Actually, the volunteers should have used the silent panic alarm button, but they didn't, which could be a whole other story. Ed hollered to me, "Don't call the fucking police!" to which I mentally replied, "Yeah, right."

The police came quickly. Ed poured out his anger and frustration on them, requiring four officers to get him in the paddy wagon. He was arrested on the complaint I signed. I sadly, because I still liked Ed, had to tell him that I was permanently banning him from the property, a standard punishment for an act of violence of this nature.

A few months later, when I was at a funeral of a staff person's family member at a downtown church, I saw Ed as I came out of the service. We looked at each other, walked towards each other and hugged. He was fine or at least managed to temporarily forgive my role in depriving him of the only place he called home. I was sad.

My mind is filled with people I know who have spun through the revolving doors of our penal "system." I used to be scared of the idea of meeting someone just out of prison, but I have since met so many and have lived to tell the tale that I think my fear must have been distorted.

The common pattern—a guy (this is typically a male "opportunity") gets busted for a minor crime, does time into the county jail, gets released in an angry, desperate, deteriorated state of mind, and gets in bigger trouble. Eventually, either by his own actions or by police harassment or a combination of both, he gets convicted of a more serious crime (often a brainless caper) and eventually goes to the big house. If he didn't know how bad life could be, he'd learn there, then be released—far from rehabilitated. Many times, especially when the weather was at its Illinois nastiest, a guy would come in for the first time, standing out like a sore thumb with his prison garb on—white shirt, black pants, black windbreaker—and have to go through the humiliating experience of asking for basics like underwear and socks. I'd ask about winter clothing and the guy would point to his prison-issued black windbreaker and say, "I'd appreciate it if you had something a little warmer. Doesn't matter what size..."

These guys, ex-cons, are for some the pariahs of the community. No matter what their intentions, they struggle against insurmountable odds to re-enter society. With prison records, an ex-offender struggles to find housing, employment, public assistance, and anything else needed to survive in an intolerant society.

If any guys can thrive facing devastating adversity like this, be amazed. In this case, I fault "the system" more than I blame individuals. (Appendix 6) Prisons are a growth industry, like homeless shelters. Two key differences—the prison industry gets big bucks and they have little accountability. Most shelters scrape by on limited budgets, depend on people of faith to volunteer, strive to satisfy funders that they have met their goals, and they try to encourage people to regain their independence against impossible odds.

20. Worker Bees

"**R**ay" was an ironworker, union man, married and living in a nice house in Aurora. "I used to drive by Hesed House on my way to work and see all those bums sitting on the grass along side the building. It made me so mad that I had to go to work and they could just sit there," he related. "Now I'm one of them..." The "bum" who doesn't work probably contributes more resentment and negativity towards homeless persons than any other characteristic, real or imagined. Advocates have tried many ways to counteract that image, but it prevails.

Ray's downfall had a lot to do with alcohol. He sat on the grass while waiting for the shelter to open. He realized that his impression of who was homeless was based on false impressions and media-influenced stereotypes. Now he stood in line waiting for the shelter to open, just like the rest of the men and women who never envisioned homelessness as their future.

One of the most profound surprises for new volunteers, especially those who worked the early morning (3 a.m. to 7 a.m.) shift, was the number of wake-up calls they had to do for the people wanting to get up and go to work. Of the 94 or so guys in the men's sleeping area, probably 30 asked for early wake-ups, some as early as 3:00 a.m. They'd quietly leave the room filled with snoring bodies, get a bite to eat downstairs, then head out either to a permanent job or to one of the many temp agencies clamoring for cheap labor.

Even I was overwhelmed by what some people went through in order to earn a paycheck. In the midst of brutal Illinois winters, people would get up, grab a bite to eat, and walk—sometimes miles—to go to work. Walking to work isn't that unheard of, but most people who do it are dressed for the weather in Gore-Tex coats and shoes. Slogging through snow and slush in hole-riddled tennis shoes with a flimsy jacket, skimpy gloves and hat (if lucky) at 3:30 in the morning strikes me as impressive.

Knowing as many homeless people as I do, I smiled to myself at the irony of knowing that a clerk at a fancy department store, Marshall Field's, was homeless. Plenty of the area fast food restaurants had homeless workers. But the bulk of homeless workers headed to the temporary help agencies. They arrived before 5:30 a.m. and hoped to be sent out on a job. Some were, some weren't.

This was my dilemma. I knew work was good, but I knew these agencies took advantage of the pool of desperate workers, some of whom had advanced job skills, some had none. Some of our guys had stellar job histories, some had prison records. All of them had a burning desire to go to work; some were burned by less than ethical practices of their temp agency.

A 1995 study by the Illinois Coalition to End Homelessness on the prevalence of temp agencies, *What's Wrong With This Picture?*, indicated that temp agencies' common practices included docking workers for transportation to and from jobs, failing to assure adequate protection for those working in hazardous environments, and failure to pay medical expenses for on-the-job injuries. The report didn't garner much attention then. Since then, the astronomical proliferation of temp agencies across Aurora and throughout the rest of the country debilitates both impoverished workers and the general community.

Sociologists can identify the cost of these agencies to society. I saw the devastation wreaked on individuals who already had their share of problems. Typically, workers' minimum wage checks, less expenses (travel provided by the temp agency) were in the $35 range for a grueling 12-hour day, a net earning of less than $3 an hour. After getting up at 3 or 4 a.m., walking to the various temp offices, they'd have to sit and wait. They never knew if they'd be sent out or not. Many related that their chances were better if they kissed up to the temp office manager.

"Jack" came in excited one evening—he landed a long-term assignment with a temp agency! He was even getting $9 an hour! He'd be out of the shelter soon and back on his feet. I inquired where the job was and he told me it was at a local manufacturer's plant. The workers were on strike and the company was hiring non-union workers to fill slots. Yes, it was good he got a job, despite what I felt were issues of justice for the union. The job didn't last long, but Jack was able to move on to better things.

The cost of temp agencies to the community's quality of life seems to be discounted in lieu of the false pretext of "job creation." My impression of the growth of Aurora's day labor entities from the 1990s and into the twenty-first century has been substantiated in reports on this burgeoning industry[13], including National Training and Information Center's 2003 report, *Short Term Pay Long Term Struggle*. "Roughly 30 percent of American workers today do not have permanent, full-time jobs; instead they work on a day to day basis as laborers." I'm no economist, but when working people aren't paid a living wage, seldom get health benefits much less retirement benefits, and are vulnerable to labor abuses: "gender and racial discrimination, wage and hour discrepancies with paychecks, illegal paycheck deductions, health and safety violations,"[14] I figure the hard-to-employ are going to be exploited.

Maybe I was too over-protective of our folks, but I felt they had already endured some pretty harsh times, so when I saw them heading down a road that would make them more vulnerable, I cringed. Pete was one guy who raised my vulnerability hackles.

Nice looking, educated, non-addicted, "Pete" often had people wondering why he was homeless. I wondered too but, over the years, I observed his behavior. My guess was Obsessive Compulsive Disorder, one mental illness which doesn't always strike people as too awful because the afflicted one appears so "normal." A common example to illustrate OCD is hand washing to the extreme. The person cannot go even moments without rushing to wash their hands multiple times, even when his/her hands couldn't have gotten dirty.

Pete once got a job in a resale shop of a charitable organization. He loved it and seemed to do well. He religiously got up early, rode his bike about 5 miles to the store, and returned to the shelter with a sense of pride. He started out on a part-time basis, but eventually moved up to full-time.

I remember him coming in one evening, searching me out to show me his new health insurance card. Pride filled the toothless smile on his face. The same thing happened when he got dental benefits. He was happy to be able to address some of his more severe dental needs. Now he had a means to do it. So far, so good, I thought.

When Pete described his day at work to me, as he liked to do, I sensed some red flag issues. His way of doing things—his way, ignoring his bosses' instructions because he wanted to arrange things his way—came out in some of his stories. Hmmm, I thought. Here we go. But for a long time, Pete happily held this job. I attributed it to his having a manager who allowed Pete to do things his own way. That's good when you are dealing with someone with OCD. It works when the OCDer is someone with generally good judgment and the manager doesn't have an ego problem.

Paradise didn't last long enough. Pete met with the disastrous fate I figured was inevitable when his manager got fired and a new one came in. Unfortunately, and hard for most people to understand, someone like Pete isn't just stubborn. OCD goes beyond typical behavior quirks. When things started falling apart, Pete got totally derailed and came back one night saying he was fired. He was devastated. I was saddened but not surprised.

To his credit, he didn't give up. He found work and eventually got his own apartment. Despite his above-average intelligence, he was befuddled when it came to basics—like cooking simple things. He, with some level of embarrassment, asked one of the volunteers who was delivering some groceries, what to do with the frozen chicken someone had given him.

Good Enough to Work

Not every employer used and abused homeless employees. Some worked with people I couldn't imagine being employable. "Eddie" was one of them. Very mentally ill and a substance abuser, Eddie went to work construction almost every day. He was a laborer, grunt worker, but he loved it.

Something I didn't see in him must have kicked into gear when he entered the job site. He came back to the shelter bearing signs of hard work—dirt, paint splotches, torn clothing—and he cleaned himself up and went out again. He asked about work boots and I managed to find him some.

Eddie bought his prescription meds for his psych problems with his paychecks. He didn't have insurance. Without his meds he would become totally dysfunctional, so I gave him credit for figuring out how to prioritize his needs enough to get his meds. When he wasn't working and didn't have meds, he'd self-medicate, typically with alcohol, to still the demons inside his head.

Like many people, homeless and not, mental illness takes a toll on one's ability to hold things together. Unlike physical illnesses, which often manifest themselves with visible signs, mental illness just silently tears apart a person, much to the puzzlement of those around him or her. Eddie was no different. His family tried gallantly to get him help, but he skirted around their efforts and landed on the streets.

When Eddie self-medicated, I could immediately notice it because he was so wacky. He'd start muttering the same old thing over and over, obsessing on some point till he annoyed everyone in hearing distance. He'd talk about a woman friend of his who was allegedly double-crossed by some drug dealer. He'd not let go of the story till he almost drove me crazy.

How he managed to work baffled me. I couldn't picture him on the job site, working in trenches or in the midst of building demolitions, but he did. Perhaps his employer had personal experience with someone like Eddie in his family. Whatever it was, Eddie kept working, despite the reality that his paychecks would do little more than pay for his medication. His chance to get a place of his own was zero because he had minor criminal history, which would preclude him from any subsidized housing. Most private landlords who do criminal background checks would also reject him. No housing, no stability, no life…

Big Payoff!

One recent evening when I was at a public school event, I paid some attention to the crew of cleaners who moved about picking up after the audience. One of the crew looked at me and brightened up—"Diane, is that you?" he exclaimed. "Mike" rushed over and shook my hand.

He refreshed my memory in part—he had worked at a fast food place when he left the shelter. My hazy recollection was that I had forced his departure for some flagrant rule violation. He proudly related to me that he was doing well—not homeless, working regularly, and in the mainstream. He profusely thanked me for all the help I gave him. Gosh, I don't remember really doing anything special for him, was my unspoken thought to his gratitude.

Mike ask about staff he knew from his shelter days, sort of like asking about your old high school teachers, then said had to get back to work. I smiled and thought, "Who knew?" as I reflected on his stay and that of so many faceless workers. With a little luck and a lot of work, some people can make it back on their feet. That's good, because it somewhat eases the pile-up of bodies at homeless shelters. It also preserves the quality of life in the community, not to mention the formerly homeless person. The contribution to staff's morale, mine included, is immeasurable when we encounter a "success" story.

Jobs—we love 'em and hate 'em! Most of us take them for granted. But what we do for a living, no matter how meager, is a significant part of who we are and how others see us. Take that away and we lose a considerable part of our self-worth. Once that's gone, what do we have? And, more importantly, what do we have to lose?

Cannot this nation of opportunity put together a jobs program like we've had before—one that restores the all-important element of dignity to those who can and want to work? What's the cost? What's the cost not to?

21. Knocking on Death's Door

*D*eath and near-death episodes tend to be the way of life for too many homeless women. Women, along with children, are most vulnerable and most frequently at risk of all kinds of harm because of deteriorated health, inordinate stress and the preponderance of violence in their lives. Being a woman, I guess it hits too close to home when I encounter these experiences, even when it's through others…

On a chilly October Saturday afternoon, the homeless guys hanging around the shelter door recognized something seriously wrong when they saw it. Even to them, the scantily clad woman, dropped off by a taxi, represented the poster child of pathetic. "Elaine," a scrawny creature in her 40s, feebly made her way from the cab with a life-grip on her walker, sliding her skimpy hospital-issued slippers on the pavement, aiming for the dilapidated chair offered to her by one of the regular stoop-sitters. One of the old-timers raced around to the front door to alert me to a problem outside.

Elaine, obviously not healed despite her abruptly ended hospital stay, sat trembling in her sweater-covered hospital gown as I came out to investigate the cause for alarm. Just seeing her caused me to seethe—how could any hospital release her, much less by this taboo "drive-by-and-dump" method? I invited her inside, causing no resentment among those forced to wait in the cold for the 7:00 p.m. opening. They knew this woman was too frail to be outside and were grateful that I agreed. Elaine laboriously shuffled in and sat down, embarrassed by her frailty and state of utter dependence.

As we sat down to talk, I struggled to mask my fuming anger with the "system" that found it acceptable to expel a physically and mentally vulnerable woman to our shelter without any prior notice, in the cold, without adequate clothing, to a new and intimidating environment, hours prior to our opening. I couldn't wrap my mind around what these health care providers were thinking.

Elaine's problem—her insurance benefits expired and her safety net failed. She had been hospitalized for a number of symptoms attributed to a breakdown. Her family, the prime reason for her collapse, was obviously not a good choice for her release plan. Since she had no other resources, the hospital stuck her in a cab and sent her over. Homeless…

As Elaine opened up to me—at the time her only advocate—her story resonated with so many others I had heard. She had been working as a cashier in a gas station, married to an abusive brute, with a troubled teen-age son. Not a great life, but better than being homeless. This 80-pound woman showed me her drivers' license—where she was over 100 pounds heavier a year ago. Stress compounded her health problems, causing her collapse at home and subsequent hospital stay.

I cringed with knowledge of what homelessness would mean to her. More for my sake than hers, I asked her permission to call the hospital administration and vent my anger at the inappropriate way they treated her. She agreed, perhaps surprised to find that someone else thought it wrong. I made a series of phone calls that did little for my anger and probably would not enhance our fragile relationship with the hospital.

After getting the registration information I needed, I paired her up with one of the more trustworthy women at our shelter, not even needing to ask "Jennie" to look out for Elaine. We arranged for Elaine to stay inside after 7 a.m., a "privilege" extended to those too infirm to be sent out in the morning as volunteers closed the shelter. She was grateful, and following a bird-sized meal, she crawled onto her pad to sleep.

Elaine eventually moved into our transitional shelter, gradually piecing together at least some parts of her life. She reunited with her son who came to visit several times. Somehow she managed to build up her strength—mental and physical—to be able to go out and try again. She and another shelter resident pooled their resources and moved into a modest trailer. Their existence, fragile, but independent...

Fear Factor

The insistent pounding on our door late one Christmas Eve gave me a clue that it wasn't Santa Claus. I was right. After looking through the reinforced glass panel to see a person whose blood-caked face and battered eyes said "Big problem, help me," I cautiously opened the door. I was clueless as to the identity of this short woman standing on the stoop, her faced bruised and swollen, who immediately called me by name, "Diane, please help...."

Come in and sit on the steps seemed the only thing I could say. She hesitatingly agreed, "I knew I could come here and you'd help me." I still didn't recognize her, mostly because of her misshapen head, freshly rearranged by the iron pipe bashing from her boyfriend. "Donna," it turned out, stayed at our shelter a few years back, with grateful memories of our help. She had done pretty well until her latest choice of roommates. He was drunk and beat her within an inch of her life, again and worse than before. She somehow escaped, taking his car, heading to the one safe place she could think—our shelter.

As thoughts spun around my head, the first priority was to get her medical care. It was 11 o'clock on Christmas Eve. Fortunately, things were pretty settled inside the shelter. I knew this was going to take some time and finesse. Donna didn't want me to call 9-1-1 because they'd send the police and she "stole" her boyfriend's car. I assured her that I'd be able to take care of the police and that she REALLY needed medical care.

She finally relented, giving me the car keys to handle when the police came. We waited in the stairwell for the ambulance to come. I used the opportunity to strongly encourage her to seek help at the domestic violence shelter when she was released from the hospital. Her battered face underlined her fear—she looked at me with eyes that had seen death heading her way, and said that she wanted to come back "home" to our shelter because she knew she'd be safe. I didn't argue, knowing that the domestic violence shelter was probably filled to capacity anyhow.

The paramedics gently but firmly convinced Donna that she needed to be checked out at the hospital. They confided in me that they, too, feared for her life. The iron pipe had done major damage to her skull and the rest of her body. She was hospitalized for a couple of days and then she, head held together with stitches and bandages, returned "home" to the one place she felt safe—a homeless shelter filled with 100 men and 20—30 women and children.

No Degrees of Separation

Education and job experience unfortunately offer no barrier to homelessness. "Betty," a small, energetic woman with several years' service as a social worker after obtaining her Masters of Social Work degree, also had several years of homelessness. Her white, middle class upbringing counted for naught when her husband dumped her for a younger woman.

Her initial understandable—though harmful—response to this destroyed marriage was to hit the bottle heavily. Her MSW didn't protect her from alcohol abuse. She locked herself in a small apartment and drank to kill the pain. When her income ran out and she burned the already-dilapidated family bridges, she became one of the "helpees" instead of helper, and joined the ranks of "the homeless."

As with so many women and men devastated by shattered relationships, Betty stumbled from one alcoholic partner to another. She sought a mate who could drink with her, avoiding anyone who would challenge her to stop drinking and grasp life. She was rarely a problem at the shelter, despite her pathetic attempts to smuggle in alcohol, a rule breaker. It was inconceivable for me to kick her out into a bitterly cold night when she was too drunk to walk. I typically took the alcohol, dumped it, and let her sleep it off. Since she caused no other problem, no one had much to say about my "favoritism."

Early one fall evening, the police called, asking if "Brad," a homeless man who usually stayed at our shelter, was around. They were exceptionally concerned about finding him. I asked why. He had allegedly just tried to kill Betty, slashing open her skull with a broken liquor bottle. The cops found her downtown, blood pouring out of gaping head wounds. She was airlifted to a Chicago hospital specializing in head traumas. They offered little hope for survival. Brad hadn't shown up yet, but we were grateful for the heads-up. I alerted my co-worker and a few key volunteers. We locked the doors early and paid extra attention to who wanted to come in.

Even though we still hadn't seen Brad, the police quickly showed up in force. They searched the entire area around the shelter, figuring that Brad was so drunk he could make the mistake to return to his place of abode. That scared me, not because of what he might do, but because of what the guys at the shelter might do to him. Despite our attempt to keep the situation quiet so as not to inspire panic, word spread quickly. Everyone liked Betty, so the person who did her harm would be at great risk of harm himself.

The police interviewed anyone Brad hung with, hoping to ferret out clues as to where he might be hiding. After several harrowing hours, they found him elsewhere and arrested him, charging him with attempted murder. We were relieved that he was caught and gravely concerned that Betty might not survive.

Reports about Betty's condition were not good, to say the least. She lost a lot of blood and, in addition to her massive head injury, had other major wounds. Her shelter-mates prayed for her, and those who knew her best pondered what fate Brad deserved. I searched for next-of-kin information, which Betty refused to provide when we had registered her. By talking to her friends, we eventually located family, whom I called, but it was quite apparent their relationship was on the far side of estranged.

Betty hovered between life and death for a couple of weeks. Incredible medical care coupled with divine intervention combined to give her another chance at life. Unfortunately, this next round wasn't going to offer her any free passes. I vigorously fought the hospital's attempt to release her prematurely as long as I could. Knowing that her uninsured status would make her a prime target for a hasty, inadequate "release plan," we furtively made arrangements to let Betty recoup in our adjacent transitional shelter—a significantly more humane setting for recovery than our hectic, overcrowded emergency shelter. She'd have a real bed, only one roommate instead of twenty, and a smaller staff-to-resident ratio so people could look after her.

Part of the agreement to get her into the transitional shelter on a temporary, medical basis, was no drinking. When she first arrived back "home," drinking was still far from her mind. But once her pain medication was reduced, the dreadful memories of her trauma returned. Faced with her horrendous experience, she opted for alcohol, creatively arranging for someone to smuggle it in. Soon, she wore out her welcome at the more-structured transitional shelter, and returned to her familiar spot on the floor of the women's room.

Because the police had the alleged culprit, Brad, in custody, it would have seemed to be a "slam dunk" to wrap this case up. Betty was more than willing to press charges—an unusual stance for many abused women. Too often, after the memory of abuse fades a little, the woman tends to balance realities—stay with the abuser, who has promised not to drink or get violent again, or leave and be alone in a cruel world. Betty cooperated completely, impressing both the investigator and state's attorney with her resolute determination to follow through with the lengthy court process.

Despite Betty's and her state-appointed advocate's attempt to connect her with victim's compensation benefits, I doubt she saw any financial relief. Much to our dismay, it even appeared that Brad would be released on technicalities, which fortunately didn't happen. Betty would go to court, meet with her lawyer and spend lots of time going to doctors. Just the act of her meeting all those responsibilities was incredible, because of the logistical nightmare to figure transportation in this travel-challenged community. I slipped her a bus pass to help, an inadequate solution considering the amount of walking she'd have to do once she stepped off the bus.

Betty, for reasons known only to her, did what so many other people in her situation have done—continued to drown her pain in alcohol. Her choice of significant others improved slightly, with Jeff, a college-educated, respectable, kind, homeless alcoholic, befriending her. They made plans to get an apartment. Things always fell apart, usually because of the drinking, and they'd make plans again, numbed to failure by copious amounts of alcohol they both consumed.

As if Betty's life wasn't painful enough, she found out that she had uterine cancer. She tried, with Jeff's caring assistance, to grapple with that reality. Alcohol assuaged the anxiety accompanying this life-threatening sentence, though it did nothing for her physical status. Jeff, through family connections, helped her locate a caring physician and accompanied her to her numerous appointments. It wasn't a match made in heaven, but it was definitely an improvement from her previous relationships.

Women Power

Because our shelter served more men than women (100:20), women's stories fill proportionately less of my memories. Typically, women would endure horrible situations—abuse, violence, and abject poverty—in order to avoid homelessness. If they were lucky, friends or family would take them in, or they'd get into a domestic violence shelter.

Fortunately, most women at our shelter tended to be "low-maintenance" compared with some families and a few men. Even the women who were impaired mentally or physically tended to get along in their cramped quarters, with my worst complaint being the mess—plastic bags filled with belongings and un-bagged stuff covering every space not used for sleeping.

Women would use their often-rusty mothering skills to look out for the kids or to offer advice to an inexperienced mother. They'd figure out on their own that someone like Loretta (Ch. 25) needed help, decide what she needed and then do it, asking for supplies or assistance from me or other staff. They'd provide compassionate nursing care to someone recuperating, like Betty.

Going into the women's sleeping area at night to check on something, I'd hear soft conversations, often occasions for sharing advice about job hunts, dealing with staff or fending off interest from love-starved men, many times those at the shelter. Sure, they'd be catty, petty, and downright mean to someone, but rarely did the meanness get out of control, and more often it would be greatly overshadowed by a care for each other rarely seen in the world outside our shelter.

A variety of women came through our doors—a former wealthy matron from a prominent family who ironed her silk nightgown each evening; an infamous prostitute who had her name in the paper more than I did; an undocumented immigrant mother who considered herself lucky to be alive after a harrowing journey to this "promised land;" a timid mentally ill woman whose multiple identities confused even her; an HIV-infected, drug-addicted, street-wise, avid reader who reported everything going on with everyone else;

a classic co-dependent, mentally fragile middle-aged woman with a lousy track record in picking her men-partners; and so many more discarded beings...in every color, every age, from every walk of life and family background. Women just like me...

One of the hardest parts of my job was not seeing what happened to people, but rather seldom knowing what happened to those I had come to know and love, like Betty, who move on to points unknown. Sometimes I'd get unconfirmed reports, frequently just gossip. Occasionally someone would cross my path, a flicker of familiarity of times past, insecure in my memory's recall capacity and she would wonder if she even counted enough to be remembered...Women who struggle with survival and with knowing that for too many people they don't matter.

Those encounters, which hopefully do something to restore value to the "throw-aways," do so much to re-establish my sense of value to my work and my being.

22. Fear of 'Frankenstein'

*T*all, menacing-looking, zombie-like Harold stepped into our dining room in the mid-90s, much to the dismay of me, my staff and even people staying at our shelter. He looked like trouble, though we had nothing to base that on except his looks. OK, he looked like Frankenstein. All of us had our private thoughts that he was probably a child molester or rapist. None of us really wanted to be the one to register him. Fear because of the way someone looks…how common is that?

Not surprisingly, Harold became one of the most beloved homeless guys who ever arrived at Hesed House. His brain-tumor-ravaged, misshapen head sported about 4 strands of wispy hair and lots of scraggly scars. His deep-set blue eyes sparkled with mischief and kindness. His thick dark eyelashes were the envy of many less endowed women. He towered over everyone, especially little children magnetically drawn to him and his monster imitations.

One of my most courageous moments was not flinching when he playfully placed his hands around my neck, mimicking a strangulation that I hoped wouldn't happen. Harold, usually in the midst of a crowded room, would make his way over to me, shuffling like Frankenstein, arm extended, growling, muttering how he was going to choke me. Now, part of me thought, "I know he's just playing," while the majority of my brain cells screamed, "Diane, this is how bad things happen!" I'm still alive to tell the tale, so I guess the majority of my brain cells are wrong.

Our meager efforts to help people move out of homelessness often began with a rare moment: a couple of workers standing and talking to each other— "Hey, do you know anyone who would qualify for the transitional shelter?" We'd scan the room for someone who wasn't obviously in the throes of massive drug or alcohol use, and consider referring them. Harold finally came up in one of these conversations, which caused us to wonder what really got him here, and what would it take to help him move on to his own place. No one had really spent any time talking to him, but since the referral would need to be based on some background information, this step needed to happen.

I drew the short straw, so I asked him to sit down so we could talk. "So Harold, how did you end up here?" my opening question drew his long response that saddened as well as angered me. Many pieces are still unknown. He talked about a brain tumor removed when he was younger and several subsequent surgeries where surgeons sliced out the majority of his brain. He spoke of working in a carwash where some of his co-workers beat his already-damaged head with a pipe. It was difficult keeping him focused on our conversation—probably in part because he hadn't had someone sit and talk with him for an extended period.

My recollection of the conversation is that I was more overwhelmed than he about what had happened to him. His sweetness became evident to my previously blind eyes. I found it easier to ignore what I previously thought were his "high maintenance" tendencies, stopping me to talk at the worst possible moments...

...like Christmas Eve. Undoubtedly the busiest day of the year, Christmas Eve tested staff more than anything, and it wasn't because of the homeless people staying at the shelter, but rather the well-intentioned people in the community who felt this was THE day to do something nice for the underprivileged. That typically meant a semi-load of Barbie Dolls and Candy Land games being brought to the door all throughout the day and late into the evening. Each person bringing these gifts—well-intentioned acts that these were—wanted to talk about their gift, who was going to get it, why they were giving it, and lots of other topics that we didn't have time to listen to because...

...the phones were ringing off the hook with inquiries about our need for volunteers on Christmas Day. Door? Phone? Door? Phone? Which to answer? Not that any staff was sitting around making deliberations, because we were all trying to put the final (and most often the first and middle) touches on our Christmas Eve and Christmas Day activities.

At Christmastime, my day typically began about 10 in the morning and I'd be happy to be home by 1 a.m. Since some essentials—like planning the prayer service for the evening and getting gifts organized for our 120+ guests—needed to happen, I plowed through the building multi-tasking and stressing. So, when Harold approached me and said, "Diane, I need to talk to you," I put my hand up in the "Stop" position and said, "Not now, Harold..." as I kept racing to whatever important task my stressed self was working on.

That day, Harold must have approached me at least 100 times, requesting a moment of my time. Same response from me: STOP hand raised, "Not now, Harold..." and I'd move on. I do recall a nagging feeling of guilt as I raised my hand, blowing him off, and that thought served to kick me in the proverbial butt when later in the day I relented and said ever so sweetly, "Okay, Harold, what do you want?"

He asked me to wait a minute—oh, yeah, now I have to wait!—and he went to get something for me. He brought a neatly wrapped small package and said, "Open it. It's for you and my Hesed family." Ouch! I opened the gift and almost sobbed right on the spot. His gift, a simple plaque, bore a picture and a prayer about how Jesus died because of love for each person. "I wanted to give you something that would remind people of God's love," he humbly shared. It is without a doubt the most special Christmas present I have ever received.

Harold stayed in the emergency shelter longer than he probably should have. Some of us thought that he should get into the transitional shelter but we did some checking of police records and he had some charge, child molestation, which set off alarm bells of some of the staff. (Later we found that this charge had been dropped.) His likelihood of getting out of the transitional shelter—a sensible goal—was questionable because he didn't qualify for housing assistance thanks to some bureaucratic technicality. So he languished in the less than ideal environment of the emergency shelter and summer campground, both of which took a toll on his vulnerable health.

Harold kept us entertained with his simple, silly antics, and kept us on our toes keeping him from scaring some unsuspecting volunteers, especially the children. He never harmed anyone, and other than a few run-ins with people like Ed (Ch. 19), he was a sweetheart. His occasional seizures scared the unknowing volunteers or homeless persons who happened to witness them, but he was never trouble and guaranteed to be the source of much joy. He was a tease—and he took teasing well, feigning hurt sometimes, then laughing and patting the teaser lovingly on the shoulder.

"Sweethearts" like Harold tend to be vulnerable on the mean streets of any city or town. I never realized how much money he carried after he finally qualified for disability assistance. He never spent money for drugs or alcohol, just cigarettes, which he rolled himself, saving a chunk of money and giving him something to do. One day he happened to take his wallet out and I saw it stuffed with bills. Yikes! I asked him to come into the office and inquired about how much cash he was carrying.

Since he trusted me, he showed me his wad, over $1,000. Trying not to seem too alarmed, I offered to lock it up in the office. Amazingly, he agreed without hesitation. I took the money, giving him a receipt.

That's when he told me about June, his beloved. It seemed that he met June when he went to "work" at his sheltered workshop job, a supervised setting that allowed people with limited abilities work at their own pace on tasks they could handle. They got paid a stipend for their efforts and reaped an invaluable sense of satisfaction from their job. He described in detail the time he first saw her and that it was love at first sight. He wanted to make sure he would be able to get money when he needed it to take her to the dance sponsored by the workshop.

Trying to wrap my brain around Harold's love life gave me a considerable challenge in mind-stretching. Harold—in love??! But it was not a passing fancy. When the day of the dance neared, he asked me to help him get a corsage and boutonniere. We got into the details—what color her dress was (he'd ask and let me know), what he was wearing (could I help him find a suit in the clothing storage room?), and how much money he wanted to spend (not too much, just enough to make sure everything was nice).

Jesse took him down to check the men's suit supply and miraculously came up with something that fit Harold's hard-to-fit shape. They even found a hat, an essential for Harold's wardrobe to cover his hairless scarred head. We helped by arranging a taxi and suggesting a place for dinner. It reminded me of prom preparations. Pictures of Harold that night speak a gazillion words—a heart filled with love and happiness. They had a great time and we got the hang of these preparations for future events.

Because Harold now qualified for disability, our hope was that he would be able to get housing and other supportive services. He'd been with us long enough to erase any doubts about him being a predator, and he had a great track record going to work and behaving himself, so we asked him if he wanted to move into the transitional shelter next door. He was reluctant, for change is hard for most people, including Harold. He finally agreed, and the transitional shelter staff then had the challenge to overcome their personal reservations about someone who looked and acted so different—and scary.

Harold quickly won their hearts and became a beloved part of their household. His inimitable love life continued to blossom. Harold tried his best to cooperate with the caseworker trying to help him qualify for public housing, but his prior record and his disability not being diagnosed in time kept things almost at a standstill.

One of Harold's challenges was his health. It seemed his brain tumor or its side effects kept causing strange symptoms, causing him to lose his balance and become forgetful. He frequently fell, hitting his head, and being hospitalized, sometimes teetering near death. He always miraculously pulled out of the crisis, returning to "good ol' Harold" but causing us to be increasingly concerned about his chances for survival. We even got a roller-blader's helmet for him to wear to protect his vulnerable head from further injury. He rarely wore the helmet, much to our dismay.

All who knew him underestimated his relentless pursuit of his dream—to marry June. "Harold get married?" we'd scoff. "Ha!" But Harold and June knew that they were meant for each other. June had an apartment and it seemed to be the answer to their housing problems, but even that had complications that slowed them down.

He asked for money to buy a ring for June and took her shopping. They continued to make plans for the wedding. His caseworker relentlessly pursued ways around housing regulations to enable Harold and June to live together. They relentlessly pursued their love. He carried her picture in his wallet, proudly showing it to anyone who asked.

One of their journeys on the way to marriage was their venture to the county courthouse to get the marriage license. They traveled by city bus, landing in swanky Geneva, where the courthouse was located. Trouble started when they found out the hard way that there were two courthouses, the old and new, three bus-less miles apart. They walked to the other, at one point landing in a bank. Harold's version of the trip, related to a staff person, was that they asked someone in the bank where the courthouse was, explaining in detail as only Harold could, why they were going there.

Whether someone in the bank recognized Harold from their volunteer stint at Hesed or they just felt sorry for Harold and June we'll never know. All we do know is that people pooled together money to help them and the soon-to-be wed couple became $248 richer as they left the bank. Any skepticism about whether or not this wedding would happen began to fade when Harold showed us his marriage license.

Plans for the wedding proceeded at full speed, which when Harold was involved, meant plenty of interruptions for his "episodes" that caused great angst among the staff helping him. The police once summoned me to the back parking lot because someone dropped off by a cabbie was standing there with his wallet out, money falling around him. When I stepped outside, I saw it was Harold and I assured the cop it was OK. I brought Harold inside, stuffing the money into his wallet. I sat him down and asked him if he wanted something to eat. He was totally disoriented, but cooperative. He had no idea who I was, where he was, or where he'd been. I alerted the transitional shelter staff that he was with us and he eventually returned to his "normal" self. He was in and out of the hospital more times than I could count. Fortunately, he had Medicare, which covered the expenses, but he seemed to be losing ground and we began doubting his chances to get married.

Because Harold was so lovable, many people helped him, and soon it became clear that the wedding was going to happen NOW. Final preparations happened in a heartbeat, and two transitional shelter staff provided the transportation to the courthouse for the ceremony. They videotaped it, which was the only way anyone would have believed what a beautiful ceremony it was. The judge was obviously fascinated with this couple and treated them royally.

Their early days of their marriage were the honeymoon. Soon after the wedding, Harold was admitted to the hospital with his most serious episode ever. No one thought he'd live. Surgery, ICU, bleak prognosis, and June keeping watch over her beloved husband. Anyone at the shelter who knew him kept asking how he was doing. For weeks, it was hopeless, but people continued to pray.

Somehow I gave up thinking that anyone would die in these seemingly hopeless situations. So many times it seemed inevitable that one of our folks would die, but they didn't, or at least not when we expected them to, or they died of something unrelated to their most obvious trauma. I often was caught flat-footed when a miracle cure happened. I didn't know how, but I figured that Harold's days weren't over yet. He lingered in the hospital for a long time and eventually transferred to a nursing home specializing in brain care.

The "nobodies" like Harold and so many others have taught me valuable lessons. I continue to struggle with my prejudices and preconceived notions based on a person's appearance, and I know I'll always be pleasantly surprised to discover gems like Harold who will enrich my life more than I would ever believe possible. Harold, and people like him, fuel my passion to improve opportunities for housing, health care, and supportive services so they can live in the dignity they so richly deserve. I need to figure out how to encourage others to move beyond their fears of the Harolds of this world...

23. Ditto

Nobody loves a drunk—especially a homeless one. The same applies to a drug addict. Ditto for a drug addict-alcoholic. Double ditto for a drug addict-alcoholic person who also is mentally ill. Well, not nobody—but such people sure push the envelope.

Probably the most difficult segment of the homeless population to work with, write about or read about is the addict. Everyone knows an addict, and it takes a special person to out-and-out love them. I'm not one of those special people, although I've made significant progress with my struggle to gain insight into the addict's reasons for being on this earth.

I've come a long way in understanding what fuels addictions and how that contributes to homelessness, and even more, how it contributes to the destruction of families of all economic levels. With a family history of alcoholics and my own period of thinking that drinking heavily was acceptable, I know too well what perils pour out of the bottle. It's not a pretty picture. Rebuilding your life after renouncing an addiction is never a done deal. The demons never quite go away. Tools to cope vary from individual to individual.

Addiction to alcohol or drugs is in some ways the same, but different. Drugs and alcohol are often interchangeable, and addicts often use alcohol or drugs, whatever is available. I knew from personal experience about the mind-numbing effects of alcohol. Drugs, never a part of my circle, were less familiar to me.

In my initial foray into the social service world, back in the mid-1980s, crack cocaine had just exploded on the streets of America. I remember hearing frightening accounts of crack-crazed people, infused with this powerful narcotic, becoming out-of-control monsters. My observation over the years is that crack was the monster—highly-addictive, grabbing the user's life and not letting go. We saw crack addicts regularly, and their behavior didn't deviate from what we gauged as "the norm."

"Skeletor," a crack-addicted, wiry, hyperactive, intensely philosophical black man who has been homeless most of his troubled life, occasionally shared some of his hard found wisdom with me, "Diane, I won't tell you no lies. I do that shit. But I won't do it in here. That would disrespect what you and others are trying to do to help us." His profound musings both inspired and saddened me. This gentle man, for reasons I couldn't explain, was caught in this web of drug use, foraging scrap metals to support his habit. He insisted that he'd never hurt someone in his quest for his drug of choice. I argued with him that when he did his relatively petty theft to augment his scrapping, it hurt people. To my knowledge, Skeletor, a man of honor, never violated his promise to me.

Theory Better Than Reality

A shelter, just like a home, has limits on the amount of tolerable disruption. I've been a believer that fairly and compassionately enforcing that limit is one way to keep the peace for all involved, so I gained a reputation of "a tough ballsy bitch" when it came to my peace-keeping role. For me, it was a no-brainer—you figure out who is drunk or high, you keep an eye on their behavior, and act accordingly. Fortunately, I usually had good staff to help foster a peaceful environment and we were able to keep the lid on what could have been a volatile environment. Our regular guests helped, too, because they didn't want disruptions to destroy the only home they had. They'd surreptitiously report potential problem behavior to me or other staff, often giving us a heads up before things exploded.

When people criticize shelters for "enabling," I usually challenge them to point to realistic options for people entrenched in addiction. Show me a treatment program with open slots for uninsured clients, support services and housing for the person when they finish the treatment, and employers who are willing to work with a person with "issues." I usually don't have to raise the other challenges—care for mental and/or physical maladies, those who self-medicate because of severe pain from untreated dental or physical pain or the host of reasons people of all income brackets abuse alcohol and/or drugs.

Nevertheless, discussing theories of substance abuse fails to do anything to ease this escalating, destructive condition. People with addictions face another insurmountable hurdle: those holding deep-seated prejudices against people with addictions. Many people have been hurt by someone addicted to alcohol or drugs. Often their feelings of hatred and disgust are understandable. Psychological trauma caused by abuse, physical pain, unprocessed painful memories, excruciating realities too horrible to face, and genetic disposition create a caseload to last addictions counselors until eternity.

'Self-Medicating' to Erase Terrible Pain

"James," a Vietnam War veteran, grew up in Aurora. He fought the war from a helicopter, as a gunner who killed more people than he ever would think possible. He returned to Aurora, got a job, married, had children, and moved on with life. Unfortunately for James and his family, his wartime experiences did not remain overseas. They followed him in the deep recesses of his mind, rearing their ugly heads at the worst possible moment.

I can only speculate that his marriage fell apart because of his drinking and that his drinking was his inadequate attempt to assuage the pain and guilt from the war. Throughout this downward slide, James kept working— construction jobs that gave him an income to keep a roof over his head—for a while. His first encounter with our shelter wasn't pleasant because he came in drunk and I turned him away because I sensed a time bomb. He returned sober the next night, gave me the information I needed for registration, and listened as I laid down the rules—which boiled down to be respectful or don't come here.

We needed to tweak his understanding of how serious the rules were, and he began to understand that if he was going to get drunk he'd try to stay with a buddy. He'd apologize for slips and he managed to adhere to the rules most of the time. Since he came in later in the evening, when things had settled down, we sometimes had a chance to share a few words.

He showed me pictures of his kids, his granddaughter, and talked in general about how screwed up his life was. He assured me, "I'm not like the rest of these bums," and we let it go at that. James was fairly low maintenance and rarely asked for anything. When I was able to help by giving him a pair of gloves or boots he expressed surprise and gratitude. He always offered to help and nagged me to take him up on his offer.

One brutally cold night, James came to the door. I picked up on his intoxicated state immediately. He was REAL drunk. Big dilemma for me: he wouldn't make it inside without saying or doing something stupid and inciting an alcohol-enhanced macho battle with someone, but he wouldn't make it back to a buddy's house to sleep it off either. I bought time by asking him to sit down on the outer stairs, which kept him inside but away from the rest of the shelter. He complied gratefully.

I kept an eye on the stairwell, realizing James was a potential explosion that I didn't want to have happen. As soon as I could, I went over to try to figure out what our options were. I knew he was really drunk, but something else seemed wrong. His face, normally quick to smile, had an agonizing look to it. I asked him if he was OK—a relative term. He shared with me that today was his granddaughter's second birthday. OK, but it was more than that. The "more than that" ripped my heart out. He broke down in tears, and asked if I could sit down and talk to him. I normally make it a practice not to try to get into big discussions with someone too intoxicated to know what they're saying, but something told me this was different.

We sat in the stairwell talking. He begged me not to kick him out and not to make him go inside. So far I could agree, but I made no promises. He then reluctantly shared the pain in his heart and head, "You know I'm a Marine, right? Well, I was trained to obey orders, and I did." He then recounted his memory of orders to slay defenseless women and children, shooting them from his helicopter perch. "I could see their faces as they looked up at us flying over. Diane, they were innocent people, mothers and children, some as young as my granddaughter." He sobbed painfully and uncontrollably.

His granddaughter's birthday party ripped open his memory of faces of innocent children. I tried in vain to find words to respond. His tough veneer gone, he pleaded with me not to make him go into the dining room. I acquiesced, unofficially letting him stay in the stairwell, and got him a blanket. He thanked me and caused no problem.

I figured James probably was drunk enough not to remember the conversation, but I was wrong. The next night I said hi to him and he discreetly thanked me for cutting him a break the night before. We talked about getting help for his drinking and in dealing with his memories, but I know from anecdotes and off-the-record comments made by people working with veterans' services that help is elusive for many reasons.

James is going to keep trying to hold his fragile life together for his family. He tries to support them as much as he can. I can hope that if and when help becomes available, he will be ready to climb out of the pain-filled gutter swirling with the blood of innocents and the 80-proof cheap booze that has kept him afloat all these years.

Music From a Former Life

Sometimes help happens and sometimes it doesn't. For Mike, it's too late. He died in jail, allegedly because he needed medical care and his needs were ignored.

His intense eyes matched his typically intense behavior. His wiry frame was always in motion. Unfortunately, his motion included drinking out of a vodka bottle. Mike was an ugly drunk. He just turned mean and you could tell, if you stayed around him long enough, that he was drinking to ease some really nasty pain in his heart and head.

We needed to establish ground rules early on, so I pulled him aside when he was sober and told him the conditions of staying at our shelter meant he couldn't come after he'd been drinking. In case he thought I was making up some rule for nothing, I described, directly, my previous contact with him when he was drunk, "You're a real nasty son of a bitch when you're drinking." To which he agreed.

Most of our years of being in the same space were fairly peaceful. One evening following our "don't come here drunk" conversation, he managed to get in the door in a highly intoxicated condition. The staff person who fortunately quickly noticed his "enchanted" presence, turned him away from the shelter upstairs, and he proceeded to go down to the front office door. He rang the doorbell repeatedly. Since it was so late, a staff person answered the door instead of one of the transitional shelter residents. She didn't know him, but figured out he was quite drunk, so she tried to just send him away. By that time, he had hit his worst stage (perhaps he had continued drinking on his way down to the door) and he got real belligerent. She managed to close the front door—a commercially-reinforced glass door—and call me to alert me to this trouble. I broke away from the action upstairs and headed down to hear loud pounding and shouting as I neared the stairwell.

Mike was in a rage—kicking the glass door with all his drunken might. I immediately called the police, all the time praying that the door wouldn't shatter. The police arrested him and Mike was temporarily banned from the shelter.

Unfortunately, Illinois winters can be really hard on people, especially those forced to find non-traditional housing—bridges, forests, cars, abandoned buildings, etc. Since the front door incident, Mike and other heavy drinkers who hung around together camped out in local forests. One particularly blustery winter, Mike and one of his buddies were hospitalized with severe frostbite on their feet. The hospital social worker called asking if they could stay at the shelter. The hospital sometimes mistook our shelter for a hospital, especially with those who had no insurance or place to live.

With no other options, I agreed, with stipulations that the social worker transmitted to Mike and his buddy, Frank. When they came, I very clearly outlined my conditions—they were under "house arrest" and if they left the building, they were history. If they even *thought* about drinking, they were history. "Okay, Diane, we get it. You'll be able to trust us, we promise," they both assured me. Yeah, right!

Surprisingly, they were true to their word. At first they slept a whole bunch, ate, and slept more. They both were in pretty bad shape so walking was more than painful. When the pain subsided, they both pitched in to help by doing tasks that required little walking. He actually begged me for stuff to do, partially to keep busy but also to show his gratitude for years of putting up with him. I tried to comply by finding some of the long put-off tasks that tended to pile up. Mike eagerly plunged in and completed everything to my amazed satisfaction.

One night, a group of Suzuki violinists—all children from 6 to 16—came to perform for this unique audience. Despite the crowded conditions, the entire gathering was engrossed in the performance. The musicians were crammed in the only spot not covered by bodies sitting at tables. It meant very little walking space, but that didn't seem to be an issue during their spellbinding performance. Not a sound could be heard except the mellow sound of violins being played by kids who probably never saw a homeless person before, much less performed to a room filled with them.

As I scanned the room, I mused to myself about this unlikely scenario. Who would ever think that a room filled with "bums" could sit respectfully listening to kids playing classical music on violins? Then, as I looked around (in case someone wasn't in tune with this experience) I saw Mike. He looked like he was seeing a vision. I don't think he blinked during the performance. When the group was wrapping up, getting ready to leave, he limped over. My antennae went up and I stood close enough to intervene if necessary.

"I just want to tell you that this night was the most beautiful night I can remember," he gushed to the kids and their instructor. "I loved your music. Thanks for coming to share it with us." Phheew! I relaxed and smiled. They thanked him and headed out.

Later, Mike and I had a few moments to talk. "So, you liked that music?" I asked. His response seared an image into my brain. He painfully recounted his former life. He worked for a hotel chain in an upper management position. He was married, had kids, and owned a nice home in the suburbs. He didn't go into details about what happened to send him in this tailspin that resulted in homelessness, but he took responsibility for it. Tonight's music gave him a glimpse of what he had known, and for some reason he seemed at peace with that memory.

Mike fell out of my good graces as soon as the weather warmed up. He at least did it respectfully and self-imposed a ban from our shelter. He returned once in a while, along with his band of buddies who opted for the great outdoors. They honestly admitted to me that they didn't want to break our

146

rules about being disruptive or drinking on the premises, so they stayed outside in all but the worst weather.

Alcohol ravaged the group. Randy died of alcohol/drug poisoning. Eddie lost several toes when he ignored signs of frostbite. Mike broke some law, got arrested and died in jail. They made no pretense that this was a healthy lifestyle. They made no pretense that they were going to be able to turn their lives around. Maybe they could, maybe they couldn't.

Good 'Cop'

In the list of alcoholic candidates most likely not to succeed, "Brian" would have gotten my vote. His drinking, accompanied by obnoxious behavior, got him tossed out of the shelter more often than most in my memory.

His all-but-toothless smile and beguiling ways almost made up for his sins, but not quite. He had a sense of right and wrong when he was sober. Trouble was, we hardly ever saw the sober side of him.

Evidently, his childhood wasn't too great. Like most people wracked by alcoholism I've talked to, he had a father who was an abusive alcoholic. Brian started drinking early and often and the toll, in addition to destroying his body, was a history of poor choices in mates and destroyed relationships.

Things weren't looking too good for him in the mid-90s when he landed in the hospital. With the diagnosis of stomach cancer, he faced that ugly possibility of death at an early age—late thirties. Something inside him snapped, and in the midst of dealing with chemotherapy, Brian decided to reach for the miracle of sobriety.

His approach was Alcoholics' Anonymous, and once released from the hospital, he hooked up with the AA group meeting in our library every Monday night. His health improved and his drinking stopped. I don't know what the magic formula was, but whatever it was, he tried to spread it around his shelter-buddies. Not many grabbed the opportunity, but that didn't deter Brian.

He pieced his life back together—some of his effort, some from a higher power, some from his friends. He moved out of the shelter and into a modest trailer, paid for in part by his willingness to be a watchman at the campground where his humble abode was parked.

I don't pretend to know how good things happen, but I usually can recognize them when they do. This one was Brian showing up in a security guard uniform on his way home from work. I think my surprise—OK, shock—was matched by his pride. I do stay skeptical, so it took awhile for me to accept that Brian's reform was more than a temporary aberration.

Every Monday night he stopped by the shelter to remind me to announce the AA meeting downstairs. The routine expanded to his coming before 7, keeping an eye on the growing line outside our doors. He knew problems could occur with folks waiting outside for the shelter to open. I in turn offered him a meal when he came in to remind me to announce the meeting.

I became convinced that Brian's lifestyle changes were at least likely to continue. One night we spent a few moments chatting. He hesitatingly shared that he was happy to come back "home" and give back some of the goodness he received from the multitude of volunteers. We had no formal agreement, but whenever possible he came during that pre-opening time and hung out, looking for trouble before it started. He'd get me or another staff member to handle it, providing a stern law enforcement presence when needed. He'd also alert us to someone's unnoticed health crisis so we could call for help or bring the afflicted person inside for care.

Now I'll admit to barely believing him as he described his hospitalizations. Then I just nodded and filed in the "yeah, right" tales pile. I became convinced of his story when visiting a hospitalized co-worker, I also saw Brian in for treatment. He still struggles with cancer and continues, one day at a time, to stay sober. I'm proud of him for his personal accomplishment and for his commitment to come and give back.

More to the Story

I remember so many men and women who stumbled across my path due to alcohol addiction. As much as I'd like to blame them, I realize that such a response would be wrong and simple-minded. I've seen a few lives turned around—most often because some physical trauma gave a person a second look at the gift of life they were destroying. I've seen those who were given the gift of life due to some extraordinary medical care and steadfast support from staff and/or volunteers just throw their lives away senselessly. I've seen guys, thrown in jail because of alcohol, get lost in the system and come out after they lost everything. I've seen guys risk missing the shelter curfew because they stopped to help an intoxicated person who had fallen in a snowbank and would die of exposure if left behind.

My biggest frustration in dealing with addicts is realizing that, for many, their desire to reform their lives isn't enough to make it happen. They need to have insurance to get into most treatment programs. Programs not requiring insurance typically offer a three-day detox and hook them up with outpatient counseling. Even the best-intentioned drinker will have a difficult time staying sober as he or she lives on the streets or in shelters. The opportunity for drinking or drugging abounds, especially in unstructured settings. The encouragement for sobriety is rare, counteracted by a society that pushes alcohol (and drugs, more subtly) in every form of advertising. In depth counseling for the underlying psychological problems is just as scarce, with prescription pills to numb pain or enhance energy. Medical care for the pain eased by self-medicating is also uncommon, leaving the addicted to choose between substance and suffering, often getting both.

My hat goes off to family and friends of an alcoholic who manage to maintain a connection without enabling the addiction. When to give up? When to hold onto hope that this will be the moment that "hit bottom" means turning around one's life and grasping sobriety? When to realize, that despite one's best effort, the addiction defies your best attempt to help?

My deep respect and gratitude goes to those who work with addicts in the field of counseling or health care; their patience gets tested beyond imagination. My admiration goes to those who today have restrained the demon in their brains. My prayer is that they have the strength to continue the struggle tomorrow. My hope is that each brother, sister, aunt, uncle, mother, father, son and daughter who finds themselves in the throes of addiction will find someone out there to be there for them, who can look past the pain they've caused and into the beauty of humanity they still hold.

24. Crazy Lovables

When the curly-headed, sad-eyed, dumpy guy walked into the dining room on a night our summer shelter was open, I could tell that he was a very lost, frightened soul. I made my way over to him, offering my friendliest hello. His eyes opened wide, scanning the half-filled dining room behind me, and he grasped onto my welcome like a drowning man going down for the last time, reaching for the life preserver.

"Will" needed a place to stay, so I invited him to sit down and tell me what his situation was. He seemed eager to share and somehow we bonded, so I got way more than I bargained for in details of what brought him to Aurora.

The small town he was from, about 30 miles from Aurora, had no shelter and no safety net for someone with severe mental health needs, so he'd struggled to not become homeless, but his landlord locked him out of the motel room he'd been renting by the week.

He alluded to some severe mental health problems—depression, bipolar—but was under the care of a psychiatrist so he could get medication. His insurance from his job with an area chemical plant was about to run out because he knew he was going to be fired for missing work. His life appeared to be a very tangled web of complications that had overwhelmed him, understandably, from what I knew so far.

I explained to him our bizarre summer shelter schedule—we were only open Tuesday, Thursday, and Saturday nights—and I tried to make him feel at home. He had been living in his car and was most interested in a shower and food, both luxuries we could provide, so he was happy for the moment.

Systemic injustices against vulnerable guys like Will really fueled my anger. I have heard Will and others like him talk about their jobs in hazardous settings, where they lacked adequate know-how, much less protective equipment. They were viewed as expendable collateral. I skeptically speculated that Will's clean-up job with the chemical plant was one where they picked the least likely person to question the safety of the substances they had to remove. It made sense, in a deceitful way, to choose people with no family to pursue lawsuits if something terrible happened.

After getting cleaned up and fed, Will thanked me profusely and got some sleep. He assured me that he'd be okay, but I gave him our summer shelter schedule just in case. Summer was difficult to line up volunteer churches, so we aimed for a respite-like schedule that would provide food, laundry, and an inside place to sleep at least three nights a week for most of the summer.

Sure enough, Will showed up the next night we were open. He sought me out, his only "friend" among the dozens of strangers. He shared a little more about his pathetic life—pathetic at least to me. He seemed to be facing major crises on every front—no place to live, job loss that would end his life-sustaining insurance, no family support, no community resources to turn to, severe mental health problems, and a scary list of physical health issues.

Much like many people who stayed at our shelter, Will offered to help in return for the many kindnesses shown to him. I offered a few suggestions of what we needed—garbage cans to clean, trays to wash, kitchen to sweep—and he plunged in enthusiastically, pointing out that he had vast maintenance and cleaning skills from his part-time job at the Golden Arches University.

Will would show up each night we were open, take care of his most basic needs, and spend moments talking to me, the person who seemed like his only friend in the world. Depending on his manic or depressed state of mind, he'd either sit quietly or buzz about helpfully. As summer went on, he appeared during the daytime, offering to help with much-needed cleaning. He seemed to work well according to our over-burdened one-man maintenance worker Miguel, so I kept him busy.

Will eventually had some major untreated heart-related health problems because he now lacked health insurance. Our volunteer-based clinic opened once a month during the summer to try to triage the most serious health problems. After explaining what the Rainbow Clinic offered, I put Will on the list. He needed some encouragement, so I ushered him downstairs, introducing him to Marilyn Scott, the family nurse practitioner who helped run the clinic.

Marilyn immediately earned Will's trust because of her sensitive, gentle manner, so now he had two friends who cared about him. She began to piece together the fractured medical history he could provide and got him on some needed medication. Will was astounded that such care was not only available to him but also so caring of him. He needed more than Rainbow Clinic could ever begin to offer, but it was a start.

As I got to know some of Will's story, I cringed with the thought of him being around for our regular, fast-paced, intimidating shelter season in the fall. After I did some checking of his situation, we managed to scrape up some money to get him back into his hometown room and we didn't see him for a while. Several weeks later, I stopped at his fast food restaurant on my way through his town and saw him hard at work. He was happy to see me and paused at an appropriate moment to tell me he was doing OK, then went back to work.

Things never end so easily, and something told me I hadn't seen the last of Will. Sure enough, he showed up later that fall, adding another mouth to feed and body to shelter to our already overcrowded population. Because I knew enough about him to form some judgments, I suggested our transitional shelter program to him. He seemed to fit the criteria—a person who seemed ready to get back on his feet, needing some help, but willing to work on his situation. He reluctantly agreed, knowing that he wouldn't get to see me as much, but that he'd get his own space and he wouldn't be prey for some of the "vultures" who stayed at the shelter. Just like the rest of the world, bullies preyed on vulnerable types, either taking their belongings or taking advantage of them in any number of ways. Guys like Will could be duped into doing something stupid, like shoplifting, and made to give the proceeds to the bully. The instigator never took the rap if the plan fell apart.

Since Will was still in our building, we saw each other, at least in passing, and he was able to maintain his medical services through Rainbow Clinic. He seemed to be adjusting to life in this communal shelter, and many appreciated his exceptional cleaning skills.

His mental health issues became more apparent, and raised some concern. Sometimes I think people living in shelters are under a microscope, unlike persons living alone or with a friend or family member. Being under that microscope puts additional pressure on a person, often aggravating symptoms. At least staff could try to link him with the scarce mental health services available.

With Will, life was never simple, and his stay at our transitional shelter was filled with drama. Once he went AWOL, causing great concern among staff. He called me from his hometown, saying he needed to get money to pay off his bookie.

He gambled when he was working, hoping to hit it big and get relief from his depressing poverty. Gambling for persons in a manic state could be disastrous, only a little less than when in a depressed state. I encouraged him to return to the transitional shelter before they kicked him out for being AWOL. They cut him some slack. I'm not sure if the bookie did.

His heart problems landed him in the hospital a few times that winter, but he kept trying to focus on getting back home, trying to cooperate with staff's expectations. He struggled, probably more than we knew, and one day he asked to talk to me. He said he was feeling suicidal and wanted help. He wasn't too excited about the standard routine to get that help—psych evaluation at the hospital and the likely period of hospitalization in the state hospital—but he was willing to do what he needed to do.

In my many occasions of talking with persons suffering mental health agonies, some state they are suicidal, a red flag that I take seriously. When someone is "a danger to themselves or others," I can petition them into the state's rickety mental health system and sometimes they end up involuntarily committed. I don't do this lightly, but a suicidal tendency prompts me to start the process.

Usually the crisis worker asks for specifics—what did they say that makes you think they're serious? Did they indicate a method they were planning to use?—so I asked Will some more questions, specifically how he planned to hurt himself. He looked at me sheepishly and dug into his pocket, bringing out a box cutter. OK, that's serious enough for me. He reluctantly gave it to me and I assured him that I'd get him help.

I called the Crisis Line and spoke with "Jack," one of the most skeptical mental health workers I knew. He reluctantly agreed to come over to talk to Will. He arrived within moments, and the two of them met in a private space to see what the next step would be. Jack asked me to join them and I sat in on what seemed to be a losing battle for Will.

Jack, probably correctly, believed that Will was just trying to get attention, but when Will told him what method he had in mind and I showed Jack the box cutter, he agreed to make the call, still not thinking that Will was serious.

As we waited for the ambulance and police to come, I said I'd go outside to make sure they came to the right door, leaving Jack and Will inside. I met the ambulance crew and police officer and we headed across the parking lot to the front door. Standing in the lobby, we chatted; perhaps a bit too casually for what was going on in the other room.

"Help, come quickly!" shouted "Janet," the transitional shelter director, from around the corner. The cop's instincts kicked in and he was the first on the scene. Will was standing in the kitchen with one of the staff. He held a large kitchen knife in a menacing way, causing the cop to draw his gun and shout to Will, "Drop it NOW!"

The ensuing moments had us all scared to death. Will didn't seem to register the "drop it now" and the cop was still poised with his gun pointed at him. I remember thinking, "Oh my God, he's going to shoot Will!" The rest of the petrified onlookers held the same horrific thoughts.

After what seemed to be forever, Will dropped the knife. The officer finished dealing with this dangerous situation as he was trained. Will threw himself face down on the floor whimpering, "*Ple-e-e-ease*, don't shoot me." It was all so sad, yet it could have been worse. The staff person felt horrible—because her inadvertent presence in that space made Will's actions look even more menacing. We never could figure out if he had grabbed the knife to hurt himself or others. She didn't fear for her life—and I understood what she meant. He, in his confused state of mind, desperately wanted help.

For Will, this was his entry into the normally closed door of mental health care. Illinois, like many states, lopped off significant portions of mental health services, euphemistically stating that "community based services" would replace hospitalizations. When have we heard that before?

'Street People' Reflect Our Failure

"Community based services," the mantra of the Reagan era, inspired a rash of budget cuts to mental health residential programs in the 1980s. "Deinstitutionalization" became the buzzword feared in communities because it meant that thousands of mentally ill and/or developmentally delayed persons would be sent back to their home communities for help. Among other problems, this approach left many very vulnerable people on the streets because local government had no way to house and care for them, and/or because the person "chose" not to take advantage of what help might have been offered.

Aurora, like every other mid-sized town, found "crazies" wandering city streets, and the city leaders didn't know what to do. The recession of the early '80s left social service budgets in disarray. Severely mentally ill persons are most challenging to treat, so agencies typically shied away from trying to provide extensive services because they lacked resources, especially housing, to care for what became known as "the street people."

'Miracle' Melvin

Melvin could be a poster child for Reaganomics' approach to mental health care. His life was horrific from early on, with brutal abuse by family members contributing to his severe mental health problems. Schizophrenia was one disease afflicting this small, mild-mannered man. The demons he faced daily would keep him far from society's mainstream. Before the emergency shelter opened, he eked out his survival in ways we'll never know.

When the shelter opened in the early '80s, he became a regular, overtly scorned by others because of his crazy ways and his extremely poor hygiene. My first encounter with Melvin is engraved in my mind—a serene face, piercing eyes, bearded and robed, just like images I've seen of Jesus.

A friend of mine, Pat, who worked as a photojournalist, clearly remembers meeting Melvin, the person she credits with turning her into an advocate for homeless mentally ill persons. Stretched out on the hill outside the shelter, he watched a busload of advocates—homeless and not—heading off to Washington, DC, for an "end homelessness" rally. Pat was there to take pictures, and her keen photographer's eye spotted this poster child on the hill.

They spoke for a while. When Pat asked if she could photograph him, Melvin was willing. Pat sensitively knew Melvin didn't need to be exploited. Her poignant photo of him bespeaks his human dignity so often ignored. Their paths crossed frequently, and he became Pat's unforgotten symbol of our society's lack of care for vulnerable people.

Melvin became beloved among many people connected with the shelter. He was a delight, with eyes dancing with joy and mischief. He would chat with staff or volunteers, sometimes tracking, sometimes not. He absolutely refused to take showers, despite the pleaders' best efforts. As his past became known, his aversion to showers became more understandable because of sexual abuse that occurred to him as a child while showering.

To say Melvin was a pack rat would be an understatement. Whatever possessed him to gather and maintain the absolute junk he protected was beyond my understanding. I would have gladly encouraged his junk collecting habit if it didn't infringe on his shelter-mates, but it did, sometimes to great dismay. Garbage—old food wrappers, cans, and uneaten spoiled items— comprised his collection. He'd carry a bag of treasures/trash everywhere.

I shudder to recall my efforts to get him to clean out his tent during the summer months. We gave him his own pup tent, knowing that he would do best without tent mates. Even though he was isolated, fumes from his stuff permeated the campground, and finally I could ignore it no longer. "Hey Melvin, I need to talk to you," I hollered sweetly from outside his tent. He stuck his head out and eventually crawled out and stood up next to me, looking at me as if I was delivering his next bag of goodies.

As he stood picking at the dirt under his curled, uncut fingernails, I tried to clearly set boundaries about his stuff. Yeah, right! That went well. I would have needed to monitor his collection 24/7, a task I had no desire to do. We found a middle ground—which was more of a concession than I wanted to make—that allowed him to keep his stuff inside his tent with anything outside getting tossed. Of course, I realized that Melvin was an expert "dumpster diver" so his way of recycling anything we tossed would always keep him ahead of the game.

Somehow, a friendship developed between Melvin and Patty, a nurse who worked at the local mental health agency. One of the beauties of our shelter was the thousands of people from all walks of life who took their regular turns helping—special people like Patty.

Eventually, Melvin began to trust Patty. She worked wonders with him, getting him on meds that would calm the demons in his head, allowing for some interventions in the rest of his life—like hygiene issues—that kept him from getting his own place.

We all noticed his improvement. Although he bemoaned his obvious weight gain, an unfortunate side effect of his medication, he soon qualified for a local supportive housing program, and his life began a significant step forward. We sadly let go of Melvin, knowing he was moving into a better situation. He had become endeared to all who knew him at the shelter and with his newly found cleanliness and improved mental condition, he was even more a sweetie!

From later accounts, Melvin moved into a challenging environment. He shared an apartment with 3 other mentally ill guys. He hadn't lived in a situation where his every move would be seen (and often challenged) by someone, so he had understandable difficulties at first.

He overcame those difficulties in a stellar manner, becoming the official "ambassador" for new residents. He was in charge of making sure new residents knew the ropes, and he offered unwavering support and practical advice to help ease the transition for many people. Melvin would stop by the shelter occasionally and chat about his new living situation. Who knew that a guy this disconnected from reality could be so back on track and such a joy!

Melvin, like almost everyone who crossed the threshold of our shelter, had serious health conditions. Those untreated maladies, chronic kidney and heart problems, turned into life-shortening realities. Hospitalized several times, he received loving medical care too little, too late. He died at the age of 33, after achieving incredible milestones—a life that meant something to himself and his community.

His jam-packed memorial service served as a testimony to this sweet, loving man who overcame so much. I went, prepared to relate how much he meant to me and countless others at the shelter. As I sat waiting my turn to speak, I was overwhelmed with the loving accounts of Melvin's life that his friends from his housing program shared. Those who received his guidance and hospitality when they first moved into their program offered glowing accounts of Melvin's skilled assistance. They painted Melvin's life so accurately, describing his idiosyncrasies and characteristics so clearly, that I quietly absorbed the miracle of Melvin without feeling that I needed to add a word.

Melvin is my poster child too, reminding me that those struggling with severe mental illness and homelessness often need someone to speak on their behalf to ensure opportunities exist for them to live satisfying lives. Pat's portrait of Melvin serves as my reminder that much work remains in this community, state and nation to allow those suffering mental diseases the same access to care as those suffering physical diseases.

Melvin, maybe not so ironically, is an excellent role model.

Mental illness, when are we going to get over the stigmas that come with that disease? Since we are all susceptible to it, it would behoove us to move beyond our stunted way of regarding persons with MI as if they are lepers. Those who find themselves slipping down the slope of "Mount Survival" need the most help and find the least. We have On-Star™ for lost drivers. What about for those lost on the highway of life?

25. Geezers

The opposite of attaining the American Dream is experiencing the nightmare of homelessness, especially for senior citizens who end up with no place to live out their last years. The idea that senior citizens would be exempt from this misery falls apart as you look at the folks sitting at shelters or huddling on the streets. Most people don't grow up homeless. For the seniors who end up there, their lives typically take incredibly painful turns when they can deal with it the least.

One nasty November Saturday night, two old guys came in for the first time. I thought they came together, but they had just entered simultaneously. I took them, one at a time, to register them. The first guy, "Charles," looked really old, but turns out he was only a couple years older than I—quite young in fact—late-40s. He was a tradesman who traded his life for alcohol, much to the dismay of his local buddies he grew up with. Life on the street, coupled with addictions, can age a person faster than imaginable, as he so effectively demonstrated.

The second guy, "Ron," really disturbed me for painful reasons. Earlier that day I had called my parents, who live out of town. Both my parents, then in their late 70s, enjoyed fairly good health, due in part to their access to medical care and a comfortable lifestyle. For some inexplicable reason, my Dad and I got into a rare conversation about his World War II adventures. It was a pleasant conversation, and it showed me a side of my Dad I didn't often get to see.

When registering Ron, I asked him for his ID, which he willingly handed to me. His drivers' license showed his birth date to be the exact same as my Dad's. Yikes! He was also a WWII vet, as verified by his military ID card. Ron became homeless because the modest, affordable apartment he lived in was yanked out from under him by the landlord who wanted a family member to live there.

Ron was a gentle soul, dismayed that he needed help, ever so grateful for the kindness of taking him in and helping him out. During our initial interview, I could not help but have flashes of my Dad in his place and it made me weak. *There but for fortune...*

Ron didn't stay long. His niece in a nearby rural community got wind of her uncle being in need of help and she managed somehow to get him into an assisted living facility. He got lucky—a family member who cared, some resources to get help—so he didn't get that grizzled look that fuels stereotypical portrayals of homeless guys.

Out of Place, Even For Us

Single women of all ages found themselves at our shelter. Most were younger, some were addicted to alcohol or drugs, and others were victims of poor choices frequently inspired by abusive pasts. But homelessness knows no age limits...

An infirm woman in her late 70s, "Loretta" had been living with her loathsome son "Mack" in a motel following their eviction from a nearby apartment. They soon lost that meager roof over their heads and stood in line one evening waiting for our doors to open. Mack, by all impressions a ne'er-do-well with abundant problems, tried to appear to care about his mother, but soon his frequent disappearances gave us all reason to doubt him.

Loretta looked woefully out of place at the crowded dining room table, surrounded by people half her age. Her matted gray hair, combined with her ashy puckered skin, made her look years beyond her 70s. Her bulky frame posed a challenge when nature called, necessitating a bathroom trip. Mack carried her down the stairs to the women's bathroom like a broken-down bride, lugging her through the women's sleeping area into the cramped bathroom.

The first night, I decided that once she got downstairs, she needed to remain there. Having someone to carry her up and down the short flight of stairs scared me. Loretta wearily agreed, cowering in her sleeping space, a specially arranged stack of several pads so she didn't need to stoop to floor level. Her lack of mobility was one pressing issue we needed to address in our inaccessible shelter. Tomorrow...

Loretta represented an unwelcome challenge to our community's senior service agencies. One agency I called said she had to have a home to get assistance. They didn't do house calls to a homeless shelter. Another required family members to intervene with her. Her Social Security benefits would be diverted to her new "home" if she even wanted to go into a nursing home, which she didn't.

She believed her no-account son with his promises of great things in the future. He spent a few moments each day feigning care for his mother, then he disappeared, leaving her to be carried up and down the stairs by strangers—homeless men who saw Loretta as painful, pathetic reminders of their own neglected mothers. These men, who had witnessed horrendous violence on the streets and in prisons, treated her gently, respectfully.

In the meantime, we struggled to figure out a solution to this unacceptable situation. The wheelchair we scrounged up sort of helped—except for the trip up and down the stairs. Senior services started to kick in gear—thanks to a compassionate caseworker willing to overlook agency policies. However, Loretta still held out hope for Mack's grand scheme.

After a few days of Mack's disappearing act, I laid down the law upon his return. His mother needed to be his Number One priority. He needed to work with us to get a place to stay. No more disappearing. He argued, saying he needed to find work to pay for a place to stay. His alcohol-enhanced condition belied his concern for his mother's welfare. His focus on her Social Security check's pending arrival convinced me that his interests did not include his mother's best interest. I turned up the heat on the senior service angle, making the "elder abuse" charge[15] against Mack.

The local senior advocacy agency was able to kick things into high gear with that allegation, substantiated by their contact (and lack thereof) with Mack. They came in one afternoon and transported an unwilling Loretta to a senior care facility. I booted Mack out when he responded with drunken threats to my staff and me. The rest of the shelter residents were ready to dismember him, so his departure was for his own good.

'Grandpa' Ray Roars

Ray was a grizzled geezer poster child—toothless with a weathered face and tobacco-stained fingers, he was skinny as a rail with skin darkened by dirt and sun. He was in his 70s when I first met him.

He didn't stand out from the crowd. He was polite to talk to, and didn't get too demanding. When he got his Social Security check, he'd head to a neighborhood tavern, often joined by a cadre of shelter mates who realized it could mean free drinks for them. Word was that Ray would treat, becoming more generous as he became more inebriated. Upon his return, he'd occasionally be "enchanted," my euphemism for intoxicated, which caused him to be a little rowdy in a harmless sort of way.

He'd often come back by cab, helped from the vehicle by some of the folks hanging around the shelter waiting for the 7 p.m. opening. Some would help themselves to whatever cash Ray had precariously stuffed in his pockets. He'd sit in a chair, smoke his Camels, and blather on and on to anyone within earshot. His alcohol-enhanced courage would inspire him to snap impatiently at the young bucks hanging by the door. He couldn't tolerate their stupidity. Despite his antagonistic rantings, they seldom retaliated with anything but words.

Folks would help him into the dining room to "Ray-Ray's seat," the corner seat closest to the door. His rank as senior member entitled him to privileges and respect. When sober, he'd avidly read or carry on thoughtful conversations with his tablemates, generously sharing cigarettes with those who asked. When intoxicated, he'd do his share of barking at anyone who even thought of crossing him, even me. Somehow, most of us realized that letting Ray have his way fared better than trying to get him to go along with someone else's ways. Fortunately, his ways weren't too far from what I thought was acceptable, so we didn't have to battle much.

I never paid him much attention at first. He blended in with the 100+ other shelter residents until the first of the month following his initial appearance, when some desperate drug addict somewhere between the bar and the shelter robbed him of his Social Security money. He was bruised and mad, because he now couldn't afford to buy his Camel cigarettes and his occasional nip of whatever he drank.

Some of the other folks were incensed about the crime, feeling defensive for this frail senior. "Nobody should take advantage of someone this old," was the overriding sentiment expressed by more than one of the guys. They began alerting me when Ray had money on him. Eventually, I tried urging him to let me hold his money, a process we came to jokingly call "Rolling Ray." I'd ask him to come to the office, have a seat, and offer to hang onto his cash so no one else would get it. Depending on his level of enchantment, my request would meet with either a "No thanks, sweetie, I can take care of it," or a prolonged procedure of him reaching into his many pockets with his tobacco-stained fingers, pulling out wads of crinkled money, and painstakingly counting out every bill, licking his fingers so he could separate the sticky beer-covered currency. That could take forever, but I felt it was worth it because many of us were worried that he'd be killed in a robbery.

If we were lucky, I'd roll him when he still had the bulk of his cash left so he would have something to spend as the month went on. The only trouble with that was the times Ray came to the front door to claim his stash. He'd scare unknowing staff to death with his insisting to see me and get his money with gruff words that typically boiled down to "Goddammit, I want my money NOW!" They'd hurry to find me or call me at home. Even times I was immersed in some important project, I'd respond immediately because I knew

Ray was more than persistent and no one would have peace until he had his money.

I struggled with his—and others'—choice of how they spent their money. Naively, I reasoned that he could have rented a room and provided for his own needs. Truth be told, he'd probably never find a room that he could afford that would also leave enough money so he could eat. Even more, he would have given up the community that our shelter offered. Many people, upon moving out of homelessness, returned because they were too lonely. Ray was a community sort of guy and he loved the interaction among his fellow guests, the volunteers, and staff. It didn't take long for me to get to love him too.

One of Ray's front door "I want my money" visits gave us an opportunity to talk. I asked him where he came from, what he did for a living, and did he have any family. He told me he had an ex-wife and a couple of sons. They weren't in contact any more. He went into detail about his one son's nice home in a warmer climate and the fact that he could join his son at any time, but he didn't want to. He had worked construction in the area most of his life. His ex lived in a nearby town and she too would be willing to help. He expressed sincere gratitude for what the volunteers and I did for him but he didn't bite on my offer to help him find his own place. He asked if I would call a cab, and hobbled off to wait for it.

Ray's stature as "honored senior citizen" improved with the years, but his health did not. He showed more signs of frailty, walking with difficulty even when sober. Eventually, he became a charter member of our "geezers and gimps" club, the unofficial name given to those lucky few who could stay inside when everyone else had to leave the shelter at 7 a.m. He usually availed himself of that privilege and was grateful for the reserved sleeping pad nearest the bathroom in the men's sleeping area.

One of Ray's shortcomings was his hygiene, or lack of it. He didn't often see the inside of the shower area and never without encouragement from me or another brave staff person. Even though he had a locker, he didn't have much of a wardrobe, so when his bladder failed, as it often did, especially when he was imbibing, one of us would head to the clothing storage room to find a pair of 32 x 32 pants and the assorted items of clothing that might fit him. Typically, I got the job of encouraging him to head to the shower because he respected me the most. Sometimes that respect didn't mean squat, and I recognized that trying to get him cleaned up would be futile.

His relentless, lifelong smoking took a toll on his quality of life. He could have been the poster child for the anti-smoking campaign. He was having trouble breathing and getting around, accompanied by a terrible cough, so I asked one of our volunteer nurses to make a house call to Ray-Ray's dining room perch and take a look at him. She was more than comfortable doing so but he needed convincing. He finally relented, lifting his shirt up so she could check his lungs and heart. Much to the dismay of the volunteers, many of whom were high school kids helping their first time at the shelter, Ray's skin was noticeably blue. To no surprise, he suffered from cardiopulmonary obstructive disease, which only would improve if he quit smoking, which would not happen.

Ray's infrequent showers made him prime target for body lice and scabies, which unfortunately visited the shelter too often. With the high numbers of homeless people and the small number of staff, it was difficult to keep up with hygiene (and many other tasks), so the critters took their toll, causing logistical nightmares for staff and physical suffering for those inflicted by the highly mobile varmints. Ray was the equivalent of a luxury hotel for the bugs looking for some unwashed place to visit. They'd cause incessant itching which would keep the unwilling host awake scratching until the bites bled.

One Christmas Eve, following a serene Christmas service attended by many of the guests and volunteers, Ray had his customary seat and seemed to enjoy the brief ecumenical service. As the last notes of "Silent Night" wafted through the dining room, I heard an insistent pounding on the outside door simultaneously with Ray's very loud shouting, "Godammit, these bugs are driving me crazy!" I prioritized the crises and chose to answer the door, going by Ray and telling him I'd get back to him in a moment. The other crisis (Ch.21) took way longer than I expected—a woman at the door with her face beat in by an iron pipe—so Ray went to bed with his lice. We eventually caught up with him, persisting at getting him to use the non-toxic lice shampoo.

Age, poor health care, and bad habits ravaged Ray's stamina, causing him to become more frail. The winter months were perhaps kindest to him because of his "geezer" status. The summers found him in Tent City, (Ch. 1) organized campground behind Hesed House that accommodated almost 100 people, mostly men. The tents, sleeping bags and mattresses provided by the churches were major improvements over the alternative—life on the streets during the 5-month hiatus when the seasonal emergency shelter was closed.

Ray took to camping, thanks in part to those who looked out after him. He shared a tent with three other guys, and came inside when a staff person opened up each evening for showers and meals. He endured this grueling arrangement because he had to—other options weren't available. His fellow campers would look out for him by making sure he had one of the few seats in the shade or by offering him whatever food was available. We tried to alleviate everyone's suffering in really hot weather or during severe storms by opening the building to let campers come inside, but for most of the time, it was outside living, complete with bugs, heat, skunks, raccoons, possums and human pests.

One summer, Ray, whose health had deteriorated throughout the winter, collapsed as he was walking back to Tent City. The ambulance hauled him to the hospital and he was admitted into the intensive care unit. One of the paramedics, a friend of mine, called me to report that Ray "coded" on the way to the hospital and that he was on life support. Broken-hearted, I went to see my buddy. One of the ICU nurses told me that he was going to be taken off life support and asked if I knew how to contact his family. She shared that she had a warm spot in her heart for our guys and would make sure he'd get good care.

I returned to the shelter and dug up Ray's son's name and number that he had given me a few years back. I called and left word that his dad was seriously ill and that the hospital needed to talk to a member of the family. His son, talking to me a few years ago when Ray had been hospitalized, made it clear that he wanted nothing to do with his father. The underlying message was that Ray had been less than a kind father, something that caused estrangement from the entire family. I wasn't sure how my message would be responded to and I went the next day to say goodbye to the comatose Ray.

Walking into ICU, I headed towards Ray's room, hearing his voice. "Godammit, I'm hungry!" he shouted to the nurse. "I haven't eaten in three days!" In the act of devouring a turkey sandwich, he brightened up when I came in. I was astounded—and yet not—to see him alive and sort of well. Ray went from near death to life, but it was clear that he needed medical care far beyond what we'd be able to offer.

The good news and the bad—it often takes a severe medical trauma like this to get a person into an assisted care facility, which means they leave their "home" and their friends to move into a nursing home. Ray, unlike many other younger homeless persons, had Medicare, which would pay for his nursing home. He had previously refused to leave his "home" for an assisted care nursing home. Now he was ready, but he was more than peeved that it meant a $30 a month budget, which had to include his cigarettes.

On my first visit to his new residence, he asked for his reading glasses and some candy. He despised his roommate, an invalid who did nothing but sleep all the time. When I returned with the glasses and candy, I had to go looking for him. He was scooting about in a wheelchair, heading down to the smoking area. He'd already made friends and had several visits from his shelter buddies who reported to me regularly on Ray's condition.

Ray lasted another year and a half. My consolation was that he had a safe, warm place to stay, medical care, reading materials, sweets and friends to chat with whenever he wanted. We remembered him at a memorial service we held at the shelter every year for Homeless Persons' Memorial Day, the first day of winter. I think of him when I hear the calming verses of "Silent Night."

Aging is scary enough without factoring in the possibility of homelessness. Anyone giving this serious consideration might do well to get involved in finding solutions to geezers living on the streets. That stereotypical "grizzled geezer" is someone's grandpa. That hunched-over bedraggled old lady is someone's grandma...

PART 6 —

ANY TIME NOW...SOONER RATHER THAN LATER WOULD BE NICE!

"If you are neutral in the situation of injustice, you have chosen the side of the oppressor.

"If an elephant has his foot on the tail of a mouse and you say you are neutral, the mouse will not appreciate your neutrality."

Bishop Desmond Tutu

26. The Challenge: Keep Hope Alive — Against Precipitous Odds

*H*opelessness kills. Allowing homeless persons to sink further into despair, removing any hope for people to regain independence, or denying that society has responsibility to work toward solutions of homelessness wreaks havoc for those in the hopeless situation—and from my perspective, for the entire country. Rather than destroy hope, we would all be better served by channeling resources and energy to restoring opportunities for people to become productive, starting with access to housing and supportive services.

Since the mid-1980s, homelessness has steadily increased, but has escaped all but minor attention of the media, policy makers, or the general population. My favorite but overused analogy is the comparison of a lobster being either dropped into a pot of boiling water (where it might be inclined to react by jumping out); or an unsuspecting crustacean being placed into cold water that has the heat turned on. By the time the water boils, the lobsters can't do anything because the heat has sapped their strength. Poverty and homelessness weren't caused abruptly by one policy or one president. It's the culmination of years of decisions to cut back life-sustaining support. And few political leaders seem greatly concerned. Nor do some embittered or unenlightened citizens. Media pay scant attention to the underlying causes of homelessness, rather grabbing the sensational and/or distorted stories that reflect, often inaccurately, the surface of homelessness. The "Man Dies Under A Bridge" report generates less attention than "Whales Die On the Beach" story. Those most motivated to bring about systemic change are a handful of advocates and most homeless persons themselves—not a powerful lobby in the halls of Congress.

A workable, comprehensive strategy to address poverty, the proverbial elephant in the middle of the living room, doesn't exist. Political candidates don't touch the topic. Religious leaders may urge charity, but rarely take the unpopular stand of urging their congregations to push for systemic change or accountability from government leaders. Few business and corporate executives exhibit a social conscience to demand an end to homelessness. They are too busy bolstering profits by shipping jobs overseas and slashing workforces, raiding previously untouchable pensions while reaping rewards from unknowing or conspiring boards of directors. A stereotypical homeless-looking man I sat next to in a diner struck up a conversation with me not long ago. He asked me what I did, and raised his eyebrows when I said I worked with homeless families. I politely asked what he did, and he said he was a retired financial raider. He described how he engineered takeovers of corporations, reaping huge profits for himself and his partners. I raised my eyebrows. He had no apparent sense that his actions created "business" for people like me. He seemed unashamed, even proud that he did what he did. I didn't begin to try to point out what I considered the error of his ways. I wondered how many more are like him?

Too many people would have to admit that they're stealing from the poor to become rich. No one wants to do that! But who wants to turn down huge profits from the sale of illegally inflated stock or to decline proceeds when the distorted housing market reaps huge proceeds for lucky owners?

Greed conflicts with poverty. Greed causes increased poverty and suffering. Greed supports a nation's justification to change priorities, ignoring explosive poverty while insulating the haves and have-mores with tax cuts and opportunities to further amass riches.

In the meantime, substantial human service budget cuts at federal and state levels shred the all-but-destroyed safety net for those who need life-sustaining help. Advocates, rendered practically voiceless, co-opt in order to survive. They ignore systemic issues and place Band-Aids on gaping wounds of poverty and homelessness. They realize that government funding depends on them being "nice" and not challenging the policies and practices that create the problems. So instead of decrying the lack of decent housing for impoverished families, you open a homeless shelter that quickly fills up with the families that should be in their own homes. Instead of challenging policies that limit support for families seeking adequate daycare services, you open a program to counsel kids in the juvenile justice system, kids who had inadequate supervision while their parents worked at low paying jobs.

The shrinking middle class often fails to see what's happening until it's too late, perhaps a result of being too busy coping with increased housing and energy costs, struggling with increased health insurance premiums, or worse—trying to get medical care without insurance.

Under the guise of saving money and fostering independence, government priorities have shifted away from the main purpose of government, caring for those most in need of help, and have successfully ensured the fiscal well-being of those with already adequate resources. Instead of creating policies to ensure survival of the most vulnerable and success for those who need some help to get back on their feet, federal policies make more people poor while making it harder to be poor. At the same time, special interest groups and politicians have increased benefits of being rich and developed policies to ensure their financial well being.

Regions previously untouched by devastating poverty are beginning to be hard hit by plant closings as jobs get shipped to other countries where labor is cheap and environmental responsibility is unheard of or at least easy to ignore[16]. Western Illinois, a quiet mostly rural area, had a few industrial establishments, which have recently closed their doors. The free legal service for poor persons, Prairie State Legal Services, reports a huge upsurge of foreclosures on the heels of the factory closings. What a surprise....My fear for people hit by this economic devastation is that homelessness is not far behind. And this area has no homeless shelters and very few motels, so where do people go?

People who know me would agree that I've paid my dues in this field of social justice. I've spent two decades trying to repair this collateral damage in the war against the poor by embracing men, women and children who have been tossed to the streets. I've sat on countless task forces; participated on gazillion committees; written and read innumerable reports and recommendations; protested and demonstrated against injustices; testified to policy-making committees; written newsletters, letters to the editor and news articles; shared my thoughts on radio and television; spoken passionately to federal, state and local legislators, and urged thousands of homeless persons and volunteers to advocate also.

My fellow advocates have done the same. Some old-timers remain, some have died, some have stumbled away disillusioned and disgusted. Some have been destroyed physically and/or mentally by the pressure of doing the impossible and being scorned and thwarted by political self-interest and corporate greed.

For those unfamiliar with the issues that fuel the fury behind my criticisms of government and societal failures, some prime examples illustrate the point:

- **Lack of medical care** for economically disadvantaged persons destroys health and personal financial stability while undermining the fiscal health of a community. Show me a community with rampant poverty and I guarantee you'll find a disproportionate number of people in poor health and lacking health care options.

In the 20 years I've been in social services, as the number of uninsured persons burgeoned (currently, over 45 million persons without insurance in our country), health care costs have skyrocketed, causing providers to ration medical care. I've seen medical bills in the thousands of dollars for treating a simple injury such as a broken arm. Hospitals have recently been criticized for charging "retail" rates to uninsured patients while discounting care for those with insurance. At best, the financial end of the medical industry needs a major overhaul. Providers often benefit by increased premiums, soaring drug costs and profitable ancillary businesses to manage the out-of-control health care industry while millions go without health care or become saddled by debt because they lack insurance.

My first memorable encounter with medical inequities was when "Sharon," a short, pleasant black woman staying at PADS, collapsed at our shelter and went to the hospital by ambulance. She had a brain tumor the size of a tennis ball. Doctors removed it and returned her a couple days later to our shelter, despite my outraged pleas for her. She didn't have insurance. (She drifted away, dependent on anyone who would take her in, even her alcohol-crazed significant other, a guy we banned because he stabbed someone in an argument.) The hospital couldn't afford to keep her. That's when things were "good," back in the early '90s.

> • **Lack of affordable housing** continues to wreak havoc for not only very poor households, but also for middle-income workers. By misleadingly equating "affordable housing" with slums, community leaders have been able to fend off efforts to create a variety of housing options for the variety of people in their community, including the working poor. Ignoring this basic necessity—a safe, affordable place to live—sabotages productivity in a community. Workers should be able to live near their work. If not, businesses struggle to attract employees, traffic problems increase, and family pressures escalate.

In the early 1990s, I was a key "conspirator" of a movement to develop a nearby abandoned industrial warehouse into what was called SRO housing, single room occupancy. The man who proffered the idea was a third shift (3 a.m. to 7 a.m.) shelter volunteer who witnessed the hordes of guys getting wake up calls in order to go to work. He rightly felt that if so many people were willing and able to work they should have a better place to live. He offered to be the developer of the renovation project if we would provide our know-how in creating the services end of the project. A decent, affordable room coupled with supervision and assistance for those who needed it would have probably allowed 50 or more adults to move out of the shelter. What a great plan! It met with a proverbial buzz saw, culminating with the then Mayor David Pierce practically throwing us through the window of his office, vehemently rejecting the plan, even before he knew the details of it. Our inability to pull off this worthwhile project stung, convincing me that homelessness would continue to escalate until we could change community attitudes and priorities. Unfortunately, as our numbers kept exploding upward, I realized that this was a challenge I'd have to ignore so I could deal with the immediate problem of too many people, too little space in our shelter. What a dilemma…

Every administration claims painful decisions need to be made in order to balance the budget. Housing options—affordable to people of all income levels—allow a community to thrive. A thriving community generates positive economic benefits. What's wrong with that? Generous government housing subsidies pour into the pockets of the wealthy in the form of income tax refunds based on property taxes paid. Why should people get tax benefits for owning two or more houses when some people have no home because the government doesn't have enough money? Is it because those with multiple houses are writing the laws that give them the perks?

Some of us see the government's choices as—bombs or housing, tax cuts for the rich or housing for the poor, superfluous spending on pork barrel projects or housing for the poor. In 2004, federal homeless assistance grants were funded at $1.241 billion, a cut of $19 million from last year's level— the first cut to the program since 1995, one that bodes ill for growing numbers of families and individuals seeking to escape homelessness.

> • In addition to reduced support of shelters and services, homeless people are feeling the squeeze from yet another cutback—**legal services**.

Often the cause of homelessness has several layers to it, including problems requiring legal advocacy. Often persons get evicted, many times illegally, and to make matters worse, their credit record gets saddled with negative credit reports, making them less than desirable applicants for future housing. If you want to help someone get back on their feet, working with them to clear their credit record and previous legal problems is the way to do it, but that typically requires time, money and an attorney.

Significant changes to public housing, credit and banking laws create significant obstacles for many homeless (and even non-homeless) persons seeking housing. Often, my co-workers and I desperately scanned the dining room with its point-in-time capacity 70+ bodies, trying to figure out who would have the least barriers to getting their own place to stay. We'd eliminate someone with an active drug/alcohol problem. Scratch those who just got out of prison. Delete those too mentally ill to live on their own. It never failed—when we came up with someone, we'd talk to them about getting extra help to move out, they'd respond favorably, and when we sat down to talk specifics they'd hit the barrier of bad credit and legal problems.

Bad credit, often from unpaid rent, can perpetuate homelessness for some people. "Gretchen" had lived on her own for years following a divorce. She had a modest apartment, worked regularly at a decent paying job, until mental illness pulled the rug and rest of the house out from under her. She fell behind on rent, eventually was evicted and landed on our doorsteps. Her pride, coupled with her inability to mentally process her reality, kept her from asking her brother for help. It took several years of coaxing her forward to get her to be able to trust us enough to help her. When she finally shared details of her demise and asked for assistance, we checked into her credit record. This grandmotherly woman, for most of her life a productive member of society, was stuck in homelessness because of a past debt to her landlord of less than $1,000.

She was ineligible for public housing because of her credit record, a result of legislative trickery designed to increase profit for property owners at the expense of unknowing tenants. Changes made in Washington to public housing laws, under the guise of improving the quality of life for tenants, created this major "Catch-22" where homeless persons with bad credit couldn't be considered for public (a.k.a. affordable) housing because they had bad credit. Good idea that needs some major fine-tuning.

Fortunately, Gretchen managed to inch forward in her ability to trust. One of our volunteers, Debby, managed to coax her along by patiently relating to her as a valuable human being. They laughed, chatted, and eventually shopped for clothes together. We managed to gather resources to pay off the old debt and clear Gretchen's credit record. Debby and her friend checked out the senior high-rise apartment building that Gretchen was finally eligible to apply for. Slowly plans fell into place—the application was approved, her police record check passed, her brother reunited with his sister, household goods were gathered, and Debby engineered the move. After years of sleeping on a thin pad on the floor during winter months and crawling into a sleeping bag during long Tent City seasons, Gretchen finally had a home. I strongly believe that if Congress could see the faces of people like Gretchen and hear her story, they would craft wiser laws and policies. I'm unrealistically thinking that they'd ignore the banking and for-profit housing lobbyists urging more greedy, self-serving regulations.

Bill, a mountain of a man, fell into the abyss of homelessness for myriad reasons, including major health problems. With incredible fortitude on his part and steadfast assistance from a number of volunteers and staff, he climbed to the edge of the deep hole, almost ready to get into public housing for seniors. He not only wanted a place of his own, he really needed one. His breathing problems and other health issues required him to sleep sitting up, an accommodation we strained to make by soliciting a recliner which we squeezed into a corner of the dining room.

He eventually was ready to apply to the housing authority. The process required a police background check. His turned up an arrest from 20-plus years prior for breaking windows. That caused him to be denied for housing, despite the fact that his life had been crime free since the shattering of glass shattered his future. He was assertive enough to invoke a higher power, this time Congressman Denny Hastert's office. The matter was cleared up, allowing him to move into his own place. Sadly, he died in his own place shortly after moving in. His massive health problems developed during his homelessness/doctor-less-ness.

I could fill countless pages with examples of tragic effects of government cuts. Resource-deficient advocates seeking justice and equality battle powerful special interest groups for access to government leaders. Doors open to those who can contribute to election campaigns or offer quid pro quo. Money eliminates any sense of fair play. It closes the door to honest dialogue about caring for millions of persons in need across this, the richest country in the history of the world.

Advocacy on this slippery slope takes enormous time, energy and money. Competing with well-funded special interest groups with little understanding or appreciation for the poor and homeless persons in this country is almost senseless. Homeless and poor persons become an acceptable trade off in the quest for affluence.

Some leaders pay lip service to religious values and moral obligations to care for the poor and vulnerable, feigning compassion and a spiritual responsibility to those in need, as they turn the impossible job over to faith-based ministries with minimal government support, inadequate staffing and program offerings and even less outrage from either the general public or religious leaders. Faith-based groups can't possibly shoulder this massive burden alone.

Things are a mess—current government priorities have created multi-layered problems for millions of vulnerable families and individuals across the country, including:

- a critical shortage of decent, affordable housing
- greatly limited access to legal assistance
- a largely-failing public education system
- slashed financial support for those too disabled to work
- scarce quality, affordable child care
- a dearth of health care.

Despite these daunting hardships, some "lucky" families and individuals manage to crawl out of the perilously deep hole of homelessness and regain some semblance of independence and normality. Those folks give the rest of us hope that keeping people alive may lead to even more people regaining a meaningful existence they deserve.

Escaping from this insidious condition is definitely not easy. Simplistic, judgmental prescriptions abound: stop using drugs/alcohol, return to your spouse (abusive or not), work harder (for minimum wage), behave, move into that affordable (but substandard) apartment, leave your spouse, get medical treatment (without insurance), find a place you can afford (on minimum wage), go back to school, move back in with your parents....and those solutions often require life-changing choices, which often require financial resources, non-existent services, unrealistic options and a strong support network.

In the years I spent running shelters, as I came to know people who stayed with us, I struggled mightily with the dilemma of offering false hope or not holding out expectations for them. A person's current predicament was usually more complicated than they shared with me. Knowing my optimistic penchant for believing every problem has a solution, I would typically feel conflicted—encourage someone to fail? or not motivate them to improve because I knew how cruel the world is? Hmmmm....it's a wonder to me that anyone gets out of the grip of homelessness.

It's Not All Bad...

One of my favorite "success" stories, Beth and her kids (Ch. 15) have grabbed a piece of the American Dream, thanks very little to government, but in great part to her mother who enabled her to buy a "farmette" in northwestern Illinois. They took in a homeless goat, "Mike," three homeless horses, and learned that life does not need to be crisis-centered. Hopefully, the kids and their mom are getting back to "normal" after years of abuse, homelessness, and abject poverty.

Lynda and her family (Ch. 14) continue to make it—paycheck to paycheck. Her daughter, Meg, now a confident and capable 21-year-old, has begun work to ensure access to school for the suburbs' estimated 20,000 homeless students. Her passion for this job will no doubt be fueled by her experiences—good and bad—throughout her homelessness.

Invisible and uncountable, others will climb the shaky ladder towards self-sufficiency as they leave their homelessness behind. A good paying job; capable and compassionate caseworkers; caring family members with access to resources; and a compilation of good luck, hard work and human kindness will help lift others off the streets. They, in turn, will provide hope and example to those looking up to them. Those who get back on their feet often reach out, sometimes clandestinely, to help those in a homeless situation, perhaps risking their fragile independence, e.g., letting someone move in with them to escape the streets that eventually could cause the landlord to kick them out for violation of the lease prohibiting additional residents.

When I run into guys like Michael (Ch. 20), who had troubles enough for five guys but somehow straightened out enough to get his maintenance job at the local high school—and keep it for a few years—I ponder his success and try to figure out how a guy like him could make it. He has a roof over his head and an amazingly upbeat attitude, even towards me, the person who had to kick him out of the shelter more times than either of us wanted.

His secret of success? My strong belief is that, in addition to some unseen inner strength, maybe we kept him and thousands like him alive during some bad times, bolstering him with hope and love when no one else would. It's human nature to remember those who stuck with us in bad times. The indescribable level of care and support that staff and volunteers extended to our homeless guests undoubtedly helped some bridge the gap between feeling useless and feeling loved. Without that knowledge, they would not have courage to try to stand on their own again.

One Way Out—Death

Such hope and example is essential, but it won't do much good for those too infirm to take advantage of opportunities for improvement. The lack of health care for too many homeless adults puts them on a fast track for premature death. Death continues to remove many of my homeless friends from their suffering. The pattern typically is: severe medical crisis, hospital, nursing home and death. Death, despite the sadness that accompanies it, is often the only escape for some people stuck in the despair of poverty and homelessness.

Spiraling Trip Downward

Gary represents many people with similar situations we saw. He arrived at our door a few days before Christmas, reluctantly asking for a place to stay. He shared with me that he recently broke up with a woman who got tired of his drunken stupidity. He admitted as much, adding that he had previously lived in a large home along the Fox River made possible by his hard work and good salary in a union construction job.

Gary was emotionally touched by our generous gift-giving spree at Christmas. This tall gruff guy participated in our Christmas Eve service, designed to minimize the pain of holiday memories and to maximize a sense that hope exists for even the most hopeless. He pulled me aside to tearfully thank me for his gift of socks and gloves. His story of devastation came out in bits and pieces, augmented by my observation that this mammoth drywaller had an even larger drinking problem. Geez, he was obnoxious when he drank! I could understand how someone could lose patience with him.

One relatively quiet evening, I broached the subject of his drinking with an at-the-moment sober Gary. He was painfully honest, acknowledging his alcohol consumption and the behavior it fueled were the source of his problems. No argument from me. At some point he mentioned some serious health concerns he had and I told him about our Rainbow Clinic, making sure he'd get on the list for the next night it was scheduled. Taking my hand in his construction-roughened grip, he promised to quit drinking; an oath I figured would be hard for him to keep.

Subsequent visits to the clinic unearthed Gary's massive health issues—including a damaged heart that caused our medical professionals great concern. Gary's time with us went through a predictable pattern: awareness of an addiction, attempts to address it, medical crises to interfere with his plans to get back on his feet, relapse, return to sobriety, move into the transitional shelter (usually more for medical reasons than a person's pending return to society), periods of good behavior intermixed with relapse, and medical crisis resulting in hospitalization.

Gary had more than his share of medical problems and received well-intentioned assistance from paid and volunteer medical professionals. The irregular care coupled by his inability to kick the bottle eventually killed him. We were stymied in our attempts to move him into a nursing home when his breathing required an oxygen machine. His inability to quit smoking made us very nervous—oxygen tank and spark—dangerous at best, and we knew he'd be able to sneak smokes. Multiple hospitalizations and near-death experiences failed to convince him of his vulnerability. Perhaps he held onto his death-defying habits as his only vestige of his former independent life-style. He died after ensconcing himself in the hearts of many people who loved him for his charisma and genuineness.

Broken Bones, Broken Spirit

Jeff also went the way of the medically-challenged alcoholic who endeared himself to countless persons. His almost lifelong reliance on copious amounts of cheap alcohol prevented people from getting to know the real Jeff, a kind and loving man.

My first clear recollection of talking to him was interviewing him at the beginning of a PADS season. We asked people what they thought was their cause of homelessness. Jeff quickly replied, "I lost my job," with his alcohol-tainted breath almost knocking me off my chair. I gently pried deeper, perhaps to satisfy my curiosity of his awareness of his situation. "Well, my wife kicked me out when I lost my job," he explained. When asked to elaborate, he revealed that his drinking might have had something to do with it. *Just a little, I sadly mused to myself.*

Jeff had his ups and downs, related to his drinking. He'd be hit by a car because he was too drunk to know he was staggering in its path (undoubtedly causing trauma to the person who hit him). Jeff would be hospitalized and in the process experience sobriety. He'd return to the shelter, sober and unable to wander the streets because of his cast, so he'd offer his help around the shelter. At first I was skeptical of his ability to render any useful assistance, but he proved me wrong. His elf-like appearance with his leprechaun smirk and his twinkling blue eyes embodied his true lovable character. The weather-related creases on his street-worn face enhanced his frequent smile. It was good to see this side of him, although we both subconsciously knew that it was probably short-lived. It was. Once his injuries healed, he heeded the internal call of all alcoholics—follow the path to the bottle. He had no safe haven and was surrounded by his drinking buddies, so it was back to his destructive lifestyle.

Jeff once worked, and whatever caused his downward spiral I'll probably never know. His life on the streets, heavy drinking, incalculable mostly self-healed fractures which caused him no end of pain, and his mental instability made the theory of him being a traditional working member of society less than plausible. Without a place to call home, he did what too many other people do, hang out somewhere and drink to kill the pain.

One blustery winter afternoon I was summoned to the adjacent nature trail because Jeff fell and was supposed to have been injured. I figured he had just passed out and looked hurt. Quite annoyed, I grabbed my coat and went to investigate. As I was led to the scene, about a quarter of a mile down the ice-covered trail, I got more aggravated with every frosty step. "He'd better be hurt," my steamy breath colliding with the frosty air, thinking of the many false alarms I'd been dragged out to investigate.

When we finally found him, he was stretched out across the trail, motionless. "Jeff!" I shouted at him with pent-up impatience. His eyes slowly opened and he looked up at me as I towered exasperatingly over him.

"Aw, Diane, I'm sorry," he sputtered. I looked at the disjointed sack of humanity and realized that even for Jeff, with prior multiple breaks of almost every bone in his body, his leg below his knee had a weird bend to it, probably broken. I used my cell phone to call for an ambulance, directing the paramedics to the nearest roadway. They had to drag their equipment down a steep, snow-covered hill. They probably were as annoyed as I because they, too, had to frequently deal with Jeff at his worst drunken condition.

They hauled him to the hospital. I went back to my administrative minutiae. Jeff required surgery and an extensive period of rehabilitation that fortunately landed him at a local nursing home. Various visitors returned with amazing stories about Jeff's sober behavior and helpful nature endearing him to the residents and staff at the facility. I went occasionally to visit him, astounded with his success in adapting to a sober lifestyle.

He mailed me a newsletter featuring how he was named "volunteer of the month" for his efforts. One of the staff shared with me how much he helped, and how loved he was. I was pleased that he was seemingly permanently housed in a supportive environment where he could contribute something for his stay. His ability to patiently deal with difficult patient/residents earned him accolades from staff and deep respect of fellow residents. He seemed set, with his injury requiring ongoing medical care.

At some point, likely tied with a visit by one of his old street cronies and a bottle of cheap vodka, Jeff was kicked out of the nursing home. I'd got word of him and his buddy living in a small apartment downtown, too close to a liquor store. I could guess the end of the story.

He showed up one late afternoon, meeting me in the parking lot as I was going out to Tent City. He had a cab waiting, and he looked good considering how I've seen him look. "Diane, I figured I'd catch you," he said. He knew my routine and knew I'd be heading out back to inspect the campground before opening up the dining room. He reached into his pocket for his wallet, where he pulled out four crisp hundred-dollar bills, probably the remainder of his Social Security check. Handing them to me, he stated, "This is for what you've done for me." I protested, saying that it wasn't just I that helped him, that I don't take money for doing what I do, and that he'd need it more than I.

He stubbornly refused, and as he did so I could detect alcohol fueling his insistence. He hopped in his cab, winking and waving, and left me with the money and a deep sadness that he would not be with us for long. I was right. Soon after, he was found dead of alcohol poisoning. I never learned what pain pushed him to deaden it. I was glad that I got to see the other side of him, realizing that beyond his drunken façade he had a goodness that made him valuable to me and those who still believed in him. Jeff's $400 went to help another person get into an alcohol treatment program, a fitting legacy.

So Poor, Yet So Rich

My "gold watch" after years of involvement with people, most of whom were embedded in bad times, is running into them in the grocery store, seeing them at their work place, getting an occasional call or email, or just waving as they walk through downtown. Members of our secret club, "the Hope Sharers," treasure life more than most. We've seen death, sickness, violence, injustice and shattered dreams. We've kept treating each other like the human beings we are, worthy of respect and dignity. It's a select club, entered into by the unknowing, much like myself, who cross that invisible line, believing something should be done, and the circumstances were right.

My crossing the line, going into this world beyond what I could have ever imagined, taught me more than I can ever realize. I've seen a side of humanity written off by too many people, and have been astounded by the quality of life and love that my homeless brothers and sisters experience and share. I humbly realize that it is not what I give them, but what they so abundantly give me that is invaluable. My walk to the other side of life enabled me to see what life really is—how we are supposed to treat others, and how we are supposed to unite to keep hope alive. The richness of this lesson is incalculable for those who have yet to venture to the other side of that line.

One of my favorite myth-breakers is to talk to a group or individual about stereotypes. I would describe our unique summer pseudo-shelter, Tent City, with 80 to 100 people living in a commune behind our building. It never fails—the listeners' eyes get wide and I can almost hear the thoughts screaming in their head, thoughts they are too polite to utter, "Oh my God! You mean all 'those' people sleep in tents in the same area without supervision?!"

Yet, in my 13 years of overseeing this seemingly insane arrangement, I saw huge amounts of "neighborliness" and relatively little unacceptable behavior. Sure, guys got drunk and stumbled into tent ropes; some had unauthorized visitors and used illegal substances. However, these same scenes play out countless times day and night all across our country—in mansions and tenements, in boardrooms and crack houses. Denying the existence of wanton behavior would be ludicrous.

Assigning blame to those living on the streets and in communes such as Tent City is unenlightened at best, hypocritical at worst. Writing off this significant segment of the population because of their "sins" is unconscionable and flies in the face of so-called religious-based values that form the basis of the condemnation. I maintain that persons who can relatively thrive and be respectful in a setting such as Tent City should be able to make it in their own place to live. They, and their communities, would be better off. When people are treated with respect, they tend to act respectfully. My years of interacting with people who responded to being treated respectfully make me somewhat of an expert in the subject.

My sentiments about alcoholics and other "problem people" changed early in my social service experience. I learned that persons mired in addictions, and those hurting so much physically and mentally, had few options other than self-medication to escape their incredible pain.

Sad Stories Beyond Stereotypes

"Red," one of my oldest "sweethearts," exemplifies this issue. In addition to being, in his words, a "lousy drunk," he also is a nice guy with massive health problems, some caused by him drinking, some not.

Many years ago, when we reached a point where we could be honest with each other, he asked me to help him get into a program so he could quit drinking. I deemed his request serious enough to work with him. Try as I may, we could find no place willing to take him.

Part of the problem was he lacked insurance or any means to pay. The bigger problem was that places, even our local religious mission-shelter, wouldn't take him because of his health problems. It strikes me as ironic that someone who sincerely wants to sober up can't find a program to accept him because everyone is afraid of him having a medical emergency in their program, so let's leave him on the streets or at the shelter so he can die there. Red caught the irony and figured he deserved to suffer, an assessment I disagreed with.

But getting sober isn't all it's cracked up to be for those "lucky" enough to get into a program. They find it's usually a three-day detox and then back onto the streets. "Brad," another long-timer, bounced in and out of sobriety. His moments of hope—getting his life back together—kept him focused on reaching for the sobriety he deeply wanted and somehow, with dogged help from a caring caseworker, he got into a program, sometimes even a 21-day program (his mother would pay), and come out resolved to make it.

With Brad, as with so many addicts, internal demons may be temporarily silenced, but when they scream inside his head, he needs more support than can find in a homeless shelter or walking the streets with his drinking buddies. He needs, among other things, a community with supportive services, including frequent AA meetings (or other support group), quality counseling, and a place to be where alcohol isn't jumping out from every corner. I can offer assurance that the environment of most homeless shelters is not the place to achieve a high sobriety success rate.

Imagine, if you can, wanting something with your entire being, taking the risk to reach for it, and tasting victory, then having it crumble and vanish before you, and being blamed for failure, time after time. Brad, and so many like him, lives that nightmare on a daily basis. Struggling with addictions is hard enough. Being homeless and struggling with addictions and rejection and more has to be beyond painful. Persons in this situation who manage to retain any semblance of humanity constantly awe me.

Taking newly acquired sobriety and stability for granted soon became a casualty of my profession. I can remember time after time rejoicing because some person with an obnoxious alcohol/drug problem got "clean." When they stumbled "off the wagon," it devastated them and greatly disappointed me. Little did I realize all the complications of the trip to and from sobriety. In over-simplifying the journey, I did a great disservice to the traveler. "All you need is to get sober, get a job, get a place, get a life..." and when it falls apart for any number of reasons, not only does the backslider get hurt, but the person who held the unrealistic hope for success—like me—also suffers, exposed to the devastating disease called cynicism.

"Hector," a personable Hispanic bike-riding guy, personified the up-down syndrome. He like so many others became homeless because of his drinking. He lost his license, but had enough determination to get back on his feet that he became a consummate bike rider, putting as many miles on his pedal-powered two wheels as some of us do with our gasoline guzzling four wheels.

He seemed resolute in his efforts to get his own life back together. He'd leave early, hopping on his bike in all kinds of weather. He'd return from his labor each evening happy, proud of his efforts, and soon he'd say, "Diane, this is my last night here. Thanks for all you've done to help me."

I'd sort of forget about him for a while and months or years later he'd show up again, repeat his pattern of biking to work, and then he'd be gone again. Sometimes, his unemployment was not due to his drinking, but the changing climate of the economy. Sometimes, he'd confess that he slipped back into his old habits, and it cost him his job. He'd always seem cheerful, respectful and incredibly grateful. I was always amazed at his resilience; he never got caught up in the escalating destructive behavior I'd see in others. He managed to remain hopeful, gleaning his attitude from those who provided the roof over his head. He was gone when I left my shelter job. I can only hold out hope that he managed to maintain his positive attitude. I finally figured out that Hector's drinking was the same as countless others who had the walls of their homes to hide them from judgment. Guys like Hector were, because of their circumstances, more visible, therefore more honest about their problem.

Sadly, we all suffer from that destructive mental condition of despair at some time. Hopelessness mixed with homelessness can be lethal, for the one being helped and the one trying to help. I've seen it affect me. I've watched co-workers destroyed. I've witnessed attrition of volunteers. I've listened to cynical politicians and police officers. I've read essays and books by those who believed the "unworthy" would never be worth anything. I've realized that once we give up on others, we give up on ourselves. I don't want to go there.

Some of my brightest moments occurred when I'd get a note, phone call or visit from a "graduate" who felt moved to thank me for being kind to

them. When I was able to allow myself to process the motivation behind the message, I marveled at the possibility of change—even for just a moment. I delight in thinking that I had played some role in a person's metamorphosis. I am awed at their determination to make the effort to thank me, usually for some very insignificant part I played in their reconstruction. Knowing how seldom I've ever thanked someone who believed in me when it was difficult even for me to believe in myself humbles me.

27. Beyond Shelter Doors—YIKES!

J ust in case you think shelters have the homelessness situation all under control, think again. As one who spent many years running shelters, I always felt that every homeless person from east of the Mississippi, and a few stragglers from west of the Big Muddy, lined up at our door. As overcrowded as we were, we just had the proverbial tip of the iceberg. The rest, especially families, were elsewhere...

One of my biggest shocks of my "post-shelter" days (and nights) is finding that homelessness abounds throughout suburban areas surrounding Chicago—and most homeless families are not in shelters. Actually, my shock got a reality check—for the worst—because I knew families turned to the local shelter as a last resort.

Since leaving my job at Hesed, I created and directed a new program funded by the federal government. Project REACH (Restoring Educational Access to Children who are Homeless), served as the lead liaison for the State Board of Education in the 8-county area surrounding Chicago (Ch. 30). We assisted homeless families and unaccompanied youth when they encountered barriers to enrolling in school. We also worked with educators, teaching them about homelessness, and advising them in situations when homeless families try to enroll their kids. Another part of our job was to coordinate the need for supportive services between agencies and/or schools and families needing help.

In speaking to hundreds of families, social service staff and educators throughout the suburbs, it was alarmingly apparent that homelessness, especially for families, had reached epidemic—yet unrecognized— proportions. Overcrowding was the norm at our shelter. I had no idea how pervasive it is outside our shelter doors.

My standard line while orienting new shelter volunteers who looked with horror at the overcrowded family room was, "If every homeless family in Aurora showed up at our shelter tonight, I'd kill myself." That may be an extreme and inefficient solution, but the burgeoning numbers of families (and individuals) just kept overwhelming us.

We'd hit our max, figure out where else we could wedge bodies, and repeat the cycle all over again. We did four major capacity-building phases in my 13 years at Hesed House—and still didn't have enough space. The guys were accommodated—loosely speaking—by giving them a spot at a table in the dining room with the caveat—"don't sleep on the floor or stretch out on the tables." They'd get uncomfortably creative, and at least they were warm and safe for the night. The dining room often reminded me of a scene from *Gone With the Wind,* with bodies of soldiers lying everywhere. Our bodies were casualties of the war on poverty.

Families proved to be more challenging because they have greater needs for safety, privacy, and structure. Myriad dilemmas face homeless families as they weigh their extremely limited options of whether to come—or not—to area homeless shelters. Some realities:

> • Most communities don't have shelters. In Chicago's suburbs, geographic areas may have overnight emergency shelters during winter months. Most rotate sites—a logistical nightmare for the "average" homeless person, much less an overburdened parent with kids.
>
> • Transportation to the shelter site; where to hang out while waiting for the shelter to open and/or after it closes (usually 7 p.m. to 7 a.m.); job and school communications and travel arrangements; how to carry all the family's "stuff" including clothing, important papers, medicine, toys, etc.; are just some normal ordeals facing the overburdened family.
>
> • Summer presents a painful challenge for families faced with shelters' seasonal schedule, the first being no place to live. The end of winter means shelter staff aggressively tries to get families placed SOMEWHERE. Too many families, too few options…
>
> • Not all shelters allow male children, or restrict admission only to younger boys with their mothers. Splitting up the family may be the only option.
>
> • Families traumatized by abuse (typically at the hand of a male household member) understandably aren't too keen on moving into a "household" with 100+ males living under the roof.
>
> • Often family sleeping areas at shelters are giant dysfunctional slumber parties—on a good night. Too many families in too small space; standard and more severe behavior issues; lots of single women with their own problems sleeping in nearby space; everyone sharing a severely inadequate bathroom area (our standard ratio was 25:2); scarce storage for immense piles of stuff…creates an environment ripe for disasters. Just think about

the last time you visited relatives without enough room to accommodate you and your family…

• Female heads of homeless families are just like those of housed families—they want companionship. Sometimes they make good choices in mates; often they don't. Stay with an abusive mate or try to find a shelter. What a choice.

• For any parent with a job or seeking employment, using a homeless shelter's address guarantees a negative reaction from employers. Balancing work and "home" life while homeless also makes life difficult to say the least. Wardrobe problems, insufficient sleep, justifiable worries about family issues; unstable housing; irregular phone and mail access; and countless more quandaries face the working parent.

• Since women's financial situations are often fragile at best, credit problems—or lack of credit and money management skills—sabotage their attempt to find a place to live. Even publicly subsidized housing requires credit checks. My bemused response to that piece of bureaucratic red tape is, "How many homeless people do I know who have GOOD credit? None!"

• Perhaps the biggest fear of homeless parents is losing custody of their kids. That fear causes families to be very secretive about their situation, which often raises red flags with school officials and other authority figures.

• Larger families have all sorts of extra challenges beyond more mouths to feed. Who wants to take in a mom with a bunch of kids? Even families with as few as four kids face daunting ordeals trying to convince a family member, friend, or potential landlord that her larger family won't pose difficulties.

• Despite the best attempts of the shelter staff, family sleeping areas tend to be breeding grounds for head lice, the common cold, pink eye, chicken pox, measles, mumps…you get the picture. Why would any parent with options—even bad ones—want to expose their kids to that?

I could go on, but you get the idea: homelessness + family = disaster. With families continuing to fuel the growth of homelessness, someone better figure out solutions fast! The more kids who experience homelessness, the worse it is for all of us. The rapid upsurge of homelessness, now estimated to include over one million children out of more than 3 million homeless persons, has done nothing but increase since this country began serious efforts of enumeration in the 1980s.

So, what does the desperate homeless mom (in most cases females) do when faced with sleeping on the streets? She will beg family members or friends for a place to stay, doubling-up[17] in their home. Depending on family dynamics or quality of relationships, this can work for a while, but tends to fall apart quickly, sometimes burning valuable bridges. Instability takes a toll on the entire family. School attendance—or even trying to enroll in school—becomes extremely difficult.

Often host families live in government-subsidized units (those most in need know what it's like to be desperate and will generously offer to help despite their limited resources). Many apartments or communities have occupancy limits. When the landlord notices the overcrowding, the entire menagerie can easily lose their place to stay.

Some branches of government don't consider doubled-up families homeless, putting them into the "hidden homeless" category. "Homelessness? Not a problem in our community," is a sure sign of a clueless elected official, especially as he/she wonders why so many kids are causing so many troubles in their community. Hmmm, could some be kids of parents struggling to find a place for their family to sleep? The parents might be slightly distracted and maybe fail to properly supervise their kids.

21st Century Shelters

Homeless families may turn to another precarious option for a place to stay—motels. This expensive option is fraught with complications. At first glance, many people legitimately wonder how a homeless family can afford the motel, typically costing $50 or more a night. Remember—some parents work or may receive disability payments.

Parents faced with having their kids sleep on the streets are desperate—and will do anything to avoid that. Sometimes the "anything" is legal; sometimes not. Some turn to legal—but unscrupulous—loan sharks, pawning valuables, like their car, to get enough money to survive day-to-day. A Chicago teacher explained her ill-advised strategy of writing checks to pay for their motel or other vital expenses and being willing to pay the overdraft fees when they inevitably bounce.

No credit checks or background checks are needed to rent hotel or motel rooms. However the money is attained, it only needs to be in daily or weekly increments. If the parent is working, the typical minimum wage paycheck barely covers the cost of the room, but at least it's a place to stay that offers some autonomy and sanctuary.

When I recently contacted a DuPage County school superintendent regarding a homeless family staying in a local motel, she matter-of-factly replied, "Our district has over 20 homeless kids now living in motels." What made that even more significant was that her entire one-school district, in an affluent community, had 380 kids.

Homeless families turn to motels out of desperation. Motel owners see this choice as a source of income. Filled rooms are better than empty ones. From an anecdotal look at motel rates in our 8-county area, they ranged from $200-300 a week. Many moms double as desk clerks or housekeepers at these 21st century homeless shelters. Dads do security or maintenance. Too often, they work for chump change—and have to race like the proverbial hamster in the cage to keep up, never getting ahead, sacrificing the kids' need for parental supervision with predictable outcomes.

The kids play in motel parking lots, privy to the comings and goings of prostitutes and drug dealers using some motels for business. Studying and other basic household activities become nearly impossible in the small rooms. Meals are catch-as-catch-can, often causing fire danger by the forbidden use of hot plates. Hygiene and personal appearance suffer greatly because of crowded living conditions. Health care tends to be unattainable, and families tend to turn to the emergency room as their source of medical services. Such "togetherness" compounds stress, with predictable outcomes of health problems, shattered relationships, and/or violence.

Denial Is Not A River

Sweeping these families under the rug of ignorance and denial does nothing for anyone. A reinforced safety net that provides for families who need the most help—and at the same time, assists families at risk of homelessness to prevent their falling into this dark, deep hole—is essential.

Beleaguered social service agencies and non-profit housing providers need reinforcement, not budget cuts. Counterproductive housing policies need revamping to become more beneficial for those who need housing assistance the most—homeless families. Reluctant legislators and policy makers need to become sensitive to the plight of the population struggling for survival—for everyone's good.

190

Ensuring permanent housing and support services for homeless families makes economic, as well as common, sense. Assisting a family with housing and providing supportive services would save money and provide a conducive atmosphere for the family. What's wrong with that? Evidently it's not a priority…

28. THIS MESS: How We Got In It, How to Get Out

O n my good days, I don't think Americans are obtuse or hard-hearted, not across the board anyhow. My unenthusiastic judgment of Americans' characteristics reflects my puzzled state of mind in trying to answer a troubling question: *Why, in this land of plenty, do homelessness and poverty abound?*

I'm not naïve enough to attribute this societal inequity solely to a national malaise of callousness or cruelty. I've met too many enlightened "do-gooders" who have done, and continue to perform, immense amounts of loving kindnesses that dispel myths of hard-heartedness and compassion fatigue. Government is not the entire source of the problem of indifference to homelessness, nor are homeless people themselves. The answer lies, I believe, with our utilization and prioritization of our nation's resources.

Inventory of National Resources and Some Painful Questions

Across this nation, in virtually every town and village:

- *Religion abounds,* with worshipers professing beliefs that include seeking justice for the oppressed and loving one's neighbors. Without generous donations of volunteer time and money, the immediate "band-aid" emergency shelter, often a 2-inch foam pad on a church floor, would not exist. But resources far beyond religious-based contributions of time, talent and treasures will be required to reduce the magnitude of need and eventually prevent homelessness. Aggressive policies and practices—combining government, private organizations, religious entities, and the corporate/business world—must be implemented.

Does religion, ironically and unintentionally, enable our nation to perpetuate poverty and homelessness by giving a false impression that they have everything under control? Is it fair for government to turn over care of poor and homeless people to religious organizations, with challenges inherent to the population, without adequate resources? What happens when "feeding the hungry, clothing the naked, and sheltering the homeless" lulls many people into thinking they are solving poverty? How does anyone confront thriving oppressive systems if the voiceless remain silenced? How many religious leaders challenge systemic causes of poverty? What direction are faith communities taking—acts of mercy or seeking justice? How many congregations know the difference between charity and putting their energies into challenging unjust policies?

• **Wealth abounds**—at least for some people. People of this country blithely spend over $4 billion a year on potato chips[18]. Non-essential pet care products sales reap a healthy $31 billion[19] each year. Gamblers in the U.S. collectively toss over $500 billion a year onto blackjack tables and into other forms of legalized gambling[20]. The 2004 presidential campaign exceeded $1.2 billion in spending[21], ironically the amount the federal government sets aside to alleviate homelessness[22]. "We don't have the money" falls flat.

> *DO THE MATH:*
>
> *$600 monthly income**
> *-500 rent =100*
>
> *$100 balance*
> *-50 transportation*
> *50 remains for food, phone, medicine, clothing, and incidentals*
>
> **represents "extreme poverty" monthly income for household of 3.*

What's wrong when the President proudly boasts a connection with the "haves and have mores[23]" while the "have nots," those at or below poverty level, find their ranks reaching 35.9 million[24] and not a word of awareness or concern is uttered? Do our nation's leaders exhibit a callous disconnect when over 15 million[25] people find themselves mired in extreme poverty[26]? Do political candidates even think about poverty and homelessness, much less formulate policies to alleviate these conditions? Do many people, especially policy makers, understand what the term "extreme poverty" means to those enduring these conditions?

Can someone in leadership explain how we can have symbols of thriving prosperity such as upscale malls, high-end car dealerships, classy restaurants, high-stakes casinos, pricey subdivisions springing up in rich agricultural land, while extreme poverty explodes? How can a family of three survive, much less thrive, on an extreme poverty monthly income of

$670 which requires a modest $500 for rent (includes utilities), leaving $100 for food, and variables such as transportation, medical expenses and clothing? Deficit spending is something the government can get away with, but households with little money and bad credit don't get the same leeway.

• **Housing abounds,** with massive single-family homes keeping the home building industry busy and providing more-than-adequate shelter for the "lucky" families who live in these modern castles, in Chicago's suburbs many of these mega-houses cost in excess of $500,000. The homebuilding industry is probably delighted to accommodate the desire for more square footage in new homes. Since 1984, the median size of houses has gone from 1,600 sq. ft. to 2,200.[27] In 1970, over 60% of new houses built were less than 1,600 sq. ft. In 2003, 23% were modest. In addition to size, pricey features such as in-home theaters and whole house audio systems add comforts while security systems (over 50% of new homes now add this feature) make sure residents are protected. Some families have two and three homes, with significant tax write-offs, while some have no home, and have little need for tax write-offs.

How can we allow millions of units of semi-affordable housing to disappear each year (urban/rural decay and the rampant "tear-down" mentality), relegating truly affordable housing to a scant memory? What's behind the imbalance in new home construction, with the median cost of new homes sold in August 2004 at $208,000[28] at the same time that persons with limited incomes have an increasingly difficult time to find a place they can afford? What justifies slashes of government-subsidized housing in the past 20 years, with a shortfall of almost 5 million units reported during 2000[29] at the same time housing tax credits for the wealthy are protected?

When are we going to have truthful declarations of what is happening to this country's "affordable" housing stock? When will the government clear up common misconceptions about "public housing" that give people the idea the government has everything under control for low income renters? Additionally, how can we require government subsidized housing applicants to pass a credit check and a criminal background check without options for those who fail those tests? If low-income people need to pass a credit check and criminal background investigation to get a place to live, why not apply that standard to all housing applicants, rich and poor?

• **Government resources abound**—at least in some categories. Federal, state and local governments find money—to the tune of an estimated $3.1 billion dollars of pork spending[30] in the FY '05 federal budget. [i]

What will it take to sensitize federal and state legislators to priorities and values of the albeit-too-silent majority? How does a government with a pledge of "liberty and justice for all" rectify its practices aimed at making life exceedingly difficult for the powerless? How can we send soldiers to fight in foreign countries, but not help them survive when they return to our own land by assisting them with access to housing, health care, mental health services and job training? How can we justify bombing countries, rebuilding them and not putting the same passion into rebuilding our own cities and towns?

Insight Into Government Policies

the arrogance of those who ~ typically combine w reason 3 in powe[r]

I sometimes shake my head in wonderment at the counter-productive policies our federal and state lawmakers put into place. My most enlightening—and dismaying—political experience was back in 1996, as a colleague and I met with the aide to the respected Republican US Congressman Harris Fawell from our area. This young woman was polite, but as we sat on the couch in the lobby of the DC office, I thought I'd end up being carried away by the Capitol police. We began expressing concerns about pending changes to the nation's welfare policies and what they would mean to families in poverty.

She wondered why we were concerned about families living in poverty since the Congressman's district was quite affluent. "There's no poverty in our district," she almost proudly proclaimed. I almost jumped across the couch to grab her and shake her. My colleague, Judy, witnessed the exchange in awe.

The perception—that no poverty existed in this congressional district— obviously was earnest. The aide didn't convey any disdain for the poor, just surprise when we assured her that poverty and homelessness were thriving in the Congressman's district, with the homeless shelter running over-capacity and under funded in this affluent county.

This encounter stuck with me. I realized that true policy makers in Washington typically were aides who acted as eyes and ears of their bosses. If they understood the existence and plight of poor and homeless people in the district, they'd likely convey this concern to their bosses. If they were unenlightened, they would simply not mention homelessness. Unless these aides happened to be exposed to these problems, either by researching poverty back in the district, or they had a "cross the line" experience where they actually went into an impoverished area and absorbed what people were experiencing, then they'd be the blind eyes and deaf ears representing their boss, the congressman or woman whose responsibility is to vote on life-sustaining (or destroying) issues for impoverished constituents. Sadly, too many deaf and blind staffers walk the halls of Congress.

Priorities and Power

Today's hot topic—the Iraqi war, with mega-deficit-causing Pentagon spending—clearly pits the needs of poor and homeless persons in this country against the need to bomb homes of Iraqi citizens. Rebuilding homes and businesses in Iraq is a multi-billion dollar non-appropriated, unregulated U.S. government expense. "Terrorism-prevention," a growth industry in the U.S., sucks up billions of dollars for contractors (often without a bidding process).

In the meantime, poverty abounds in the United States and budgets of programs that could ease suffering caused by homelessness are drastically slashed[31], supposedly justified by the "no money" argument. Getting ahead in this country only applies to those who have some wealth to begin with. Aside from the fluky "got-rich-quick" by pulling myself up by those indestructible bootstraps lucky stiffs, the bulk of the impoverished population in this country would think they were lucky to find a pair of boots that didn't let the icy puddles freeze their toes as they walked to work their inadequately paying job.

Those of us who work with income-challenged populations, including those without homes, look at the above realities and scratch our collective heads. "We're a wealthy nation. How can we have so much homelessness? It's crazy!" observed Nancy, a formerly homeless Hispanic teen in a documentary on homelessness[32], "Give Us Your Poor," which ironically has yet to raise enough money for production. She and her mom and brother became homeless when her Anglo dad divorced her mom, leaving this shattered family unit to cope with a new country and homelessness. This family, through gritty hard work and lots of help, made it, buying a "fixer-upper" house that is now their mansion. Both kids succeeded incredibly in

196

school, and their mom endured grueling hours of work in a factory to keep the roof over her motivated children as they soared academically.

Nancy, now a pre-med student at the University of Illinois, shared her personally learned wisdom as part of a national "flower-roots" campaign (the multi-year effort that used forget-me-not flower seeds as a symbol and gathered hundreds of homeless and non-homeless students at the U.S. Senate's Hart Building) to raise Congress' awareness of homelessness. When asked by a reporter if homelessness was something she could do something about, Nancy astutely replied, "Yes, it's my problem. It's everyone's problem. We're like a wealthy country. It's crazy..."This unique "Forget-Me-Not" campaign at the turn of the century enabled Nancy and other courageous homeless teens to lead a successful campaign to—of all absurd things—make it easier for homeless kids to get a public education!

Until the Homeless Education Assistance Act passed in 2001, many schools routinely turned away students who, lacking a permanent address due to homelessness, couldn't even get into schools. Following the passage of the law, at least they have the right to public education, although school administrators keep the school doors closed if they don't know the law or they prefer to pretend that they don't, perhaps fearing that any homeless student will bring down their school's test scores.

The ultimate price we all pay is much greater than lower performance on tests—it's kids who grow up without an education who will tax society's resources by requiring corrective measures to deal with their problems.

EPILOGUE—

IT AIN'T OVER TILL IT'S OVER!

"Cautious, careful people, always casting about to preserve their reputation and social standing, never can bring about a reform. Those who are really in earnest must be willing to be anything or nothing in the world's estimation, and publicly and privately, in season and out, avow their sympathy with despised and persecuted ideas and their advocates, and bear the consequences."
Susan B. Anthony

29. Every Day's An Adventure!

I vehemently complained to the Illinois State Board of Education's homeless education coordinator when he told me about the state's plan to add another, in my words, "layer of bureaucracy" to its homeless education program. He was proposing to assign a "lead liaison" to each of the seven geographic regions of the state as divided by the Illinois Association of Regional School Superintendents.

That was in October 2002, shortly after more federal money became available to help states implement the vastly improved McKinney-Vento Homeless Education Assistance Act of 2001. As things go, following my untimely dismissal at Hesed House, I swallowed my pride and chewed vigorously on my words in January 2003. I needed a job, and that seemed like a perfect fit for me.

After approaching the Kane County Regional Office of Education to ask if it would sponsor the program, I wrote the grant application describing how I would implement the newly proposed lead liaison program for homeless education for Area One. Yup, that was the same program I decried just months earlier.

My proposal was successful and from June 2003 to June 2005, I directed this pilot effort in an 8-county area outside Chicago. Our territory encompassed 305 school districts, over 1,500 schools, more than 800,000 students, with an estimated 20,000 homeless school-age children, some in school, some not.

I have been fortunate to hire some great co-workers, all of whom I knew and/or worked with in my days of running the shelter in Aurora. We've taken on a challenge that no sane people would consider: to enforce federal and state laws that direct schools to immediately enroll homeless students. We've added to that challenge the mission of doing aggressive outreach to find homeless families and unaccompanied youth not staying in shelters.

What makes this so challenging is schools are facing severe financial challenges, as is the state. Property tax caps, combined with inadequate federal and state funding, cause budget woes. Add to all that, the widespread mandates from the federal No Child Left Behind legislation hold schools to higher performance standards, jeopardized, some believe, by admitting homeless students. Adding even more to our challenge is the reality that Chicago recently tore down thousands of units of public housing—without making sure that the former residents had a place to move. To no one's surprise, homelessness in the nearby suburbs has burgeoned, especially for families.

These families are doing what any family in a similar situation would do—look for someone to take them in. Often, it's a plan "scotched-taped together" as my colleague Karen Turk aptly describes it. The families who hop around from family member to friend to whomever exasperate the residency checkers who think the families are trying to sneak into their districts for the purpose of attending their fine suburban schools, a big no-no. Most such families don't describe themselves as "homeless," although most clearly are by definition[33] and reality. This makes it even harder for schools to sort out, and some don't even try.

In fact, most families are just trying to survive. Sending their kids to school is amazingly a priority in the midst of the chaos and crisis they face in their very real survival drama. Resources—shelters, affordable housing, rent assistance, etc.—are scarce. Often one family member agrees to let a friend or relative move in with them, in the process jeopardizing their own housing because of violation of lease rules aimed at preventing overcrowding. Families can't prove residency, resulting in the school doors being slammed in their faces.

That's where Project REACH (Restoring Educational Access for Children who are Homeless), our lead liaison project, came in. We'd get calls from desperate homeless families seeking education for their kids. We fortunately were fairly successful getting the kids in right away. The McKinney-Vento Act[34] and the Illinois Education for Homeless Children Act[35] are good, clear laws. I helped write them and get them passed so I know them well. My co-workers are passionate and knowledgeable about their work. They respect educators and the families we work with, know a lot about the communities we cover, are well-versed on the law, and are compassionate, streetwise professionals. It was great project! (Ch. 30)

This project allowed me to utilize my knowledge of homelessness and educational rights of homeless students, to direct my energies to bring about systemic change, to empower homeless families and youth to seek their rights, to educate educators and administrators on their obligations and their need to be aware of homelessness, to encourage human service agencies to coordinate with schools in meeting myriad needs of homeless families, and most importantly, to continue my quest to work with people who mean so much to me.

Each day brought me new awareness of what families face when they lack a place of their own. Their stories overwhelmed me and my colleagues. Although the sagas all have a common element, homelessness, they were each unique. The Chicago public high school teacher with massive stress-related health problems, her self-employed husband whose recent minor stroke and broken kneecap slowed him down immeasurably, their brain-damaged adult son, and their high school senior honors' student daughter fell prey to a predatory loan company that kicked them out of their suburban home when they fell behind on a few payments (even though they made up their deficit). They turned to a motel, at $50 a night, and stayed there for months hoping for some miracle to spring them back into their home, or any home. The motel, a few blocks outside the high school district where they lived for years, gave the school officials what they mistakenly thought was good reason to refuse to enroll the daughter for her senior year. Fortunately, one of the mom's co-workers knew of our project and gave her our number. She called, told me their plight, and asked for help. Instead of just making a phone call, I decided to go in person.

Seething, I made my way to the school, one that has repeatedly defied laws to educate homeless students. The administrator knew of the family's plight and assured me they were just "checking" facts. I reminded her of provisions of the law that allow families to enroll without proof of homelessness or residency, and asked what questions they would have since the family had been longtime residents of the district. I expressed dismay at the need to interrogate the mom, in front of her daughter, to the point of tears and a later stress-induced physical reaction. The administrator had no good answer.

The student enrolled, as she was entitled. Her mother shared with me that her daughter suffered because of her family's trauma, the related stress of the school's initial barrier and the attitude conveyed by school officials. Her grades tumbled, her self-confidence wavered. The family found a 2-bedroom apartment to rent as they try to rebuild their lives. After five months in a 200 sq. ft. motel room, their new abode seems luxurious.

I am constantly in awe of families' phenomenal efforts to ensure their children's ongoing education, despite incredible obstacles. I am honored to be able to assist them in this endeavor.

One of our enjoyable tasks was to conduct training sessions with educators and agency personnel about the laws governing homeless students' educational rights. Karen was always quick to point out what I might miss as I focus on our objective—by far, most educators and administrators are eager to learn about the law and willingly comply. Many good, caring education professionals—principals, teachers, social workers, health care providers—go way beyond the call of duty to help kids without homes to have a better life. At our trainings, we got to reinforce such behaviors while pointing out the many reasons they wouldn't want to ignore the laws. By far, most educators are decent persons, sometimes trapped in dysfunctional systems. They expressed appreciation and admiration for our efforts and recommitted themselves and their schools to better serve homeless kids.

Real Unclear on the Concept

Nothing starts my day off better than crisis. My shrill ringing cell phone shattered my peaceful drive to work. Cathy, who worked at the Lake County shelter, had a Hispanic woman in her office facing a residency hearing in 1½-hours to determine if her son could remain in his school. Cathy knew the law but felt it was time to call in a pro. My route through this upscale Geneva neighborhood contrasted with the realities of homelessness facing this mother and all too many more families...

Cathy handed the mom the phone so she could tell me her sadly typical story. Evicted, they lacked other options, so they moved nearby into a cousin's house. Someone at the school got suspicious and instigated a residency investigation to determine whether or not their 10-year old boy had a right to continue at his school. I scribbled notes on a piece of paper scrounged from my car's back seat.

The story seemed clear cut to me—and it angered me that schools would spend this much time and money to try to illegally push a homeless kid out of the one stability he had left—his classroom. Since nothing seemed questionable, I assured the mother that the district would see that they made an error after I called. I didn't think she'd even have the scheduled residency hearing when I finished explaining things. By this time I had pulled up in front of our building. I told her I'd make a call and then call her back.

I was able to contact the assistant superintendent who was conducting this investigation. At first he couldn't accept that *maybe* they erred in their actions, but he seemed to slowly absorb the reality of what I was saying—the family is homeless and is entitled to protection under federal and state laws[36]. Maybe he didn't know about those laws...I even halfway apologized that we hadn't been able to train all 305 school districts in our area the way they needed to be trained. Our conversation wound down with me suggesting that he could call his attorney and tell him his services weren't needed because they didn't need to hold the hearing.

We ended our discussion amiably and he said the school district's attorney would probably give me a call, an opportunity I welcomed because many lawyers don't know the laws governing homeless students—laws that I helped write and get passed. After awhile, not hearing from the attorney, I called the mom to let her know how the call went. Since it was about 15 minutes before the hearing time and she wasn't far from the school, we agreed that it would be best that she go over to show her good faith—and confidence—in her status as a bona fide resident of their district. I encouraged her and said she could call me if she encountered any problem.

Ringing phones can either be good or bad—and so far that day mine were clearly bad. The next call was the mom saying they agreed to put me on speakerphone so I could be a part of the scheduled residency hearing. Not a good way to represent "a client"...but I agreed. The "suits" included the attorney, assistant superintendent, residency "cop." Our team was mom, whom I had barely spoken to, and me by my least favorite way of representing someone—speakerphone.

I managed to immediately endear myself to the attorney by introducing myself as the lead liaison for homeless students for the Illinois State Board of Education. I proceeded to try to let him off the hook by explaining that many attorneys didn't know the laws regarding homeless students' rights. He assured me he did—of course; he needed to convince his client that he was worth the $175 an hour they were paying. I assured him that this was not a residency issue, it was a homelessness issue, and thus they didn't need to be conducting the residency hearing. We sparred over that one, and he finally asserted his law degree by saying the hearing was going to continue, with or without us. That went well....

They went first—the tale of how this family came onto the school district's radar screen sounded like they were on the alert for Mideastern terrorists, not a struggling Hispanic family making sure their little boy got to school while keeping a roof over their heads. Someone spotted a car and felt they were dropping off a kid to catch the bus—the last time I checked this was not a crime. The "cop" tailed people, photographed cars, license plates, and houses. He called landlords and spoke to neighbors—all confirming their suspicions that the family was no longer living at their reported address. He "found" them living in a different place—horrors!—outside district boundaries.

After he was finished, the mom started telling her story. She and her husband had money problems and were evicted. They moved in with a cousin who lived in the district. It was a crowded house and they were sleeping in the basement. *Uh oh,* I thought. Knowing how some Hispanic families live when they are trying to help their countrymen and women survive in this new land, I didn't want her to go into detail about the living arrangements in this setting. Earlier she had shared with me that her cousin was undocumented—and I guessed that others under that crowded roof were too. Too much information for these suits to hear...I interrupted, my strategy to keep her from being questioned further about who and how many were living in the house. I asserted she had provided enough information to verify they were living in an inadequate nighttime place of abode. Then they brought up another can of worms that I didn't even know was on the shelf...an apartment rented by the mother outside the district.

At that moment I realized that we could either step deeper into a snake-filled swamp or I could call a timeout, which I did. I asked to talk to the mom in private and they agreed. She picked up the phone. OK, what are they talking about, I asked. She then explained that she and her older son, who has the same name as his dad, rented an apartment that she and her kids stayed at occasionally. The older brother would sometimes drive his brother to the bus stop.

She then got into the personal stuff—she and her husband weren't getting along (which I read as domestic violence)—so she and the boy would stay at the cousin's—an uncomfortable situation in a household full of mostly male strangers—or the son's apartment. The school must have investigated thoroughly enough to find the lease and utility information at her son's place. As juicy as the information was, it didn't cloud the fact that the family still fell under the definition of homeless. I assured her that I would respect the privacy of those details and that we were still fine. She called the suits back in and we had Round Two.

I took the offensive and let them know that I had heard the details of the second residence and it only provided temporary confusion, but it didn't change the position I started out with—the family is homeless. They were hot to pursue their questioning, but I called a stop to it saying that I felt that this residency hearing was in error and the mother should consider filing a dispute-hearing request to determine homelessness. The mom followed my lead and said that she would give them the written request for the hearing.

This hearing would have an element of fairness to it—a definite lack in the present one. The Regional Office of Education is responsible for conducting the hearing within five school days. The mother also had some rights, which I pointed out to the school people... When the mother came in and said they were evicted, the family was likely in a homeless situation, which should have triggered a referral to the district liaison for homeless students. They failed to do that. In the event they felt the family wasn't homeless, they were supposed to direct her to resources for legal assistance. None of that happened. Ooops!

Since Mr. "I-know-the law" lawyer didn't have much more to say, we thanked them and I indicated that I would make the arrangements for the hearing.

Mom called me as soon as she got back to her son's place. I couldn't help but congratulate her for her incredible courage in that trying situation. She profusely thanked me for my help. She expressed deep concern that her cousin and his many brown-skinned housemates would encounter fallout because of this conflict. I couldn't dispute the possibility, but I assured her that if that happened I would not sleep until I brought the wrath of God upon the school (via the Illinois Attorney General's Office Civil Rights Bureau). We ended the conversation with my stressing that if ANY problem was apparent to them—how her son was treated in school, strange white men taking pictures or hanging around, or anything that could be construed as harassment, to call me on my cell phone immediately.

We would get to meet on Tuesday at the regional office. I couldn't wait to meet this courageous woman. She probably couldn't wait to meet this fool who, with just the most basic facts, challenged a bigwig lawyer who doesn't know beans about homelessness.

Before our hearing, I wanted to have my ducks in the proverbial row. The mom and I talked—which helped me clear up some confusion in my mind. Her details and her willingness to fax me supporting documents gave me great confidence. I tried to bolster her spirits without sounding overconfident. We agreed to meet at noon to go over any loose ends before the 12:30 session. I managed to get a good night's sleep—a sign that I wasn't too worried about the hearing.

My two-hour drive to the Lake County Regional Office of Education was actually pleasant since I didn't have to deal with rush-hour traffic. I got up to the area in time to drive around the community where she lived. I saw her son's school but I didn't have a map of the area so I couldn't find her neighborhood. Most of the community is comprised of expensive housing, but evidently those who do the grunt work have some areas where they can afford to live.

The assistant regional superintendent would conduct the hearing—her first. She wanted some guidance as to how she should proceed. I deliberately tried to avoid tainting her mind in favor of the mom, but it was clear that the school's position annoyed her. We ate and chatted about our project's challenges. My associate, Karen, also detoured from her previously scheduled meeting so she could add some moral support while witnessing her first dispute hearing. The mom arrived promptly at noon and we met in the conference room.

Meeting the people we're working with is a rare occurrence. Most of our work is done by phone. I'm not sure who was happier to meet whom…but we didn't have time for small talk. I could tell that this mom would be able to hold her own, but she was understandably nervous. I had a few questions to clarify some loose ends that occurred to me on the peaceful drive up. The answers only strengthened my resolve. Karen asked if the mom had a picture of her son. She pulled one out—attached to a bookmark that her son had made—a poignant reminder of the purpose of our efforts. *Bring 'em on!*

Two school representatives showed up at 12:30, including the same guy I had spoken to the day of the residency hearing. Their district homeless student liaison, who hadn't been involved previously, came along. I was amazed that the attorney didn't come with them. The "Judge" entered and began by asking the mother why she disputed the school's decision, to which the mother firmly replied, "Because we are homeless and my son wants to continue at his school."

Sadly, the district's assistant superintendent fit my stereotype of an incompetent bigot. He whined about the fact that I had only called him minutes before the residency hearing. He whined about how hard it was to keep people out of the district when they had no right to be there. The judge brought him back to reality by asking what proof they had that the mother wasn't homeless. It got pitiful from there…

They didn't have any proof and figured they just had to show up and they were going to get told that the boy could stay in school. He practically whimpered. I tried to contain myself. Karen and the mom shared my feelings. The judge retired to her office to make her decision. Interesting enough for us was that the two school representatives began chatting and asking questions about what they need to do to avoid mishandling things in the future. The liaison even said she recognized my name from when she lived in Aurora. She couldn't make it obvious that she agreed with me, but she managed to offer a look that bespoke her dismay.

In a few moments, the judge returned and pointed out that the facts of the case compelled her to rule in favor of the mother who, at that, let out a huge sigh of relief. The school folks wanted more information from the ROE and from us, so they went down the hall to the office, leaving the three of us to celebrate this victory. Big hugs—that's what we work for! And that's what we got! The mom was exuberant! We were pleased. I wasn't too surprised that we won because we were right, and this law makes it easier for those who are right to win.

The mom clearly remembered our talking to the school representatives about what assistance her son was entitled to—tutoring, free lunches and fee waivers being on the top of the list. Evidently, the school folks forgot. We later learned that there had been no follow-up.

At the end of the school year, the mom left several panicked messages for us on our voicemail. We tried catching her, and when we finally did, my anger spewed. The Friday before Memorial Day weekend, the mom attended the end-of-school-year conference. She was told her son needed to attend summer school and was given an application. She took it home, read the form and saw it was due on Memorial Day. She also saw that the cost was $130. On Tuesday, she brought the form into school, where the secretary efficiently and effectively berated her for being late. Pointing out that she just got the form on Friday and that Monday was a holiday, she asked if her son was entitled to a fee waiver because of their economic condition and their homelessness. Mom remembered our describing a homeless student's rights for waivers.

When the efficient and effective secretary said no to the fee waiver request, the mom asked if she could have more time to come up with the money—a virtual fortune for her. No again. The mom found out that, despite what we had assured her—that her son would be able to get free lunches—he had not been granted that right and had gone lunch-less, unbeknownst to her, and now faced the significant barrier to school success by not being able to afford to attend summer school. That's when she called our office.

The mom finally caught up with me and halfway apologetically told me why she was calling. When she described the situation, I fumed. I assured her that this, like the initial injustice, could be corrected. I called the liaison—who still seemed like a nice person—and she assured me the district would correct the situation. How anyone could correct the wrong of this kid missing lunch for months was beyond me...but it made me hyper-aware of this type of thing happening with other families.

This district seemed to have caught on to its obligations under federal and state law to educate homeless students. We wonder how many unreported and unresolved similar situations are out there. Much work remains to ensure educational rights of homeless students. It would be easier if schools were willing to learn...

It's that kind of experience that keeps us going. We know, despite evidence to the contrary, more people care than not. Our goal is to stoke that care into a movement that calls for an end to homelessness. It would be cheaper to accomplish and, gosh, better for the families, unaccompanied youth, and our communities' quality of life.

My hope, and the prayers of those who know these and other cool kids who happen to be homeless, is that someone will be there for them when they need help. These kids need to be needed, nurtured, and encouraged to claw their way out of the deep hole of homelessness. With a lot of luck and sheer determination, they could be the next generation of street-smart counselors and shelter directors...or lawmakers.

30. Easier Done Than Said

With all my years of working with homeless people, undoubtedly one of my most troubling realities was knowing how close to the edge most of us are when it comes with facing the likelihood of homelessness ourselves. Even me. Just writing those words causes me to shudder.

Always skirting disaster with ill-advised financial decisions, knowing that social services pay and retirement benefits offer no protection from myriad disasters hovering over my head like a wrecking ball with a frayed cable, experiencing "you're fired" way too often for comfort, having my worst fears about this nation's health insurance inequities butt up against my inability to afford COBRA payments in those periods of my life when employment was a memory...homelessness hung over my head like a ever-darkening storm cloud.

Taking the job as director of Project REACH didn't remove my fears of homelessness vulnerability. Actually, as each spring came around, I realized how fragile my position was. State budgets seemed to have politically-fueled delays each May. Competing proposals threatened our program's continuity. Disgruntled superintendents targeted the very existence of our program. Dysfunctional bureaucrats dismissed our efforts as disposable.

At the end of March 2005, Project REACH's sponsor, Clem Mejia, Kane County Regional Superintendent, waged the latest assault to my fragile sense of security. In the Aurora Beacon News article about his proposed restructuring of our program, our efforts were at the same time lauded and disregarded. *Although Project REACH has "done a very good job," Mejia said. "The new model would place the help 'closer to the clients.' Regional superintendents have a long history of being advocates for the homeless," Mejia said. "We believe that if we move some of the responsibility, regional superintendents can tailor the program to meet the needs of their area."* With those words, Mejia planted the kiss of death on our project. At first we figured the IL State Board of Education would not let this happen, but our dismay grew when we uncovered their apparent disregard for enforcing the McKinney-Vento Homeless Education Assistance Act and the IL Education for Homeless Children Act. We immediately realized that this plan would jeopardize school for countless homeless kids in our 8-county area. An implicit message from ISBE that McK-V compliance wasn't required of districts would slam school doors in the faces of families and youth without the prerequisite residency proofs that provide barriers to homeless and non-homeless students alike.

Beyond the families we serve, the reality of what this action means sunk in quickly on an all-too-close personal level. No job means no paycheck. No paycheck means no insurance. No insurance means any health problem becomes the bank-breaker (seeing as the "bank" has so little in it to begin with). Losing this job also means I'm at a point when I need to face the "what do I want to do when I grow up?" dilemma, at age 55, in an area that boasts few jobs of interest that pay what I need to keep a roof over my head.

My fiscal vulnerability is only matched by my ever-growing cynical outlook toward employers who can, capriciously it seems, toss a person (or in this case 8 persons) into a tailspin. This is a good "Homelessness 101" lesson that needs to be shared with the rest of the country. At a time when job security is at its frailest, those who rely on a paycheck to keep a roof over one's head and to maintain health insurance, firing a person should be done for good reason, not for anything else.

"You're Fired!" Donald Trump's phrase *de jour,* means a lot more than old Donald could imagine from his ivory Trump Towers. It means more than most people realize until the words come in your direction. Having heard these words more than I'd care to, I realize that each time I experienced the trauma I also somehow survived. My family support network being intact probably means I'll survive this latest assault on my peace of mind. I hope so, because peace of mind is hard to maintain in the face of losing the opportunity to perform the service to so many families and teens needing help getting into school. Having done a fair amount of reading about the tie between peace of mind and good health, I painfully realize how easy it is to let this job, or loss of it, make you sick. That would be a disaster! I can't afford to be sick. My recent wellness visit to the doctor, with my health insurance, left me financially reeling and quite befuddled with the co-pays and the insurance no-pays. My good health, something I try not to take for granted, must be protected, job loss be damned.

One reassuring aspect of these hard times is to realize how supportive friends can be. Mine are the best, perhaps because I've kept them busy practicing how to be reassuring to me when I go through these traumas. Not surprising to me is the passionate support we are receiving from the families we work with who found out about our plight. They'd do anything to help, and I do believe "anything" means anything. Their anger with how we are being treated reflects their anger at how they were treated by their schools. I can only reflect that what we're going through—the betrayal laced with confusion about our future, the uncertainty of our options, the fear that comes with pending loss of income, the realization of our bleak situation on so many levels—all this and more is typical for homeless families who encounter ignorance and prejudice when trying to get their kids into school.

Talking to my long-time friend Ken (Ch. 31) about our plight brought me to ask him how he was doing. This dad, whose wife's job recently was downsized, with their 4 year-old, realizes how hard it is to make a living. Ken's entrepreneurship and his technological skills make him a hot commodity in an industry that's grown colder as the economy founders for the non-Donald Trumps of this world.

His tech business now keeps two or three guys from homelessness, just barely. These guys work for Ken, who believes in paying people fair wages. Ken is torn between getting a job for himself, working for someone who may or may not respect what he brings to the workplace, or struggling to maintain and grow his own business. He shared that he's talked with many others in the same boat—trying to stay afloat with tsunamis slamming them in the form of outrageous health insurance costs, ever-increasing expenses to doing business in a world that demands cost-cutting, and an increasing number of techies looking for work following their layoffs. Ken knows what he's doing. He knows others are struggling too. His customer rounds give him plenty opportunities to hear from other beleaguered small business owners who see bankruptcy peering in their business windows.

I don't know that I want to know that economic struggles are burgeoning in the middle class. Knowing what faces me is overwhelming enough. I'm dealing with my own deep resentments at the apparent disregard of federal and state laws that I helped craft by bureaucrats who apparently don't understand how important getting into school is for homeless kids. I'm pondering my next job...whether or not I can keep my home, how can I afford health insurance...and knowing all the while that this dilemma plays out too many times for too many people. My co-workers face similar worries.

Sadly, this dilemma plants the seeds of homelessness: the gradual erosion of my financial foundation, combined with immense stress, which will only take another catastrophe to topple the all-too-fragile survival that I've managed to hang onto.

Oh, too close for comfort...go away insecurity...time for my favorite author Anne Lamott's frequent prayer, "Help! Help! Help!"

31. Postscript Filled With Gratitude

*P*eople frequently ask me how I keep going in this line of work. It's a fair question, because, especially when running a shelter, life can be more than hectic. Working with schools and homeless families to eliminate barriers to enrollment can be exhausting and frustrating. Aside from the fact that I like a job that's not boring and that challenges me, I can also point to the people I work with as a bonus. In no way is this "go it alone" work. I learned early on that if you have competent co-workers good things happen even in bad times.

I was shocked when I first needed to hire someone to help me operate a shelter that anyone actually would want the job. My long-time friend, *Jill Skole*, responded wholeheartedly back in the mid-80s, and greatly assisted me in starting Will County PADS shelter in 1987. She capably took over the Joliet shelter for me when I left for Aurora. She now heads an agency devoted to helping persons with AIDS.

Without going through the entire list of my capable, incredible co-workers, some notable cohorts deserve mentioning, in addition to those already included throughout this missive. They all share qualities so necessary in this type of work, or ministry: street-wise yet compassionate. They thrive on the unknown and unexpected, reacting appropriately when confronted by situations that would cause lesser humans to run for the exit.

Jesse Hernandez, my longest co-worker, right hand and dear friend, defies description. His reliability, integrity and compassion make him unique in this world. I could fill a book with our adventures. His bilingual ability and his anal-retentive neatness, his demented sense of humor and his respect for—and willingness to work toward—my goal of establishing a safe, respectful shelter will keep him in a category all his own.

Nichole Marcusson, an idealistic young woman studying social work at a local college, had volunteered at our shelter with her parents through their church. Despite her youth, (she was 19 when I hired her) she gave competently and selflessly for many years, gaining a firsthand education to augment her college courses. Her compassion and humor enriched me. Those who knew her regarded her as the benevolent "big sister" who best not be crossed.

Kay Pepiot, the "Queen of Composure," constantly amazed me with her ability to look inconspicuous and yet know everything going on. I hired her right out of high school, after watching her as a teen volunteer with her church—capable, caring and calm. Her actions reflect a deep commitment to the "have-nots" of this world. Her willingness to extend kindness to even the hardest-to-love guest astounded me. She still works there, steady, caring, calm...

Beyond Honorable Mention

I had plenty of experience fending off well-intentioned first-time volunteers' offers to do the world and all for us. Being at Hesed House would bring that quality out of most people—seeing the good that some people can do and seeing that so much needed to be done. From persons with access to goods, services, or personal skills that could improve life for us, we'd get scads of offers. Sometimes the offer would pan out, sometimes not, occasionally with unexpected results.

Ken Johnson made a generous offer on a Friday night during my first years in Aurora. Tall, naïve-looking, blond and white, Ken was from down the river in Oswego. He made a flippant remark about our fairly useless phones, saying he could replace the system for less than what we were paying to lease the equipment. "Beware of offers too good to be true," my standard practice, led me to think this sounded like one of those offers.

I found out we could drop our current lease for a nominal charge, so I pursued Ken's offer. At the time we probably had 20 phones scattered across our 40,000-square-foot fortress of a building. This engineer by trade, and crazy man by practice, gave a detailed breakdown of savings by owning our own system. OK, go for it, Ken, was my final answer.

Instead of seeing a project fall apart because of myriad reasons—too impossible, too costly, too much trouble, etc.—he persisted, doing it after his other "real job," computer and electronics systems work. Soon we had a new, very functional phone system.

Ken and I became friends over the years. When he was out of work when I needed a part-time staff person, I hired him. His streetwise nature sometimes seemed to overtake his compassion, but he capably handled the challenge, including what was becoming a more insane task—dealing with severe overcrowding, especially with families, which posed more of a challenge than we first realized. Ken was my salvation, and damnation, during this episode.

When you are THE person facing the impossible task of fitting the moms and kids in the tiny family sleeping room, it makes you crazy. I can remember standing in the middle of the sea of bodies and bags of stuff agonizing, "God, what are we going to do with this crowd?" and other such frustrated thoughts, punctuated by profanity. Since this logistical nightmare was getting to be a regular occurrence, I knew we had a big problem.

Ken, the problem-solving engineer, helped me develop a few potential solutions that we presented to the board. We examined several possibilities, all of which would inconvenience some of the other programs in the building, but would give us more space to accommodate the growing numbers of families seeking shelter. Suffice to say, our solutions were resented, but eventually we got the go-ahead to proceed on a multi-stage construction project that would significantly expand the women's and family sleeping space. I began "dialing for dollars," my euphemism for fund-raising, while Ken began lining up workers and contractors (who were going to donate services).

Ken offered to use his expertise to manage the project, a welcomed offer to me because: a) he knew what he was doing, b) I knew very little about this work, c) I had no time to even oversee taking out the trash, and d) he needed the job. He would also save us thousands of dollars—money which I needed to find to do this project. He was also superb at organizing crews of our homeless guys to help. They did the lion's share of the beginning work, under Ken's nurturing supervision and side-by-side labor.

Along the way, this project set the stage for my impending departure from this place I had grown to love. Ken and I knew things were getting tense, but we tried to focus on the project at hand—doubling the family sleeping space. He elicited amazing performance from some of our guys who were willing to volunteer their time in such a loving and wholehearted way that it inspired us to ignore the growing tension with the executive director.

Ken, despite his incalculable contributions of time, talent and treasure, was fired from this mostly volunteer job on a technicality—his psuedo-volunteer efforts weren't covered by insurance. His massive contributions were disregarded. His self-worth remained intact only because he knew he tried to do the right thing and that the guys he worked with knew he had been shafted. I knew it too, and it wasn't long before I found myself in the same plight.

'Good Bad and Ugly'

To be kind, running a non-profit organization is challenging at best. It wears people down, especially those who struggle with personal problems. It can burn out paid staff, volunteers, clergy members and advocates. One thing can be said, when it gets ugly in the non-profit arena, it's as ugly as or sometimes uglier than in the for-profit, dog-eat-dog world. It's sadder, too, because some people have expectations, somewhat unrealistic, that religious-based programs should have some element of "religion" in their day-to-day operations. But these organizations are just like people—good, bad, and sometimes ugly. Justice, kindness and respect can be in extremely short supply when dealing with personnel issues. I have painfully learned this lesson.

As Ken's saga unfolded, I needed to replace him STAT! I needed someone knowledgeable, street-smart, compassionate, and hard working. Throw in the most important element—humor. *Tom Aguilar*, the king of humor, happened to pop in and say he was looking for a job. I knew Tom for 15 years as an outstanding volunteer with his church, who possessed physical presence, street smarts, desire—and sense of humor. When he said he wanted and needed the job—Wow! I hired him and was awed at what he brought to the job.

He still hangs in at Hesed House, despite being battered in my ugly departure. Tom, an imposing figure with an enormous heart, could find something funny in the most bizarre circumstances. This model of cynicism could cook for hundreds on a moment's notice, organize a disastrously chaotic storeroom, spot a hidden bottle of vodka under a bulky coat, comfort someone who is going through a major crisis, and find something funny to say to me as I was on my last nerve. His liability—he cares, and he's outspoken.

At about the same time that my demise as shelter director was playing out, we hired a woman to assist our homeless guests with finding the services needed to move out of homelessness. *Karen Turk* had no idea what she was getting into—with her job or the ancillary drama swirling around Hesed House. An immensely qualified social work professional, Karen's reputation in Aurora's human service arena was impressive, even to me. I had little to do with hiring her, but she quickly figured out that she had stepped into a snake pit. The destructively dysfunctional environment made her job as service coordinator—an incredible task at best—became even more impossible as time went on.

Karen sifted through the controversy and eventually chose to align with me. At first, she just sought advice on how to do her job from me, someone known to know what was going on. We eventually became friends, and her insights and wisdom pulled me through many impossible moments. She was fired for her allegiance to me. (I recognized a silver lining and hired her for my new venture, Project REACH. Following the turn of events in Chapter 30, she may decide to choose a less vulnerable career next time around.)

In addition to my beloved homeless brothers and sisters with the unpredictable richness they'd bring to me each day and the delightful volunteers, with their chocolate chip cookies and complete dedication to our ministry, my co-workers brought me constant joy. Without their competency, I would never have had time to even breathe, much less pause to get to know the human side of the sea of bodies facing us each night. Their goodness filled my days and nights with immeasurable joy.

It's humbling to reflect back on the people who make the impossible possible. My opportunity to do what I did in my years of working at Hesed is unmistakably tied to the talents and efforts of many people, those I have mentioned and so many more unmentioned. I will forever hold them in my heart.

I have come to acknowledge that the "love of my life" is loving those deemed to be society's "unlovables"—homeless men, women and children. I know I can't help every one of them by giving them what they need most—a safe, decent place to stay, food, medical care, and a friendly ear to listen to their stories—but I can use my energies to try to level the playing field. Improving the system that often creates or perpetuates homelessness will eventually reduce the flow from a flood to a trickle. Hopefully this book helps...

APPENDICES

APPENDIX 1

Federal Definition of Homeless

(McKinney-Vento Homeless Education Assistance Act of 2001)

`Homeless children and youth'—

(A) means individuals who lack a fixed, regular, and adequate nighttime residence (within the meaning of section 103(a)(1)); and

(B) includes—

(i) children and youths who are sharing the housing of other persons due to loss of housing, economic hardship, or a similar reason; are living in motels, hotels, trailer parks, or camping grounds due to the lack of alternative adequate accommodations; are living in emergency or transitional shelters; are abandoned in hospitals; or are awaiting foster care placement;

(ii) children and youths who have a primary nighttime residence that is a public or private place not designed for or ordinarily used as a regular sleeping accommodation for human beings (within the meaning of section 103(a)(2)(C));

(iii) children and youths who are living in cars, parks, public spaces, abandoned buildings, substandard housing, bus or train stations, or similar settings; and

(iv) migratory children (as such term is defined in section 1309 of the Elementary and Secondary Education Act of 1965) who qualify as homeless for the purposes of this subtitle because the children are living in circumstances described in clauses (i) through (iii).

APPENDIX 2

IL Education for Homeless Children Act, a.k.a. "Charlie's Bill"

(HB3244, signed 9/9/94, amended on SB881, signed 1/24/95)

AN ACT in relation to schools and government, amending named acts.
Be it enacted by the people of the State of Illinois, represented in the General Assembly:

ARTICLE ONE

Section 1-1. Short Title. This Act may be cited as the
Education for Homeless Children Act.

Section 1-5. Definitions. As used in this Act:

"School of Origin" means the school that the child attended when permanently housed or the school in which the child was last enrolled.

"Parent" means the parent or guardian having legal or physical custody of a child or youth.

"Homeless person, child or youth" includes, but is not limited to, any of the following:

(1) An individual who lacks a fixed, regular and adequate nighttime place of abode.

(2) An individual who has a primary nighttime place of abode that is:

(A) a supervised publicly or privately operated shelter designed to provide temporary living accommodations (including welfare hotels, congregate shelters, and transitional housing);

(B) an institution that provides a temporary residence for individuals intended to be institutionalized; or

(C) a public or private place not designed for or ordinarily used as a regular sleeping accommodation for human beings.

Section 1-10. Choice of Schools.

(a) When a child loses permanent housing and becomes a homeless person within the meaning of Section 5, or when a homeless child changes his or her temporary living arrangements, the parents or guardians of the homeless child shall have the option of either:

(1) continuing the child's education in the school of origin for as long as the child remains homeless or, if the child becomes permanently housed, until the end of the academic year during which the housing is acquired; or

(2) enrolling the child in any school that nonhomeless students who live in the attendance area in which the child or youth is actually living are eligible to attend.

Section 1-15. Transportation to the school of origin. Subject to the provisions of Article 29 of the School Code, if a child becomes a homeless child or if a homeless child changes his or her temporary living arrangements, and if the homeless child's parents or guardians decide to continue the child's education in the school of origin, the parents or guardians shall make a good faith effort to provide or arrange for transportation to and from the school of origin, including authorizing relatives, friends, or a program for homeless persons to provide the child with transportation to and from the school of origin. If transportation to and from the school of origin is not provided in that manner, it shall be provided in the following manner:

(1) if the homeless child continues to live in the school district in which the school of origin is located, the child's transportation to and from the school of origin shall be provided or arranged by the school district in which the school of origin is located consistent with the requirements of Article 29 of the School Code; and

(2) if the homeless child's living arrangements in the school district of origin terminate and the child, though continuing his or her education in the school of origin, begins living in another school district, the school district of origin and the school district in which the homeless child is living shall meet to apportion the responsibility and costs for providing the child with transportation to and from the school of origin. If the school districts are unable to agree, the responsibility and costs for transportation shall be shared equally.

If a parent or guardian chooses to have the child attend the school of origin , that parent or guardian, a teacher of the child, and the principal or his or her designee from the school of origin may meet at the option of the parent or the school to evaluate whether that travel is in the best interest of the child's development and education as compared to the development and education available in attending the school nearest the child's abode. The meeting shall also include consideration of the best interests of the homeless family at their current abode. A parent may bring a representative of his or her choice to the meeting. The meeting shall be convened if travel time is longer than an hour each way. (Source: P.A. 88-634, eff. 1-1-95.)

(105 ILCS 45/1-20)

Sec. 1-20. Enrollment. If the parents or guardians of a homeless child or youth choose to enroll the child in a school other than the school of origin, that school immediately enroll the homeless child or youth even if the child or youth is unable to produce records normally required for enrollment, such as previous academic records, medical records, proof of residency, or other documentation. Nothing in this subsection shall prohibit school districts from requiring parents or guardians of a homeless child to submit an address or other such contact information as the district may require from parents or guardians of nonhomeless children. It shall be the duty of the enrolling school to immediately contact the school last attended by the child or youth to obtain relevant academic and other records. If the child or youth must obtain immunizations, it shall be the duty of the enrolling school to promptly refer the child or youth for those immunizations. (Source: P.A. 88-634, eff. 1-1-95.)

Section 1-25. Ombudspersons; dispute resolution; civil actions.

(a) Each regional superintendent of schools shall act as an ombudsperson to provide resource information and resolve disputes relating to the rights of homeless children under this Act, except in Cook County, where each school district shall designate a person to serve as ombudsperson when a dispute arises. If a school denies a homeless child enrollment or transportation, it shall immediately refer the parent or guardian to the ombudsperson. The child shall be admitted and transported to the school chosen by the parents or guardians until the final resolution of the dispute. The ombudsperson shall convene a meeting of all parties and attempt to resolve the dispute within 5 school days after receiving notice of the dispute.

(b) Any party to a dispute under this Act may file a civil action in a court of competent jurisdiction to seek appropriate relief. In any civil action, a party whose rights under this Act are found to have been violated shall be entitled to recover reasonable attorney's feel and costs.

(c) If a dispute arises, the school district shall inform parents and guardians of homeless children of the availability of the ombudsperson, sources of low cost or free legal assistance, and other advocacy services in the community.

Section 1-30. Homeless Children Committee. There is hereby created a Homeless Children Committee composed of 24 members, 18 of them shall be appointed by the State Superintendent of Education after consultation with advocates for the homeless and private nonprofit organizations that advocate an end to homelessness, two of whom shall be members of the General Assembly appointed (one from each chamber) by the Governor, and 4 of whom shall be members of the General Assembly appointed one each by the Speaker of the House of Representatives, the Minority Leader of the House of Representatives, the President of the Senate, and the Minority Leader of the Senate. Of the 18 members appointed by the State Superintendent of Education as provided in this Section, 6 shall be homeless and formerly homeless parents or guardians, 6 shall be providers to and advocates for homeless persons, and 6 shall be school personnel from different geographic regions of the State. Members of the Committee shall serve at the pleasure of the appointing authority and a vacancy on the Committee shall be filled by the appropriate appointing authority. The Committee shall have the authority to review and modify the current and future State plans that are required under the federal Stewart B. McKinney Homeless Assistance Act.

Section 1-35. Application of the Act. The provisions of this Act apply to all school districts organized under the School Code, except that provisions that relate to transportation with respect to school districts organized under Article 34 of the School Code shall be phased in during that 2 year period, school districts organized under Article 34 shall continue transportation programs serving homeless children.

Section 1-40. Federal obligations unaffected. Nothing in this Act shall limit the obligations of school districts under the Federal Stewart B. McKinney Homeless Assistance Act.

(105 ILSC 45/1-45 new)

Sec. 1-45. Penalties. No person shall, under the provisions of this Act, enroll or attempt to enroll in a school other than the school of origin a child who he or she knows is not a homeless person as defined in this Act. No person shall knowingly or willfully present to any school district false information regarding the homelessness of any child or family for the purpose of enabling that child to attend a school other than the school of origin. Any person who violates this Section shall be guilty of a Class C misdemeanor.

APPENDIX 3

10 Confusions About Educational Rights of

Homeless Students

(created by Project REACH, 2003)

In general, most confusion is caused by the belief that someone already "knows all about the rights of homeless students." Experience shows people often work with incomplete or outdated information. *So if you think you already know—think again!*

It may be helpful to realize common school guidelines for enrollment do not apply for homeless students. Federal and state law override school and district policies: *provisions for homeless students must be followed despite whatever policies exist for non-homeless students in the school or district. School policies may not act as a barrier to enrollment or success of homeless students.*

The following are true statements:

1.   Being "doubled-up" with friends/relatives because a family lost their housing *is* homelessness.

2.   Homeless families often do not say "homeless" outright because of fears, shame, or not seeing themselves as homeless (as when doubled up with someone). If homelessness is suspected, it is the responsibility of school staff to <u>discreetly</u> inquire, preferably taking the family to a private area where they may feel safer to talk about their living situation.

3.   The right to choose to go to the school of origin (where student attended prior to homelessness or student last attended) or to the school where student is now staying is up to the homeless family/youth.

4.   Homeless students have the right to remain in their school of choice for the length of homelessness and may finish the school year at that school *even if* they become permanently housed before the end of the school year.

5.   Transportation to the school of origin must be provided if needed. Cross-district transportation arrangements and cost are arranged between involved districts.

6.   "Immediate enrollment" means enrolled and attending without delay! Schools are responsible for acquiring school records/IEP plans, or for referring the student to free/low cost physicals. Fees are automatically waived and homeless students qualify for school lunch/breakfast programs.

7.   Requiring proof of residency, a barrier for homeless students' enrollment, is illegal. The school may not require leases, bills, or other proofs

often required for ordinary enrollment. <u>School officials may not contact the landlord, zoning board or housing authority!</u> This violates the student's right to privacy under Illinois Law. Such contact could cause both the homeless family and the "host family" to lose their housing. The parents can be asked for emergency contact information.

8. "Unaccompanied youth" in homeless situations (teens not in physical custody of a parent or guardian, including runaway youth) have all the rights of other homeless students, and the right to be immediately enrolled on their own without proof of guardianship or signatures/permission of parents, or proof of "emancipated minor" status. A "Caregiver's Authorization Affidavit" available through Project REACH can make things a little easier but is not required. All youth (including homeless youth) have right to enroll in or attend school beyond age 18 if they will be able to graduate by age 21.

9. Kindergarten-age homeless children have all the rights of other homeless students, even though never previously enrolled in school. Although kindergarten is not mandatory school attendance, the homeless parent has the right to choose to have the child attend kindergarten, with all the rights described for other homeless students, including the choice of where to attend (school of origin or school in current attendance area).

10. Homeless preschool-age children have the right to be assessed for the need for preschool programs (the right to attend preschool is need-based for all children, and is not universally provided). Homeless preschoolers have all rights of other homeless students.

The above "Common Confusions" reflect the intent of the McKinney-Vento Homeless Education Assistance Act, the Illinois Education for Homeless Children Act and Illinois State Board of Education policies.

*AUTHOR'S NOTE: Schools, too, have rights with regard to educating homeless students. Protections are in place to prevent abuse of this legislation. More information about the McKinney-Vento Act and the Illinois Education for Homeless Children Act can be found the Opening Doors web site, **www.homelessed.net**.*

APPENDIX 4
A CRASH COURSE IN PRISONS

Unfortunately, Illinois Department of Corrections (IDOC) and most other prison systems typically fail miserably at "corrections"—the word that supposedly defines their purpose. I realize they have an incredibly difficult challenge. I also believe some people are so incapable of living in society that they should be kept locked up forever. Those are the ones most often released, tragically directly to the streets.

During the '90s, Illinois released over 6,000 persons a year like "Buddha" right into homelessness. A friend of mine who worked as a parole officer confirmed my worst fears. The release plan typically mandates things like anger management or job searches but the parole and probation officers, their ranks thinned by budget cuts and their attitudes jaded by bureaucratic bungling, struggle in vain to keep tabs on their growing roster of ex-offenders. Other little known facts about ex-offenders—those who have completed their sentences, paid their debt to society:

- Employment, at least socially acceptable and life supporting kinds, is extremely challenging because more and more employers do criminal background checks.
- Housing—an essential for all humans—becomes hard to get for the ex-offender. Again, criminal background checks weed out those with prisons in their pasts.
- Public housing—government subsidized—is often off limits for men and women with criminal records of a more serious nature.
- Voting, or participation in the civics side of society, is frequently forbidden, depending on the state.

Horrendous Ripple Effect

Families with parents in the prison system face their own grueling challenges. It is estimated that on any given day over 2,250,000 children in this country have a parent in prison. Tens of thousands of children end up in the foster care system because of having a parent incarcerated.

The website, www.asentenceoftheirown.com, contains disturbing information about the senseless destruction of families which contributes significantly to homelessness and abject poverty. Filmmaker Edgar Barens chronicled an all-too-typical family's downward spiral in his poignant film, *A Sentence of Their Own.*

APPENDIX 5

Suggestions for Involvement

- **BECOME AWARE of HOMELESSNESS in YOUR COMMUNITY**
It is my belief, along with "experts" in the field of homelessness, that homeless persons are in virtually every community. Sometimes they are visible, but often they blend in with the fashionable and fashion-challenged individuals making their way through malls, libraries and city streets. Tune into the people around you, talk to co-workers or friends who know someone who has lost their place to live, read the local paper—you'll start realizing that homelessness is everywhere. Good books and movies can offer a valuable starting place for understanding homelessness, including:
Where Can I Build My Volcano?, Pat Van Doren. 1999. Self-published children's book (great for adults, too). Order through Anderson Books, **www.andersonsbookshop.com**, or email Pat, **patvandoren@earthlinks.net**

Homeless to Harvard: The Liz Murray Story. DVD. Lifetime TV Productions. 2001.

- **VOLUNTEER AT A SHELTER**
From my experience, I'd emphasize:
  o Most shelters are desperate for volunteers, especially for the late-night or early morning shifts.
  o Don't feel rejected if your ideal time doesn't mesh with their needs. They can only have so many people at one time. It can be considered a "test" of your willingness to serve if you exhibit some flexibility.
  o It's good to go with someone who has volunteered before—a buddy system.
  o Take an open mind, knowing that your eyes will be opened—for good and bad—by what you'll see.
  o Don't just call at Christmas time or other holidays. Those are probably the worst times because of the increased level of activities.
  o Remember, the "do-gooder" attitude needs to allow for accepting realities other than yours. Not everyone has (nor wants) the safe, secure middle (or higher) class values you do.
  o You can't fix everyone's troubles. Nor do people want/expect it.

o Most homeless persons, as well as those with homes, are happy for a smile, a recognition of their personhood, and whatever kindness you can offer.

- **OTHER WAYS TO HELP**

In addition to hands-on volunteer service, most shelters need support to keep their doors open. Money works! Regular small contributions can be as valuable as the big ones. Matching dollars from your workplace can double your donation. It's great to involve kids in supporting a local shelter's operations too.

Also, supplies from Apples to Zip-lock bags are needed. Again, ask the program what they need. Don't assume they need a truckload of something, even though it might be an essential supply. It's often a matter of storage. On behalf of recipients of your donations, make sure the items are new or gently-used. Avoid the "It's good enough for who it's for" attitude.

Again, kids can become involved gathering essential, yet inexpensive items like socks and underwear. Kids can come up with creative ways of collecting supplies to feel like they are doing their part.

Many communities are becoming involved in sponsorship or mentoring programs, where homeless persons are linked with trained, caring individuals to support the journey to independence (often called transitional shelters/programs). Some faith communities rent an apartment, and let a social service agency refer a family to live there. Coordinated efforts are needed to ensure the family's success. Some families have lots to deal with—bad credit, under-developed life skills (budgeting, cooking, cleaning, etc.)--while some families are able to be self-sufficient. A good model of transitional programs in our area is Bridge Communities, **www.bridgecommunities.org**.

Hiring or renting to homeless individuals can also be a great help, but it requires some know-how (just like with non-homeless persons). Check with a reputable agency to see if your offer meets their needs.

- **ADVOCACY ORGANIZATIONS**

Changing policies that cause or perpetuate homelessness makes sense. Several states have advocacy agencies designed to focus on systemic change. National groups also spend considerable effort to stem the growing tide of homelessness.

Their premise, which I can wholeheartedly endorse, is that most voters don't have much knowledge about homelessness and poverty. When information is shared, most voters will support the move to create more just policies and government financial support. When voters speak up, legislators listen.

Homeless persons have a hard time with survival, much less negotiating the halls of Congress or their Statehouse. Persons who believe changes need to be made can, and should, communicate with legislators. Don't underestimate the power of, "I voted for you, and I am asking you to change (policy, etc.)..." To locate the name and contact information of your legislator, go to **www.house.gov** and **www.senate.gov** and follow the prompts.

APPENDIX 6

DAY LABOR INFO

According to the National Training and Information Center's 2003 report, Short Term Pay, Long Term Struggles, day labor, a.k.a. temp work, has burgeoned in this country. They state that from 1995 to 2001, temp work has increased 135%.

Among issues this type of employment may cause:
- Temp work pays less, typically less than poverty wages.
- Fewer benefits, if any.
- Rare opportunities for advancement or permanent job.
- Unregulated work environment leads to many types of abuse—illegal deductions, discrimination, health and safety violations, etc.

Homeless adults often turn to day labor as a stepping-stone into the work force. The surge of temporary help agencies, rarely-reported economic news, shows the deterioration of economic security of the working class.
For copies of the report: **www.ntic-us.org**

APPENDIX 7

Web sites to visit for information

National Law Center on Homelessness and Poverty, **www.nlchp.org**
National Coalition for the Homeless, **www.nationalhomeless.org**
National Center for Homeless Education, **www.nche.org**
National Association for the Education of Homeless Children and Youth, **www.naehcy.org**
National Center on Poverty Law, **www.povertylaw.org**

Most sites have lists of links to lead you to information, resources, and personnel that can hopefully enlighten.

The website for my new project (7/05), HEAR US (Homeless Education Awareness Raising in the US) can be found at **www.hearus.us**. Email: bookinfo@hearus.us.

APPENDIX 8

Hesed House and Tent City Diagrams

Below a rudimentary sketch of the facility known as Hesed House and the layout of Tent City, often referred to in this book.

The layout of the building is incomplete, omitting reference to Aurora Area Interfaith Food Pantry and Aurora Soup Kitchen, both located at Hesed House. Also not depicted are the PADS (Public Action To Deliver Shelter) sleeping areas, space for up to 180 men, women and children to sleep on an emergency basis. The playground is also missing.

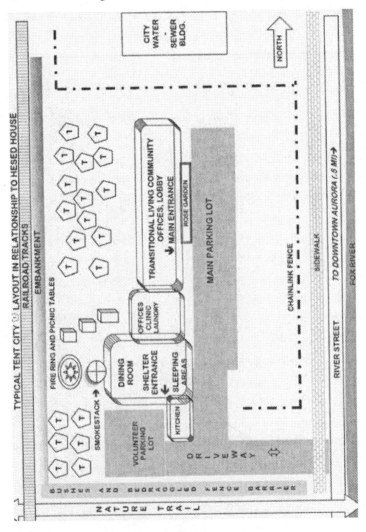

Endnotes

[1] An estimated 3 million people, 1% of the U.S. population, will be homeless in a year, with 39% being children. Urban Institute, 2002

[2] Illinois PADS programs operated in DuPage Co., Elgin (northern Kane Co.), Lake Co., McHenry Co., south Cook Co., west Cook Co., southwest Chicago, Freeport, Ottawa-Peru and Joliet/Will Co. They operated independently, subscribing to the overall mission of PADS, Aurora, the original program begun in 1982.

[3] DeNavas-Walt, Carmen, Bernadette D. Proctor, and Robert J. Mills, U.S. Census Bureau, Current Population Reports, P60-226, *Income, Poverty, and Health Insurance Coverage in the United States: 2003*, U.S. Government Printing Office, Washington, DC, 2004.

[4] *People Just Like You*, A report on suburban homelessness. Illinois Coalition to End Homelessness. Joseph Clary and Diane Nilan. 1996.

[5] Pat Van Doren. Self-published. Contact her at 630/355-5859, or Anderson's Bookstore, Naperville, www.Andersonsbookshop.com.

[6] "The Safety Net Delivers," Center on Budget and Policy Priorities, 11/16/1996. "Scapegoating Rent Control: Masking the Causes of Homelessness." John I. Gilderbloom. Journal of the American Planning Association. Journal of the American Planning Association, Vol. 57. No. 2. 1991.

[7] Aurora, like many communities, experienced a proliferation of temporary help agencies, also called day labor. They prey on the hard-to-employ (Appendix 6).

[8] Illinois welfare cash assistance levels rose slightly in 2003 after over a decade of level funding, e.g. $377 increased to $396 for single parent, 3 children.

[9] Sergeant Shriver National Poverty Law Project, Chicago-based advocacy and policy review, www.povertylaw.org

[10] Federally funded housing assistance that guarantees payment of rent by the government and requires the family to contribute one-third of monthly household income to the total rent.

[11] Illinois Education for Homeless Children Act, passed Sept. 1994 (Appendix 2)

[12] Established in 1998 in memory of André E. LeTendre, husband of Mary Jean LeTendre, former Director of Compensatory Education for the U.S. Department of Education, the LeTendre Education Fund for Homeless Children provides scholarship assistance to students who are homeless or have experienced homelessness. (www.naehcy.org)

[13] *Short Term Pay Long Term Struggles,* National Training and Information Center, 2003.

[14] Ibid

[15] "Elder abuse" is a criminal charge in IL that triggers an immediate investigation. **(320 ILCS 20/) Elder Abuse and Neglect Act.**

[16] Interview, western Illinois area ISBE lead liaison Eileen Worthington, 1/7/05.

[17] When families or youth lose housing and move in with another household, i.e. double-up, they are considered homeless when it comes to the kids' rights to attend school (Appendix 1 and 2).

[18] Snack Food Association

[19] World of Dogs

[20] Speech by Senator Paul Simon, *The Explosive Growth of Gambling in the United States,* Senate - July 31, 1995

[21] Center for Responsive Politics

[22] HUD Press Release 12/19/03

[23] Governor George W. Bush, thanking donors at a New York speech, October 20, 2000.

[24] U.S. Census Bureau report, 8/26/04

[25] Center for Budget Priorities, News Release, 8/27/04

[26] "Extreme poverty" in the U.S, is defined by government as below 50% of poverty level, $8,000 for a family of 3.

[27] US Census Bureau Report, http://www.census.gov/const/C25Ann/sftotalmedavgsqft.pdf.

[28] US Census Bureau Report, CB04-165

[29] *Losing Ground in the Best of Times, Low Income Renters in the 1990s,* Nelson, Treskon, Pellatiere, 2004.

[30] Citizens Against Government Waste, www.cagw.org

[31] National Alliance to End Homelessness newsletter, Nov. 22, 2004

[32] *Give Us Your Poor,* scheduled for release in 2001, as of 10/05 still seeks production funding. www.guyp.org

[33] The McKinney-Vento definition of homeless includes: persons, due to loss of housing or other crises, who are doubled-up, in motels, shelters, or other substandard housing (Appendix 1).

[34] The federal McKinney-Vento Homeless Education Act of 2001, 42 U.S.C.11431 et seq. (Appendix 1)

[35] Illinois Education for Homeless Children Act of 1994, 105 ILCS 45 (Appendix 2)

[36] Illinois Education for Homeless Children Act (105 ILCS 45/), and Subtitle B of title VII of the McKinney-Vento Homeless Assistance Act (42 U.S.C. 11431 et seq.)

Printed in the United States
65337LVS00003B/176

9 781591 138365